FAUX's Dexterity

ALSO BY RICKY JAY

•

Cards As Weapons

Learned Pigs & Fireproof Women

Many Mysteries Unraveled:
Conjuring Literature in America 1786–1874

The Magic Magic Book

JAY'S JOURNAL *of* ANOMALIES

JAY'S JOURNAL *of* ANOMALIES

CONJURERS · CHEATS · HUSTLERS
HOAXSTERS · PRANKSTERS
JOKESTERS · IMPOSTORS · PRETENDERS
SIDESHOW SHOWMEN
ARMLESS CALLIGRAPHERS
MECHANICAL MARVELS
POPULAR ENTERTAINMENTS

RICKY JAY

FARRAR STRAUS GIROUX

New York

Farrar, Straus and Giroux
19 Union Square West, New York 10003

Distributed in Canada by Douglas & McIntyre Ltd.
Printed in the United States of America
First edition, 2001

Library of Congress Cataloging-in-Publication Data
Jay, Ricky.
Jay's journal of anomalies : conjurers, cheats, hustlers, hoaxsters, pranksters, jokesters,
imposters, pretenders, side-show showmen, armless calligraphers, mechanical marvels,
popular entertainments / Ricky Jay.— 1st ed.
    p.   cm.
Includes bibliographical references and index.
ISBN 0-374-17867-4 (alk. paper)
    1. Entertainers—Biography.   2. Curiosities and wonders.   3. Abnormalities, Human.
4. Impostors and imposture.   I. Title.

PN1583 .J375 2001
791'.092'2—dc21
[B]

2001016200

Frontispiece art from a lithograph of Lionel, L'Homme-Lion, Friedlander,
Hamburg, 1914. Author's collection.

Designed by Patrick Reagh and Ricky Jay

for Chrisann

CONTENTS

JAY'S JOURNAL *of* ANOMALIES

JAY'S JOURNAL *of*
ANOMALIES

VOLUME ONE, NUMBER ONE   SPRING, 1994   PUBLISHED QUARTERLY

The Faithful Monetto & The Inimitable Dick

THE NINETEENTH CENTURY, not so unlike those which preceded and succeeded it, was rich in showmen who appropriated the acts of more illustrious and innovative rivals. As a performer, I can think of no more opprobrious behavior. History, however, affords us a retrospective view which, on occasion, can transform the fatuous into the farcical. When the perpetrator of act-stealing is animal rather than human, our willingness to smile instead of chide is increased, particularly when the performing repertoire can be antedated by many dog years, indeed.

The subject apotheosized in the woodcut below is Monetto, the time-telling, tail-wagging, signifying, studious, and faithful dog presented by the felicitously named Mr. Hoare. The animal was in deed and spirit, although not in appearance, an imitator of Signor Castelli's justly celebrated Munito.

In an era rich in examples of animal scholarship, Munito was a star. Some called him the "Isaac Newton of his race." A highly manicured poodle, he appeared at Laxton's Rooms, New Bond Street, London, in 1817. To commence his act, he was introduced into a circle of pasteboards on which were printed various numbers. With his teeth Munito picked up the correct cards to solve problems in addition, subtraction, multiplication, and division. For inquiries in the disciplines of geography, botany, and natural history he selected appropriate alphabet cards. He could identify colors and objects and was adept at dominoes, often winning against celebrated competition. He seems to have captured the public's imagination as no other canine star before or since.[1]

Listing the impressive patronage of the Prince Regent and the Duke of York, who not "only beheld him with Astonishment, but gave him their most unbounded Applause," the dog's trainer boasted his ward had "qualifications

MR. NICHOLAS HOARE, THE CELEBRATED CONJUROR,
AND HIS FAITHFUL DOG MONETTO.

almost beyond human credibility."[2] As a keepsake of the exhibition, one could purchase an *Historical Account of the Life and Habits of the Learned Dog Munito, by A Friend to Beasts.* Such was the poodle's fame that a translation of his memoirs was available in Dutch, and likenesses of him appeared on souvenir prints and on china plates which were sold in London, Paris, and Amsterdam.[3]

After his initial success in England, Munito traveled to the Continent, no doubt to fulfill contractual obligations. When he returned to London, advertisements cleverly announced his "having been abroad for some time to finish his education." Actually, it was his newly found endurance which was most impressive, as Munito was now appearing every hour from twelve until five o'clock at No. 1 Leicester Square (previously at Laxton's Rooms he had shown only at three and seven o'clock). Even though Munito had in the interim obtained a medal from the Humane Society for "having saved the life of a lady in the most extraordinary manner," the price of admission to his revue remained one shilling. (This was a substantial sum well beyond the means of many Londoners.)

Such was the poodle's impact that forty-five years after witnessing his show Charles Dickens was able to recall Munito's repertoire. A magic fancier and amateur conjurer himself, Dickens admitted to being fooled by the dog's "answering questions, telling the hour of the day, the day of the week or date of the month, and picking out any cards called for from a pack spread on the ground."

Dickens witnessed the performance a second time and "watched more narrowly. . . . We noted that between each feat the master gave the dog some small bits of some sort of food, and that there was a faint smell of aniseed from that corner of the room. We noticed that the dog, as he passed round the circle of cards with his nose down and his eyes directed to the ground, never pounced on the right card as his eyes covered it, but turned back and picked it out. It was clear that he chose it by the smell and not by. . . sight. We recalled that each time before the dog began his circuit, the master arranged and settled the cards, and we then found that he pressed the fleshy part of his thumb on the particular card the dog was to draw, which thumb he previously put into his waistcoat-pocket for an instant, and as he passed close to us, his waistcoat had an aniseed scent. After the performance we remained until the room was clear, and then spoke to the master. He did not deny the discovery of his principle."[4]

This scenario has a surprisingly modern ring, not in the performance of the dog but rather in the interchange between the amateur and professional conjurer. In the time-honored tradition the amateur, thoroughly fooled, returns to scrutinize the show. He intuits a method which, although almost certainly incorrect (or at best providing only a partial explanation), satisfies him. He now confronts the conjurer (unlike many of his present-day counterparts, Dickens had the courtesy to wait for the room to clear) and proudly announces his theory. The performer smiles and says nothing. This the ama-

teur interprets as a sign of assent. Convinced of his remarkable powers of observation and analysis, the tyro departs, basking in the glow of self-congratulation.[5]

The most logical explanation of Munito's methods is provided in E. de Tarade's *Education du Chien* (Paris, 1866).[6] According to the author, it was Munito's exceptional sense of sound, not smell, which was exploited by his presenter. As Munito circled the cards with an "air of reflection," the trainer would, at the appropriate time, make an almost inaudible clicking noise with his fingernail or a toothpick. This would alert the dog to the proper selection. To further disguise the method, the sound was made with the trainer's hand concealed in his pocket.

Munito was presented by a Signor Castelli. There is speculation that Nief, a Dutch trainer, assumed the name of Castelli, as Italians were thought to be more intriguing than showmen from Holland in the early nineteenth century.[7]

Although the dog's fame was extraordinary, it never lived up to the prediction of the usually astute circus historian, Hugues Le Roux, who proclaimed in 1889 that "Munito... seems to have as much chance of being remembered as Archimedes the Syracusian."[8]

Monetto, on the other hand, may be remembered only by the woodcut herein reproduced. From his carriage one would imagine him more likely to point out partridge than to tell the time on a gentleman's pocket-watch. His rustic appearance is most unlike that of the elegantly coifed poodle that preceded him on the boards.

Nicholas Hoare, Monetto's exhibitor, survives in almost a dozen playbills I have seen, none of which, however, mentions his faithful dog.[9] Although Sidney Clarke in his *Annals of Conjuring* (London, 1929) dismisses Hoare in a single line as a "small fry," the showman presented a pleasing if fairly standard early-nineteenth-century magic show. Torn or burnt cards were restored, coins were vanished and subsequently reappeared, pancakes were fried in a gentleman's hat, playing cards were transformed into small animals, and a rooster was decapitated and his head then reaffixed.

Hoare's fame, what trifle exists, is due almost entirely to his exhibition of trained animals. In addition to Monetto, he presented an unnamed learned goose, and the eponymy of learned pigs, "Toby the Sapient Swine." Mr. Hoare, for all his faults as an imitative showman, was the instigator, if not the author, of one of the great examples of genre literature. *The Life and Adventures of Toby the Sapient Pig, with his Opinion of Men and Manners* (London, c. 1817) is an autobiography which, viewed with my myopic eyes, equals in stature those of Franklin, Cellini, and Robert-Houdin. It is a far better read than *The Dog of Knowledge, or Memoirs of Bob, the Spotted Terrier, Supposed to be written by Himself* (London, 1801).

Originality was a quality sought, but rarely achieved, by generation after generation of itinerant showmen. Trained dogs had been exhibited since Roman antiquity, but caused little excitement when compared to more exotic examples of brute creation. The appearance of "learned" dogs became popular in the eighteenth century, and a remarkable volume, *Tractaetlein mit Hundedressurkunststucken,* was published in Germany (c. 1730). It contained numerous hand-colored copperplate engravings showing its canine star selecting cards, totaling dice, spelling words, and returning borrowed objects to their rightful owners—almost a century before Munito mounted the stage.

Even "Bobby, the Handcuff Dog," the terrier owned and presented by Houdini in 1918 (he was, if we are to believe his master, capable of extricating himself from ropes, handcuffs, and a pooch-sized strait-jacket), had his progenitor in Emile, the Newfoundland star of a "doggie-drama" at the Cirque Olympique in Paris. One of the highlights of the French production was the dog's impressive release from the restraints which bound him and his master.[10]

ANOTHER DOG who mastered the act of a human star was the "Inimitable Dick," a talented poodle who through diligent effort re-created Loïe Fuller's "Serpentine Dance."

Loïe Fuller, a most unlikely star of vaudeville and music hall, was born in Fullersberg, Illinois, in 1862. She was a singer, dancer, and actress of no great distinction. While rehearsing a play in 1890, she held up the folds of her long and flimsy gown to avoid tripping. As she gathered and swirled the diaphanous material the spotlight bouncing off her dress created a startling effect.

Loïe capitalized on this chance discovery and choreographed a series of dances involving multiple beams of light projected through colored gels onto the folds of her costume. Often her dresses consisted of hundreds of yards of material which were enhanced with wire frameworks to aid in their manipulation. The flower dance, the mirror dance, the butterfly dance, the fire dance, and the serpentine dance brought her praise, profit, and fame. Isadora Duncan and Ruth St. Denis heralded her as a pioneer. (The approbation, however, was not universal. As one critic related, "she stood stock still and only moved her arms." Her dance, he said, looked like an exercise "routine with Indian Clubs.")[11]

She played the major European theaters, but was particularly heralded by the French, who in a pre–Jerry Lewis frenzy embraced her as "La Loïe." Her Théâtre de Loïe Fuller was the leading attraction of the 1900 World Exposition in

Paris. Her image, often much more flatteringly rendered than nature allowed, was immortalized in posters by Cheret, Pal, Meunier, Orazi, and Toulouse-Lautrec. She spawned numerous imitators, human and canine.

Under the tutorship of Miss Doré, an eccentric clown and animal trainer, the poodle named Dick appeared at the Alhambra in London doing a jam-up version of Loïe Fuller's serpentine dance. The act was a resounding success. Moving to the Théâtre des Nouveautés in the revue "Paris-qui-passe," the dog received star billing as "La Nouvelle Loïe Fuller" and "L'Inimitable Dick."

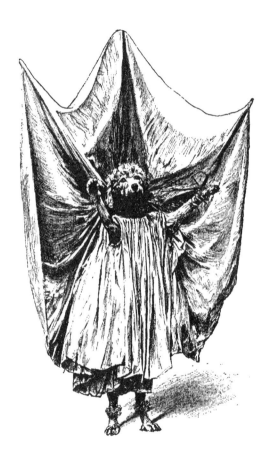

The idea for Dick's performance, and indeed Dick himself, was supplied by Pierre Hachet-Souplet, the respected animal trainer and author of the classic *Le Dressage des Animaux*. Hachet-Souplet's little black poodle was already capable of walking up four flights of stairs on his hind legs and then executing a five-minute waltz without once lowering his forepaws. Miss Doré took advantage of Dick's natural talents in her theatrical staging. The bells and bracelets Dick formerly wore on his legs were replaced with extension sticks necessary for the serpentine dance. With Dick's forepaw turned back against his shoulder, a stick positioned almost like a rifle at rest helped him to perform the butterfly dance. A light robe, fourteen meters in circumference, was draped on the dog. When stationary, he seemed engulfed in fabric, but when Dick began to waltz the garment would waft gracefully, allowing the dog to re-create Loïe's rose dance.

For Dick's French debut in "Paris-qui-passe," the master of ceremonies, M. Germain, opened with a comic tune about the serpentine dance. Suddenly a spotlight appeared stage left. As the orchestra played Loïe Fuller's signature waltz, a peculiar form, seemingly Lilliputian, appeared, wearing a gold robe and a blond doll wig. As it took mincing steps toward center stage the audience began to comprehend, some shouting audibly, "It's a dog." Dick began to pirouette while the projector changed the color of his costume successively from red, to blue, to violet. Then, with leaps of two meters at a time, Dick propelled himself toward the wings, his movements shaking free his dress so that his puffed poodle tail came into view just as he disappeared offstage.[12]

For a finale, "The Inimitable Dick" mounted a platform in a costume of light blue silk. An enormous blacksmith's bellows concealed in the framework inflated Dick's dress so that it rose in the air and fanned out around him in imitation of Loïe Fuller and in anticipation of Marilyn Monroe.

Dick proved everything but "inimitable" as, according to a Düsseldorf trade paper, he spawned imitators in four countries — some twenty different dogs tried to appropriate his highly successful act. All, it was said, were inferior to the model. Miss Kosiki, Tchernoff, Parker, and Néraguet were some of the transgressing trainers; but they all fared better than another presenter, Professor Richard. The latter advertised the serpentine dancing dog act in colored lithographs for appearances at the famous café-concert-cum-music hall, the Alcazar d'Été.[13] He was dragged to court and enjoined from using the term "creator" (of the dog Loïe Fuller act) on his advertising material. Richard was sentenced at the Tribunal of Commerce at the Seine on April 24, 1895. ◉

ILLUSTRATIONS

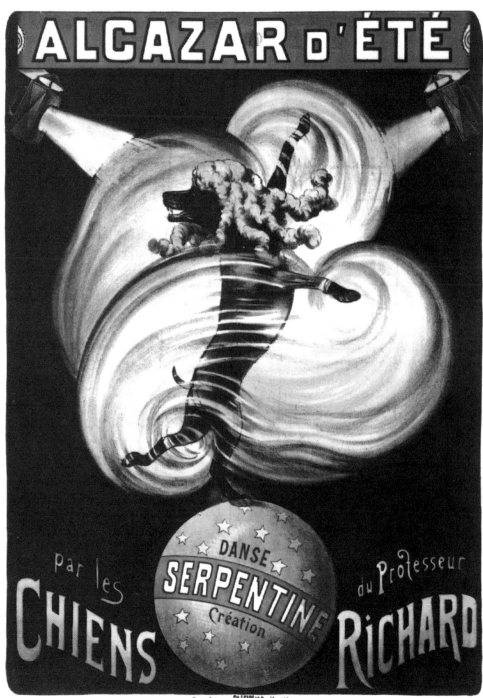

NOTES

1. Among the many canine performers who preceded Munito on the boards in England were: The Incomparable Bitch exhibited by a Mons. Radou from Paris in 1731; Le Chien Savant, or the Matchless French Dog, who appeared in London in 1751; the dog exhibited by Coan the Norfolk dwarf at the same time; The Learned Dog from Douglas, Isle of Man, exhibited by the Indian Gentoo for the Royal Family at Kew in 1784 and later in a show fronted by the conjurer Johnson in 1790; a talented dog presented by Flint and Gyngell in Cheswick in 1801; and another featured by the magician Moritz at the New Minor Theatre in London the same year. These canine stars were capable of a variety of stunts, including telling the time, answering questions, and identifying specific members of the audience.

A playbill in my collection, hand-dated 1816, features a "Russian Gambling Dog" who was advertised as playing All Fours, Put, and Dominoes. The exhibition was promoted by Signor Giraldelli (sometimes Girardelli) at 349 Strand, a favorite venue of his wife, the Signora, the beloved fireproof woman. In 1815, Gyngell featured a London performance of "The Learned Dogs, in whom the proverbial Sagacity of the whole Species seems concentrated! Their Performance... is of so varied and novel a kind; that, subjects less deserving, have occasioned most elaborate Panegyrics! But Mr. G ever averse to *puffing*, would rather please, by exceeding the Promise of his Bill, than by *a contrary Plan, force a Disappointment on his Audience*."

2. Playbill in Daniel Lysons, *Collectanea*, a series of five folio scrapbooks assembled in the early nineteenth century and housed in the British Library.

3. The most popular engraving of Munito is by Lanté from the French fashion series *Le Bon Genre*. Originally depicting richly caparisoned attendants witnessing the concert of a harpist, the print was reworked at a later date, substituting Castelli and his sagacious dog. This was brought to my attention by that indefatigable researcher of magic prints, Bob Read.

4. The *Journal of Magic History*, vol. 1, no. 2 (July 1979): 88–110, contains an informative article about Dickens' involvement with conjuring by Steven Tigner. He cites the account of Munito from *All the Year Round* (January 26, 1867), but does not include the explanation of the trainer's techniques quoted here.

5. "Good and Bad" may be a more appropriate distinction than "Amateur and Professional," as some hobbyists show far more skill and understanding of the art than many vocational practitioners.

6. I was able to locate a copy of this scarce title in the Peter Chapin Collection of Books on Dogs at the College of William and Mary. I would be remiss if I did not mention that Mr. Chapin is a cocker spaniel, or rather, in "Pythonian" parlance, an ex-cocker spaniel.

Additional material appears in Paul Heuzé, *La Plaisanterie des Animaux Calculateurs* (Paris, 1928), an important source of information for such acts.

7. This theory, while hardly illogical, has been presented as fact by Max Dif in his *Histoire Illustrée de la Prestidigitation* (Paris, 1986). It is, to my knowledge, unsubstantiated.

8. Le Roux, *Les Jeux du Cirque et la Vie Foraine* (Paris, 1889), 83.

9. I have tried to reconstruct Hoare's repertoire from playbills examined at the Harry Ransom Humanities Research Center, the University of Texas at Austin, and those reproduced in my *Learned Pigs & Fireproof Women* (New York, 1986), 17–18.

10. *The Magic Circular* (May 1986): 85–86 contains a charming account of "Bobby" by Edwin Dawes in his ongoing series "A Rich Cabinet of Magical Curiosities," and includes material on Munito and other learned dogs. The account of Emile is in Hachet-Souplet's *Le Dressage des Animaux* (Paris, 1897), 39.

The "doggie drama," in which canine stars mounted the stage in theatrical productions, was an outgrowth of the "hippodrama," in which players appeared on horseback to deliver their lines (see Arthur Saxon's *Enter Foot and Horse* [New Haven, 1968]). Animal celebrities were occasionally called upon to lift sagging box office receipts, as was the case with Carlo the Newfoundland in Sheridan's 1803 production of *The Caravan*. After the successful opening, Sheridan is said to have come center stage asking, "Where is my preserver?" When the pleased author came forward Sheridan cried, "Not you, the dog."

Other "doggie dramas" included *The Felon's Death, or the Dog of the Mountain, The Forest of Bondy*, and the unforgettable 1835 production of *Love Me, Love My Dog*. Dickens, ever the admirer of such fare, described a play in which " a dog, instead of rushing at the murderer's throat, came down to the footlights and in high good humour, stood wagging its tail and tongue at the audience. Meanwhile, the infuriated murderer was actively inviting him by suppressed threats of invitation to fly at his throat. He had eventually, in sheer desperation, to fly at the animal himself, and, as it were, lift him to his throat" (Percy Fitzgerald, *The World Behind the Scenes* [London, 1881], 81-82).

11. Harlowe Hoyt, *Town Hall Tonight* (Englewood Cliffs, N. J., 1955), 90. Material on Fuller's iconography and dances may be found in Alain Weil's *100 Years of Posters of the Folies Bergère and Music Halls of Paris* (New York, 1977).

12. Hachet-Souplet, 75-77, details Dick's performance.

13. A droll lithograph of Richard and his dog act is reproduced in Hannah Winter, *Le Théâtre du Marveilleux* (Paris, 1962), 176.

JAY'S JOURNAL OF ANOMALIES

Written by Ricky Jay and published four times a year by the author and W & V Dailey, Antiquarian Booksellers, 8216 Melrose Avenue, Los Angeles, California, 90046, (213) 658-8515. Subscription $90 per annum. ¶ Printed letterpress by Patrick Reagh using Monotype Ehrhardt with Thorowgood heads on Rives Heavyweight paper. ¶ Designed by Mr. Reagh & Mr. Jay. ¶ The author wishes to thank Tim Tobin, Andrea Braver, and Susan Green for generous assistance in the preparation of this issue. ¶ Written and illustrative material, © Ricky Jay, 1994. ¶ All images are from the private collection of the author. Any subsequent use of any text or image is permissible only with the express written consent of Mr. Jay.

JAY'S JOURNAL *of*
ANOMALIES

VOLUME ONE, NUMBER TWO   SUMMER, 1994   PUBLISHED QUARTERLY

Edward Bright: The Gazing Stock and Admiration of all People

SUPERLATIVES arrest our attention. We observe with fascination the tallest, the shortest, the widest, the deepest, the fastest, the strongest. The *Guinness Book of World Records* outsells everything in print except the Bible, itself the benchmark for superlatives (the wisest, the oldest, the most righteous…).

In mid-eighteenth-century England, the biggest, fattest man known was Edward Bright, who at his death in 1750 was said to have weighed between 616 and 622 pounds. (An estimate arrived at by calculating his food intake and rate

Printed for Caringten Bowles, at Nº69 in St Pauls Church Yard. London.

of growth, correcting for his lack of movement during his final illness, and adding this figure to his last official weight.) He was five feet nine inches tall and he measured five feet six inches around the chest. His arm at its largest circumference measured twenty-six inches and his legs "were as big as a man's body of midling [sic] magnitude." He was five feet eleven inches around the belly. According to one contemporary squib he was "suppos'd to be the largest man living or perhaps ever liv'd in this island." Indeed, no standard medical texts of the time identified anyone of greater corpulence. Although his weight would be surpassed handily in the future, Bright was, at the time of his death, the largest man on record, and a great curiosity.[1] Never a showman or an entertainer, Bright by size alone compelled such attention that he was called "the gazing stock and admiration of all people" by that quintessential chronicler of the unusual, James Caulfield.[2]

While I have long written about anomalies, in dimension as well as deed, I have traditionally placed more emphasis on acquired prowess than physical exaltation. Siamese twins, for instance, were worthy of discussion only if balanced on their heads, reciting Goliardic verse and providing their own accompaniment on violin and dulcimer.

Why then have I decided to focus on Edward Bright? I suppose there are a number of factors beyond simply expanding my horizons. Bright was remarkably well known in his day, but was subsequently almost completely forgotten, except as a footnote to the story of Daniel Lambert, his far larger and more famous successor. Despite this undeserved eclipse, Bright inspired unusual wagers, a topic that has long interested me and that indeed called my attention to him in the first place. Finally, over the years I have gathered, from the most far-reaching and unlikely sources, a small cache of prints of our protagonist, which I find irresistible and feel compelled to share.

Bright, a successful grocer from Malden in Essex, was descended on both sides from families "greatly inclined to corpulencey." Unlike Daniel Lambert, who was to succeed our subject as the heavyweight champion of the British Isles but who was of normal size until the age of twenty, Bright's embonpoint was almost embryonic. By the age of twelve he weighed 144 pounds, and he totaled 336 pounds while still a teenager.

A Compendium of
GIANT CHILDREN
Selected from the Author's Portfolio

☛ **"The Giant Baby,"** Vantile Mack, called the "Infant Lambert" by the prevaricating P. T. Barnum, who claimed the child weighed 257 pounds at the age of seven. He was said to measure 61 inches around the chest and 36 inches around the leg.[3]

☛ **Master T. R. Reed,** "The Modern Dan'l Lambert," who "has attained the remarkable altitude of five feet two inches and weighs 265 pounds," at age eleven. He was exhibited at the Boston Museum in 1843.[4]

☛ **William Price,** "The Shropshire Infant Prodigy," was exhibited in 1839. At the age of fifteen months he measured two feet around the chest, was two feet four inches tall, and weighed 42 pounds: "The mother accompanies the Child and is induced to exhibit it in consequences of the distressing death of its Father by a lamentable accident in a coal pit, whereby she has been left with a family of four children extremely destitute."[5]

☛ A **giant baby** was advertised at the Albert Palace in Battersea Park. Born in 1885, it weighed 58 pounds and was three feet tall at one year of age. A playbill states, "The Members of the Medical Profession who have seen it have pronounced it to be a most extraordinary specimen of humanity and the wonder of the World." The sex of the child is not revealed, expressing a sentiment, or lack thereof, which I well understand.[6]

☛ **Maria Loncar-Vincek,** a giant child exhibited at the Prater in Vienna in 1850 who tipped in at 126 pounds at the age of three.[7]

☛ **William Wilkinson,** "The Giant Boy," born in Glasgow on March 26, 1811, and exhibited at Bartholomew Fair at age fourteen, where William Hone judged him to be "of fair complexion, an intelligent countenance, active in motion, and of sensible speech." He weighed a modest 308 pounds.[8]

☞ That paragon of succinct description, **"The Giant Hungarian Schoolboy,"** who tipped in at 420 pounds at age eighteen.[9]

☞ The most remarkable example of prodigious progeny must surely be **Thomas Hills Everitt,** said to weigh more than one hundred pounds at nine months of age! He was born on February 7, 1779. His father was a well-respected tradesman in the marvelously specific profession of "mould paper mark maker" (a fabricator of watermarks) and worked at the mills in Endfield, Middlesex, where Thomas was born. The child was not remarkably large at the time of his birth, but by nine months he had achieved such substantial size that he was taken to a local physician, Mr. Sherwen, who measured him and found him to be considerably larger than a robust seven-year-old. Sherwen sent his findings to the Royal Society. At eleven months of age Everitt was supposedly three feet three inches tall, measured two feet six inches at the chest, one foot nine inches around the thigh, eleven inches around the arm, and nine inches around the wrist. At this time the child was taken to London and exhibited by his mother. He was said to be "comely, lively, and well-tempered," with a degree of facial expression surprising for one so young. According to contemporary accounts, however, within six months the child was "not sufficiently attractive" to draw crowds and had to join forces with a dwarf. The two were exhibited at the New Inn in Southwark for six weeks. A print of the mother and child was struck, according to Bromley's *A Catalog of Engraved British Portraits,* in 1779 (although most other sources say 1780). Some accounts say the family reunited, left show business, and were not heard of again; the more likely explanation is that the child died before turning eighteen months old.[10]

━━∿∿∿∿ค∩◉∩∩∿∿∿━━

E dward Bright was a leading exponent of exponential growth. He weighed nearly 400 pounds at his wedding at age twenty-two, and 584 pounds at his last official weigh-in some thirteen months before his demise.

Bright was said to be quite agile on both foot and horse. "He could walk very well, and nimbly too, having great strength of muscles," until illness began to plague him in his late twenties. He apparently had a large but not remarkable appetite, and was fond of beer and wine rather than hard spirits. Although his consumption of these potables was significant —"his chief liquor was small beer, of which he commonly drank about a gallon a day"— he did not drink "to an intoxicating degree." A conflicting if more credible account stated, "he perhaps drank more than prudence would have dictated to a man of his excessively corpulent disposition."[11]

Bright was widely known for his good nature and his business acumen. He was the father of five children, his wife pregnant with a sixth when he died. He was considered a dutiful father and husband. His decline was attributed to an inflammation of his leg which troubled him for some years before he succumbed to the "military fever" that was to take his life on November 10, 1750, at the age of twenty-nine. His leg, whenever inflamed, had a tendency to mortification which necessitated "scarification and fomentations." He was bled, at his request, two pounds on these occasions, and "was no more sensible to the loss of such a quantity, than another man is of 12 or 14 ounces." His last fever was accompanied by inflammatory symptoms, coughing, and difficulty of breathing. He surrendered on the fourteenth day of the siege. Even

though the weather was cool his body began to putrefy at a rate which exceeded that of the fabrication of his coffin, much to the dismay of his neighbors. Matched to Bright's height, its width was three feet six inches at the shoulders, two feet three and one-half inches at the head, twenty-two inches at the feet. It was three feet one and one-half inches deep.

Part of the house had to be disassembled to remove his body. It took a dozen men to draw the casket in a low-wheeled carriage to the funeral service. This spectacle captivated a curious aggregation of onlookers. A special engine was created to lower the coffin to its final resting place.

It was not Bright's anomalous size alone which commands our attention; he was also the subject of singular wagers in the betting-crazed atmosphere of the day.

In the mid-eighteenth century, men of rank and pleasure indulged themselves at gaming houses and private clubs. Considerable sums were staked on propositions odd, gruesome, or frivolous: the life expectancy of a friend, the virtue of a friend's wife, or which of two raindrops would first hit the bottom of a windowpane—all were considered legitimate topics on which to bet.

It is not surprising that Bright would be named in such scheming. Twice he was the principal, if unknowing, participant in imaginative wagers, once during his lifetime and again shortly after his demise.

Horace Walpole, that indefatigable compiler of social delectation, related the proposition concerning Bright and the ungainly Duke of Cumberland:

There has been a droll cause in Westminster Hall: a man laid another a wager that he produced a person who should weigh as much again as the Duke. When they had betted, they recollected not who knowing how to desire the Duke to step into the scale. They agreed to establish his weight at twenty stone [two hundred eighty pounds], which, however is supposed to be two more than he weighs. One Bright was then produced, who is since dead, and who actually weighed forty-two and a half. As soon as he was dead, the person who had lost objected that he had been weighed in his clothes, and though it was impossible to suppose that his clothes could weigh above two stone, they went to law. There were the Duke's twenty stone bawled over a thousand times,-but the righteous law decided against the man who had won![12]

Actually, there was an official weighing of Bright's waistcoat, shirt, breeches, and stockings, apparently unknown to the bettors. About thirteen months before

Bright's passing it was determined that he weighed 584 pounds. On that occasion, the aforementioned garments totaled sixteen pounds, well under the two stone, or twenty-eight-pound, limitation imposed in the wager. One hypothesizes that Walpole's indignation, and that of the defeated punter, would have been greater had they only known of these proceedings.

The house of the Widow Day, the Black Bull inn in Malden, was the site of a wager determined on December 1, 1750, less than two weeks after the death of Bright. A Mr. Hants, and a judiciously named Mr. Codd, gathered at the inn to determine if five grown men at least twenty-one years of age could be buttoned into the waistcoat of the recently deceased. The entourage took their places accordingly, and the bet was decided when not five but seven men were ensconced in the giant vest, "without breaking a stitch or straining a button."

Edward Bright was the subject of numerous representations in life as well as death. Paintings, drawings, and engravings were produced by artists and print sellers. Among those I have personally examined are a wash drawing of Bright seated in a chair by L. J. Jacques "taken from life"; an unsigned engraving of the same image; a hand-colored version printed for John Bowles at the Black Horse in Cornhill in August 1750 (see page 12); an engraving of Bright seated but sporting a hat from the Universal Magazine, *published by J. Hinton, at the King's Arms in St. Paul's Churchyard and appearing in the issue of February 1751; a similar mezzotint by Ja. McArdell of an image by Ogborne; and an engraving published by John Bowles at the Black Horse in Cornhill on January 1, 1750, in which Bright's weight is listed at 609 pounds (a later print, presumably, of the same image in the author's collection is published by Carrington Bowles at No. 69 in St. Paul's Churchyard, giving Bright's weight at 621-1/4 pounds; see p. 9). Fairburn's Accurate Portraits of the Two most Corpulent Englishmen ever known, with a Comparative Account of their Extraordinary Persons and Manners, was issued by the well-known publisher John Fairburn at 146 Minories, London, May 27, 1806, second edition. An attractive broadside with hand-colored engravings of Lambert and Bright, it sports a charming insert depicting seven men within the latter's vest (a detail from the print is on page 15). Of these many images, none is more enjoyable than the engraving published by B. Dickinson*

THE SURPRISEING BETT DECIDED.

at Ludgate Hill, April 2, 1751, to commemorate the famous waistcoat wager, "The Surpriseing Bett [sic] Decided." Beneath a portrait of our subject seven seraphically smiling gentlemen are circumscribed "with ease" in the enormous waistcoat. Two men, Codd and Hants, watch the proceedings: "Sir you'll allow that to be fair," says one; the other responds, "I do sir, & to me beyond Immagination [sic]." This image is a lasting tribute to insouciant iconography (see page 14).

NOTES

1. As humans have grown stronger and faster, breaking world records regularly, so too have they grown larger. The accounts of both men and women who have tipped the scales at more than one thousand pounds are now, if not commonplace, at least more frequent than one might imagine. My files reveal two men and three women who have surpassed the half-ton mark. The current record-holder is a woman who has recently appeared on television talk shows. Her weight is estimated at a credibility-straining 1,600 pounds, more than two and a half times the size of Edward Bright.

2. This phrase, as well as the outline of Bright's life, is taken from a document authored by T. Coe, a physician who knew the subject from childhood. It was published in the *Universal Magazine* (London, November 1753), 233–235. This is the primary source for the many accounts of Bright which are given and then repeated over centuries. The unattributed quotes in this monograph are from this article.

The literary genre of "eccentric characters" is fascinating but unexacting in its scholarship. The source of such studies can be traced to the Rev. James Granger (1723–1776), whose *Biographical History of England* (London, 1769, and subsequent editions) was intended to justify and document his remarkable collection of historical portraits. It is to this man we can trace the term *grangerized*, to signify a volume extra-illustrated with prints. It is said that Granger's history caused the market in such images, and volumes containing them, to more than quadruple in value. Although largely unknown at the time the book was published, Granger afterward achieved some notoriety. He dedicated his history to Horace Walpole, and Samuel Johnson found his liberal political views intolerable: "The dog is a whig. I do not like much to see a whig in any dress, but I hate to see one in a parson's gown," said the Doctor. Granger gave a sermon, later published, *An Apology for the Brute Creation, or Abuse of Animals censured.* His concern for animals was taken by his parishioners as defaming the dignity of his pulpit, and it gave rise to the theory that Granger was mad. When he died his collection numbered more than fourteen thousand images.

James Caulfield (1764–1826), an early champion of this literature, was especially interested in Granger's twelfth class of personalities, "remarkable characters." Already an established print seller, Caulfield began collecting and even commissioning these images, and by 1790 was publishing his *Portraits, Memoirs and Characters of Remarkable Persons*, which in 1794–95 was collected as a complete work. He was responsible for various revised editions into the nineteenth century. He also assisted William Granger, no relation to the clergyman, in his compilation *The New, Original, and Complete Wonderful Museum and Magazine Extraordinary*, which was issued in six volumes from 1802 to 1808. According to the *Dictionary of National Biography* (the source of much of this account of Granger and Caulfield), "His knowledge of English history and biography was minute and extensive, while his acquaintance with engraved British portraits was unequaled by any person of his time." He collaborated on many other books of this genre, including, on occasion, those of his former competitors.

Other rich sources of this material include: *Extraordinary Characters of the Nineteenth Century • The Eccentric Mirror • Wonderful and Scientific Museum • Eccentric Biography • Wonderful Characters • Ten Thousand Wonderful Things Comprising Whatever Is Rare, Curious, Eccentric And Extraordinary In All Ages And Nations • English Eccentrics • Fifty Wonderful Portraits • Lives Of Great And Celebrated Characters Of All Ages And Countries Comprising Heroes, Conquerors, Statesmen, Authors, Artists, Extraordinary Humorists, Misers, Mountebanks, Kings And Queens, Jugglers and Other Curiosities of Human Nature • Kirby's Wonderful And Eccentric Museum • The Book Of Wonderful Characters •* and even the recent *Tales of The Weirrd [sic]* with wonderful drawings by Ralph Steadman but, sadly, the same unwillingness to credit sources found in many of the aforenamed predecessors.

3. Engraving (New York, Currier & Ives, n.d.).

4. Playbill (Boston Museum, February 20, 1843).
5. Playbill (Bridgeworth, England, 1839).
6. Undated playbill.
7. *Schausteller Gaukler und Artisten* (Essen, 1980), 51.
8. Hone, *The Everyday Book*, vol. 1 (London, 1838), 1, 195.
9. Undated playbill (see below).

10. There are many brief accounts of Everitt in the literature; this one is taken largely from George Smeeton's *Biographica Curiosa; or, Memoirs of Remarkable Characters of the Reign of George the Third.*

With their Portraits. Collected from the Most Authentic Sources (London, 1820); and Wilson & Caulfield's *The Book of Wonderful Characters: Memoirs and Anecdotes of Remarkable and Eccentric Persons in all Ages and Countries* (London, 1869).
11. Anon., The *Heaviest Man That Ever Existed. The Life Of That Wonderful And Extraordinary Man, The Late Daniel Lambert … And Other Interesting Matter* (Stamford, England, c. 1809), 25.
12. Quoted in Timbs, *English Eccentrics and Eccentricities,* vol. 1 (London, 1866), 276–77.

JAY'S JOURNAL OF ANOMALIES

Written by Ricky Jay and published four times a year by the author and W & V Dailey, Antiquarian Booksellers, 8216 Melrose Avenue, Los Angeles, California, 90046, (213) 658-8515. Subscription $90 per annum. ¶ Printed letterpress by Patrick Reagh using Monotype Ehrhardt with Thorowgood heads on Rives Heavyweight paper. ¶ Designed by Mr. Reagh & Mr. Jay. ¶ The author wishes to thank Susan Green for generous assistance in the preparation of this issue. ¶ Written and illustrative material, © Ricky Jay, 1994. ¶ All images are from the private collection of the author. Any subsequent use of any text or image is permissible only with the express written consent of Mr. Jay.

Detail of a giant child from a nineteenth-century hand-colored
engraving, Les Extrêmes Se Touchent ou, Le Magnétisme Animal.

JAY'S JOURNAL *of*
ANOMALIES

VOLUME ONE, NUMBER THREE   FALL, 1994   PUBLISHED QUARTERLY

The Bonassus: Verbal Deception Deciphered

THE BONASSUS, according to contemporary handbills, had been captured as a six-week-old cub deep in the interior of America. It survived the long journey to the East Coast, the longer sea voyage to England, and the final excursion to central London after its debarkation in Liverpool. It was presented to a populace eager for amusement and edification, whose appetite for curiosities, both animal and human, was insatiable.

Advertisements for the unusual attraction greeted Londoners in March 1821: *A Newly Discovered Animal Comprising the head and eye of the elephant; the horns of the antelope; a long black beard; the hind parts of the lion; the fore-parts of the bison; is cloven footed; has a flowing mane from the shoulder to the fetlock joint; and chews the cud.*

"Take him for all in all, we ne'er shall look upon his like again" – Shakespeare

London Pub^d by G. Humphrey 27 St James's St. June 25 1821.

Using every conceivable method of prevarication, the playbills of the day unabashedly concealed the true identity of this "newly discovered" Bonassus, this "new genus" of the animal kingdom never before seen in England. He was none other than the American buffalo.[1] As for ne'er seeing "his like again," in 1821 the buffalo "was the most numerous hoofed-quadruped on the face of the earth."[2]

The audacity of likening the foreparts of the Bonassus to those of a bison was, if possible, surpassed by an advertisement which announced: *To convince the public of the great difference between the Bonassus and the Buffalo, he has obtained one of the latter, which may be viewed at the same time; though in its nature a very great curiosity, it is only exhibited as a striking contrast betwixt that and the Bonassus to whom it is in no wise related by gender size or habit of feeding.*

To excite the gullibility of the public, the exhibition's presenter, Joseph Earl James, a Birmingham draper turned menagerist, issued a monograph on the capture of the beast complete with anecdotes on its species and behavior. The author was listed as Captain Alfred Spooner, of New Lancaster on the Ohio River, the same intrepid hunter who led the expedition to ensnare the savage Bonassus. A reluctant author, Spooner nevertheless reveals the harrowing—and completely unbelievable—circumstances of the beast's capture. With a party of fifty musket-wielding Indians, Spooner headed west from Fort St. Louis in January 1819. His pamphlet presents gems of mis-, if not dis-, information: rattlesnakes "never attack anyone," the Bonassus "does not generally herd in flocks," and it "never makes the smallest noise, even when most irritated."[3]

After fourteen days' chase, and the death of one Indian by trampling after he had thrown a rope noose around the neck of a large female ("I have never heard of an instance of a Bonassus *full grown* being in anyone's possession," says Spooner), an exhausted young cub was trapped in a pit and fettered. The lassoing of the adult is worthy of note. Says David Mamet, "The American Indians, the greatest Hunters of all time, thought this: while it is praiseworthy to be able to shoot well, it is more deserving of merit to be able to *stalk,* to *sneak up on* the prey."[4] The long journey was made difficult by the intractability of the cub, even more difficult, however, by the circuitous route. The trip, Spooner tells us, straining

our geographic sensibility, began in the Appalachian Mountains, herein located 250 miles west of St. Louis, to end on the Virginia coast some 2,700 miles away. Rich fodder for an aberrant gazetteer.

Joseph Earl James appends some equally counterfactual remarks about the Bonassus to Spooner's narrative: "From his size and power he is classed with the elephant, rhinoceros, and hippopotamus, and his ferocity is truly astonishing: he neither fears nor shuns the attack of the tiger" (making one question once again the animal's Appalachian origin). Only paragraphs later, ferocity is transformed to docility, as the beast will "quietly receive from any hand an apple or pear, while his keen eyes express gratitude for the present made." James concludes that "the great and universal patronage he had received, is the most striking proof of this animal's excellence, whose equal is not found in Europe."

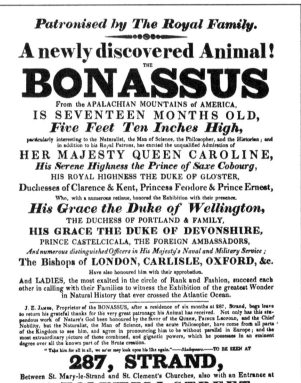

In spite of the dissemblance of the presenter, the Bonassus did enjoy impressive patronage. Playbills listed "his serene Highness, the Prince [Leopold] of Saxe Cobourg (also the dedicatee of the Spooner pamphlet),

His Royal Highness the Duke of Glo'ster, the Duchesses of Clarence & Kent, Prince Feodore and Prince Ernest, the Bishops of London, Carlisle and Oxford, the Duke of Wellington, and Her Majesty Queen Caroline" among the satisfied spectators.[5]

Queen Caroline suffered ignominy from her association with the exhibit when she appeared as the subject of a political caricature entitled *An Old Friend with A New Face or the Baron In Disguise*. This engraving, probably by Theodore Lane, was published by the London printseller Humphrey on June 25, 1821. It featured Caroline kneeling to proffer a kiss to the Bonassus, whose head bears a striking likeness to "Baron" Bartolommeo Bergami, the Queen's unpopular alleged lover. Caroline, already offending high society with her scandalous dress and behavior, added to her disrepute by promoting Bergami, a common courier, to the position of Chamberlain. Beneath the caricature the legend reads:

Altho' Bonassus does not roar,
His fame is widely known,
For no dumb Animal before,
E'er made such noise in Town.[6]

The Duke of Wellington and Lord Stowell, next to Queen Victoria the most prestigious and indefatigable patrons of curious exhibitions of all kinds, both visited the Bonassus. Stowell, slightly more parsimonious than the Duke, refused to attend attractions costing more than one shilling, the exact price of admission in this case ("working people half-price"), which included not only a viewing of the Bonassus but unlimited gazing at a five-legged calf, a dog-destroying male lion, and a Lilliputian ox, among the under-billed supporting cast.

Stowell was unsuspectingly drawn into the web of Joseph Earl James when he appeared for a return visit to the Bonassus: "The keeper very courteously told his lordship that he was welcome to come, gratuitously, as often as he pleased. Within a day or two…there appeared under the bills of the exhibition in conspicuous characters, "under the Patronage of the Right Hon. Lord Stowell."[7]

Not everyone, however, reacted as favorably to "the greatest curiosity that ever crossed the English channel." A distraught neighbor of singular literacy penned the following letter on March 28, 1822:

Gentleman,—I am sorry to trouble you but I Am so Anoyd By next Door Neighbour the Bonassus and with Beasts, that I cannot live in my House—for the stench of the Beast is So Great And their is only A Slight petition Betwixt the houses and the Beast are continually Breaking through into my Different Rooms And I am always loosing my lodgers in Consequence of the Beast first A Monkey made its way in My Bedroom next the Jackall came in to the Yard and this last week the people in My Second Floor have been alarmed in the Dead of the Night by Monkey breaking through into the Closet and are Going to leave in Consequence of this being the thrid lodgers I have lost on account of the Beast and I have been letting my Second Floor at Half the Rent—And those men of Mr. James are Bawling the whole Day Against My Window—and continually taking peoples attention from My Window—And I am quite pestered with Rats and I am Confident they came from the Exebition—And in Short the Ingury and Nuisance is so Great as almost Impossible to Describe But to be so Anoyd By such an Imposter I think is Very Hard—Gentlemen your early inquiry will

oblige your Servant—
T.W.—

N.B. And if I mention anything to Mr. James He ondly Abuses me with the most Uncouth Language.[8]

Perhaps the most revealing contemporary comment on the Bonassus is found in *Real Life in London* (a chronicle of "The Fancy," or sporting crowd, of Regency England) by an imitator of Pierce Egan, who originated the popular genre in his *Life in London*. The book's protagonists, Bob Talleyrand and Tom Dashall, visit the exhibition and, noting the large crowd and long list of noble patrons, announce, "perhaps there are more *Bon asses* than one."[9]

Thomas Frost, nineteenth-century chronicler of variety amusements and author of *Circus Life and Circus Celebrities*, *Lives of the Conjurers*, and *The Old Showmen and The Old London Fairs*, tells of seeing a Bonassus when he was a small boy. Frost viewed the attraction at Croydon fair:

I remember the excitement which was once created amongst the visitors to that fair by [George] Wombwell's announcement that he had on exhibition that most wonderful animal, the bonassus, being the first such specimen which had ever been brought to Europe. As no one had ever seen, heard, or read of such an animal before, the curious flocked in crowds to see the beast which proved to be a very fine specimen of the bison, or the American buffalo.

The Bonassus, implies Frost, so captured the public's imagination that it became part of the epilogue of a Westminster play. The beast was eventually sold to the

Zoological Society and shown in Regent's Park where, already "enfeebled by confinement and disease," it soon died. The Hudson's Bay Company replaced the stellar attraction with a young female that survived for many years.[10]

The ultimate indignity of the deception, however, lay in its cyclical nature. The Bonassus, by all accounts, was presented to a public that had already viewed a buffalo but could be lured into parting with hard-earned coin to see a remarkable amalgam of animal parts designated by an unfamiliar name. How then do we react to the news that seventy years before Queen Caroline heaped affection on the beast, a Bonasus (so spelled) was shown and advertised not only in much the same manner but also on the same street as its successor:

From the Kingdom of the Great Mogul, hunted by the Nabob several days on the Mountains of Bali-sore, and found in the Camp of the Nabob, after he was defeated by the Glorious Col. Clive, and sent to England—There is something in its Structure extremely wonderful—The lower Part of his Head resembles that of a Stag; the Forehead that of a Buffalo, He has Bristles on his Back like a Hog, and is broad on his Back like a Deer. The Horns are situated contrary to any other Animal, and his Tail in some Manner resembles that of a Ho.—In short, it is one of the most extraordinary Animals ever exhibited in this Kingdom."

This Bonasus was shown as part of "The Old Farmer's Collection," at the Talbot Inn in the Strand, in the company of an assortment of monkeys, apes, and sea monsters.[11]

The "not-so-mighty" Bovalapus.

A Verbally Challenging
BESTIARY

Space does not permit a thorough treatment of the history of the use of scientific nomenclature to deceive. Below are a few examples of a phenomenon worthy of further exploration. Among difficult-to-identify animal attractions presented by equivocating exhibitors are the following:

☞ **The Bovalapus.** Advertised as the "Mighty Bovalapus, the rarest, strangest, awfulest of all the mighty monsters of the great deep," this creature was actually a common water buffalo from the Philippines. An 1898 Walter Main playbill characterized the animal as the "Most Monstrous Bovalapus, The Stupendous! The Terrible! Horned, Hoofed, Maned, Hairless." John B. Doris, another entrepreneur, advertised on his Great Inter-Ocean Circus "The Great Egyptian Bovalapus, Positively the Only Living Specimen in Captivity. $50,000 will be paid to anyone duplicating this rare Bovalapus." It was exhibited in "the largest portable tank ever constructed."[12]

☞ **The Woolly Horse.** P. T. Barnum purchased a small horse with "a thick fine hair or wool curling tight to its skin" in 1848. The animal had no mane or hair on its tail, and Barnum believed it to be "a mere freak of nature." When accounts of Col. Frémont's disappearance and subsequent safe discovery filled the press, Barnum capitalized on the topicality of the event by linking his horse to the Colonel's Rocky Mountain Campaign. He advertised "Col. Frémont's Nondescript or Woolly Horse . . . made up of the Elephant, Deer, Horse, Buffalo, Camel and Sheep. [It] bounds twelve or fifteen feet high. Naturalists and old trappers assured Col. Frémont that it was never known previous to his discovery." In spite of protests that the Colonel had never seen or captured the horse, the attraction proved highly successful.[13] Barnum good-naturedly described the imposture in his autobiography, little knowing that he had, in all likelihood, exhibited a rare breed called the "North American curly horse." This story, which came to light almost one hundred years after the showman's demise, is related by A. H. Saxon in "P. T. Barnum's 'Woolly Horse': Truth is Indeed Sometimes Stranger Than Fiction."[14]

By PERMISSION.

Is ſhewn in a

By a COMPANY of ITALIANS,

A COLLECTION of

WILD BEASTS,

From AFRICA.

The LYCAON,

A Great MONSTER of AFRICA.

This extraordinary Animal has the head of a Wolf, the beard of a Goat, the ears of a Horſe, the nails of his fingers are like thoſe of a Tiger, his ſhoulders, breaſt, ſtomach, fingers, wriſts, knees, legs, and the reſt of his body, are like thoſe of a Man; and what is moſt remarkable, his teeth and ſkin are as white as thoſe of a human creature. He is dreſſed, and walks upright like a Man.

ALSO A

Young BEAVER,

Which grunts like a PIG. &c. &c.

From Canada.

Ladies and Gentlemen 1s.—Tradeſmen 6d.—Servants and Children 3d each.

Theſe Curioſities are to be ſeen from NINE in the Morning, till NINE at Night.

The above Curioſities are the greateſt ever ſeen in this kingdom alive.

Gentlemen may be waited on with the above at their own houſes.

☞ **The Lycaon.** Exhibited by a "Company of Italians," probably at Bartholomew Fair in the 1780s, the Lycaon was called a "Great Monster of Africa." One could view the beast as well as a young Beaver from Canada that "grunts like a pig," for one shilling (or less, if one was a tradesman, servant, or child). According to a contemporary playbill:

This extraordinary Animal has the head of a Wolf, the beard of a Goat, the ears of a Horse, the nails of his fingers are like those of a Tiger, his shoulders, breast, stomach, fingers, wrist, knees, legs, and the rest of his body, are like those of a man; and what is most remarkable his teeth and skin are white as those of a human creature. He is dressed and walks upright like a Man.

The *Oxford English Dictionary* does not acknowledge the beast, but describes a Lycopanther as "a fabulous hybrid of a wolf and a panther." One is perhaps tempted

to recall lycanthropic tales of the werewolf, as they bear some similarity to the beast here advertised.[15]

☞ **The Bactaranus.** This was exhibited by the redoubtable Joseph Earl James on the provincial playbills featuring the Bonassus: "It stands nearly nine feet high, is of the most docile nature, and with the size of the Elephant and the strength of the Lion, it combines the agility of the Horse, and the sagacity of the Dog." Only when we are told about the privations of thirst and hunger endured by the animal, and of the two fine humps on his back, do we recognize it as the common camel.[16]

☞ **The Zimbo.** Featured on a playbill issued in Jacksonville, this creature was advertised as "the only one in the United States." Supposedly captured on the "Keane [*sic*] Expedition in the Exquimoux" by Captain Gromes, it was shown for the benefit of "the Ladies of the different Religious Societies" in December 1855.[17]

☞ **The Kaamas.** According to an advertisement in the *Flying Post* of February 6-9, 1703, a male and female of the species had just arrived in London from the "Bear-Bishes." They were billed as "the strangest Creatures that ever was seen alive in Europe; being as tame as a Lamb, having a trunk like an Elephant,…and eyes like a Rhinoceros; Ears with a white Furr around them like a Sable, Neck and Main like Horse and Skin as thick as a Bouffler [buffalo?], a Voice like a Bird," and, wonderfully, "stranger feet than any creature that has ever been seen." My favorite attribute of these beasts, however, was expressed in the menacing phrase "Teeth like a Christian."[18]

☞ **The Cynocephalus.** A fabled race of dog-headed men, as mentioned by John Bulwer in *Anthropometamorphosis: Man Transform'd; or the Artificiall Changling* (London, 1653). The New York Circus of L. B. Lent announced a cynocephalus in 1871, and a "Giant Cynocephalus Monster" was featured on the S. H. Barret circus in 1885, both esoteric billings for what proved to be a baboon in lederhosen. This creature, garbed in Tyrolean dress on the Lent show, was most likely the *papio cynocephalus,* a rather common yellow baboon from East Africa. Also common in the menageries of this period were the guzzerat, coal-black tigers, and horned horses (which were featured in a recent comeback as the widely advertised "living Unicorn," the center-ring main attraction of the Ringling Brothers and Barnum & Bailey

Circus of 1985–86). In a classic example of midway puffery, the Sells-Floto Circus of 1911 advertised "specimens of nearly every animal with the possible exception of a dinosauris and ichtydon of the Eiocenan and Pleocenian periods." Disappointed dinophiles were promised "a herd or two next season."[19] The Christy Brothers Circus in the 1920s presented a biblical spectacle, "Noah and the Ark," which pictured a pterodactyl on one of the cage wagons.[20]

NOTES

1. Richard Altick's *The Shows of London* (Cambridge, Mass., and London, 1978) contains a fascinating account of the beast which whet my Bonassian appetite. *Bison bonassus* is the scientific name for the European buffalo, but it was almost certainly the *Bison bison*, or American buffalo, that was exhibited.
2. Richard Reynolds, conversation with the author, November 17, 1994.
3. Spooner, *The Bonassus, an Interesting Account of this Wonderful, Newly Discovered Animal...Describing the manner he was caught—his Figure—Diet, and numerous extraordinary Qualities, alike pleasing to the Curious, and instructive to the Naturalist, the Philosopher and the Historian* (London, 1821). This work is more appropriate, I believe, to the student of fiction than to the naturalist.
4. *The Bison Newsletter*, Baltimore (November 2, 1990), vol. 2, no. 8 [p. 4]. Revised, December 4, 1994.
5. Playbill, n.d., author's collection.
6. Dorothy George, *Catalogue of Political and Personal Satires* (London, 1952), vol. 10, no. 14192. The legend is from a much longer poetic effusion which, unattributed, graced at least one contemporary playbill (in the author's collection):

> Dark and dear the tempest rages
>   Where BONASSUS *spurns the ground;*
> *High on* APPALACHIAN *ridges*
>   *Lightnings flash, and thunders sound.*
>
> *Wrapt in clouds, in tempests tost,*
>   *Above the reach of human power,*
> *Bonassus reigns, himself an host,*
>   *And glitters in the darken'd hour.*
>
> *O'er regions he directs his way*
>   *Where never human foot hath trod:*
> *Go, reader, view this proud display,*
>   *This wond'rous work of Nature's God.*

The original continues for seventeen more stanzas (*supplied upon request*).

7. John Timbs, *English Eccentrics and Eccentricities* (London, 1866), vol. 1, p. 305; also cited in Altick, *The Shows of London*, pp. 303–5.
8. Quoted in John Timbs, *Romance of London* (London, n.d.), pp. 241–43; also cited in Altick, *The Shows of London*, p. 303.
9. Anon., *Real Life in London* (London, 1821), vol. 1, p. 155.
10. Frost, *Circus Life and Circus Celebrities* (London, 1876), pp. 78–79. Frost is considered somewhat unreliable, and I have seen no corroborating evidence for Wombwell's involvement in the exhibition of the Bonassus. H. J. Bostock's *Menageries, Circuses and Theatres* (New York, 1928) briefly mentions [Joseph] Earl James and his exhibition on the Strand, but there is no mention of the Bonassus. George Daniel, in another classic work of the period, *Merrie England in the Olden Time* (London, 1881), mentions the exhibition of the Bonassus, "whose fascinating powers are most wonderful," and a fictional Bartholomew Fair showman whom he names "Bonassus Bigstick, Esq."
11. Undated playbill, annotated by hand, c. 175?, entitled: "To the Curious in General. There are just arriv'd from most Parts of the World, and now to be seen at the Talbot Inn, in the Strand, The Largest Collection of Living Sea-Monsters and Wild Beasts, That ever were seen in England." Included was a "woman tyger," whom a contemporary viewer to the exhibition pronounced, in a handwritten annotation, "very diverting." Private collection.
12. See Chang Reynolds, "The Bovalapus Brigade," in *Bandwagon*, Columbus, Oh. (November–December, 1963), pp. 4–8. The 1898 Walter Main bill is in the Circus World Museum. The Doris poster is in the collection of the Shelburne Museum.
13. *The Life of P. T. Barnum Written by Himself* (New York [1854]), pp. 349–51.
14. *Bandwagon*, November-December, 1990, pp. 72–73. While Barnum, to my knowledge, never exhibited a Bonassus, buffalo became the subject of another of his deceptions. In 1843 he obtained a herd of these animals from their destitute owner in New Jersey and advertised a free buffalo round-up in Hoboken. He assured the public "no possible danger need be apprehended," as he provided a double railing around the threatening herd. This itself was perfect puffery as some twenty-four thousand attendees watched a tame and enfeebled bunch of calves avoid the lassos of amateur cowboys and Indians. Barnum's take for the "free" attraction, from the sale of ferryboat fares and refreshments, was $3,500 (see *Life of P. T. Barnum*, pp. 352–56). Perhaps the promoter's most famous verbal swindle was the sign posted at his American Museum in New York City. It read, "To the Egress," and capitalized on the public's lack of familiarity with this little-used word for "exit." When customers opened a door to view the unfamiliar "Egress" they soon found themselves on the street, and the Museum was ready to receive a new crowd of paying customers. In carny lingo, Barnum had used semantic subterfuge to "turn the tip."
15. The Lycaon and the beaver, you will be surprised to learn, made housecalls: "gentlemen may be waited on with the above at their own houses." Undated playbill, author's collection.
16. "Bactaranus," from the species Bactrian, or two-humped camel. Playbill (Cheltenham, c. 1824), author's collection.

17. Playbill tipped in the Wyman Scrapbook, International Museum and Library of the Conjuring Arts, Las Vegas. The Grinnell expeditions to the Arctic were headed by Elisha Kent Kane (1820–57). Margaret Fox, one of the founders of modern spiritualism, claimed to be secretly married to Kane.

18. William Ewald, Jr., *Rogues, Royalty, and Reporter* (Boston and Cambridge, 1954), p. 167. Not a scientific term used to deceive, "kaama" was apparently the local (i.e., Hottentot) name for the hartebeest, a South African antelope.

19. Quoted in Chang Reynolds, "The Bovalapus Brigade," p. 4.

20. Fred Dahlinger, the diligent and knowledgeable curator of The Robert L. Parkinson Library and Research Center, Circus World Museum, Baraboo, Wisconsin, writes, "Our search for documentation proved as fruitless as the patron's search for the beast on the show lot. Regardless, I am certain of the presence of the pterodactyl name in the 1920s." Correspondence with the author, November 18, 1994.

Some of the material in this issue was presented in a talk at the Magic Collector's Conference in Chicago, April 1991. Shortly thereafter a Bonassian Society was launched (I am told, with the ceremonial firing of ordnance dormant since the Civil War), in Turkeyville, Michigan, by Robert and Elaine Lund and Dan Waldron. I was, in absentia, designated "leader, guiding light, and undoubted founder," an honor I shall always revere.

ILLUSTRATIONS

Page 17. Bonassus, from playbill of Joseph Earl James [1821].
Page 18. *An Old Friend with A New Face or the Baron In Disguise.* Hand-colored engraving, 1821.
Page 21. Nineteenth-century engraving of water buffalo.
Page 22. Undated playbill of "Wild Beasts," c. 178?
Page 24. Trade card for Van Amburgh, Chas. Reich, & Bros. New Railroad Shows [1885].

JAY'S JOURNAL OF ANOMALIES

Written by Ricky Jay and published four times a year by the author and W & V Dailey, Antiquarian Booksellers, 8216 Melrose Avenue, Los Angeles, California, 90046, (213) 658-8515. Subscription $90 per annum. ¶ Printed letterpress by Patrick Reagh using Monotype Ehrhardt with Thorowgood heads on Rives Heavyweight paper. ¶ Designed by Mr. Reagh & Mr. Jay. ¶ The author wishes to thank Susan Green, Fred Dahlinger, and Richard Reynolds for generous assistance in the preparation of this issue. ¶ Corrections, comments, and emendations to the text are welcome. ¶ Written and illustrative material, © Ricky Jay, 1994. ¶ All images are from the private collection of the author. Any subsequent use of any text or image is permissible only with the express written consent of Mr. Jay.

The Van Amburgh-Reich show of 1885 featured a beast called "Quedah," captured in the Malay Mountains. "NOT AN ELEPHANT," they unabashedly advertised, "but a descendant of the *Prehistoric Monsters or Mammoths* that were contemporaneous with the *Ichthyosaurus and Pterodactyl.*"

JAY'S JOURNAL *of*
ANOMALIES

VOLUME ONE, NUMBER FOUR   WINTER, 1995   PUBLISHED QUARTERLY

Fact & Crucifixion

A S THE LAST CENTURY drew to a close, Tommy Minnock was singing "after the ball is over" to a wildly enthusiastic audience in a Trenton, New Jersey, music hall. Since Mr. Minnock was not known for the exceptional
range or quality of his instrument, and this selection was one of the most popular songs of the 1890s, the event hardly
seems worthy of our attention a hundred years later. I would be remiss, however, if I failed to mention that the singing
was effected while Minnock, in a supposedly hypnotic state, was impaled, hands and legs nailed to a cross, his head
hanging to one side in "similitude of the picture of the crucifixion of Christ."[1] Oblivious both to the pain and his surroundings, the entranced Minnock crooned:

After the ball is over,   *Many a heart is aching,*
After the break of morn,   *If you could read them all;*
After the dancers' leaving,   *Many the hopes that have vanished,*
After the stars are gone.   *After the ball.*[2]

"I am told by those who saw me nailed to the cross that I presented a weird but impressive spectacle," Minnock later wrote, and he continued, "every night during the week, with my hands pierced with nails…I sang this song. As the strains of "After the Ball" rolled out over the great audience the house went wild." Minnock, who worked under the aliases Thomas McDonald, Thomas Grave, and Thomas Eaton, among others, was what was known in the trade as a "horse," a subject who could endure what for normal persons would be unbearable physical pain. He was an important but unheralded and unnamed participant in experiments conducted by more famous showmen.

According to his own account, Minnock was born in Bridgeport, Connecticut, around 1870, and as a youngster traveled to Europe with his father, who was a clown in Dan Rice's circus. His father's death left him stranded in Paris. He soon found employment with Jean-Martin Charcot (1823–93), the famous neurologist, medical experimenter, and hypnotist, also a profound influence on Sigmund Freud. According to Minnock, throughout the next year Charcot systematically inflicted on him a series of tests designed to refine his nervous system, until he learned to control his reflex action and regulate his breathing. "Tom," as he was called, was a remarkable student, and Charcot used him to demonstrate his theories about hypnosis. Minnock could feign catalepsy by greatly reducing his heartbeat, withstand the thumping of his eyeball without flinching, eat vast quantities of cayenne pepper, and suffer a daunting variety of body piercings and penetrations without ill effect. In short, he may have been the perfect hypnotic subject, but Minnock rejected the very concept of hypnosis, claiming he was conscious every moment during these ordeals. He stayed with Charcot until the doctor's death and used money bequeathed to him to return to Bridgeport.[3] He then hired out to various showmen as a "horse," and over the next few years aligned himself with a variety of mentalists, faith healers, and hypnotists such as the charismatic Santenelli, who presented the crucifixion act in New Jersey. Disillusionment and physical deterioration eventually led Minnock to expose his methods to Houdini, Joseph Rinn, and other investigators of the paranormal.

A horse of another color was Evatima Tardo, a woman who had made her reputation through invulner-ability to pain. On stage she was seen to tolerate, without any apparent ill effect, the bites of poisonous snakes that sank their fangs deep into her bare arms.[4] Houdini found her even more impressive than Minnock,[5] and described her as "a woman of exceptional beauty, both of form and feature, …and a fearless enthusiast in her devotion to her art."[6] Tardo was also able to control her circulation, stemming the flow of blood and stopping her heartbeat (for up to six minutes, she claimed), and to resist the adverse effects of many different poisons. She attributed her insensitivity to pain to a cobra bite she had sustained as a child in her native Trinidad (that cobras were not indigenous to that island seems never to have been objected). Although William J. Byrnes, a physician who examined her in Minneapolis in 1897, believed her childhood snake bite strong enough to paralyze her sensory nervous system,[7] Houdini was persuaded that her "immunity was the result of an absolutely empty stomach into which a large quantity of milk was taken shortly after the [snake] wound was inflicted."[8]

Oofty Goofty, a contemporary of Minnock and Tardo, eked out a precarious living in San Francisco by letting bar patrons punch him anywhere, as hard as they could, for a dime; if they paid twenty-five cents they were allowed to strike him with a walking stick, and for fifty cents they were entitled to a mighty whack with a baseball bat that he carried for that singular purpose from bar to bar.[9] The standard disclaimer about performing these stunts at home is hereby invoked. It is probable that these turn-of-the-century "horses" exhibited a now medically accepted congenital insensitivity to pain.

In February 1898, Chicago papers heralded Tardo's invulnerability in advertisements for the Middleton Clark Street Museum: "She Laughs at Death! Poison Proof!! Bitten Hourly By the Most Venomous Snakes!"[10] Accompanying the carnival-like copy was a crude line drawing of Eva with snakes encircling her arms and legs. But in the present context we are more interested to note that during this engagement Miss Tardo was regularly nailed to a cross, to remain so suspended for more than two and one-half hours. Under the aegis of a Professor Cummings—more likely a carnival-talker than an academic—a tree was hauled on stage, and then Tardo exhibited a handful of large horseshoe nails to a physician, George H. Bangs. When no one volunteered to hammer them through Miss Tardo's appendages,

"Dr. Bangs was compelled to do the work of the Roman soldier," explained the account published in the *Chicago Chronicle*. "Before I gave the nails to the doctor I had them steeped in deadly poison," Miss Tardo was quoted as saying, "there wouldn't be any fun unless I had prussic acid on the ends." But she was not only interested in sport: "Out of respect for the tragedy enacted on Calvary, she allowed only her left hand and foot to be pierced. Miss Tardo went through the ordeal without flinching. She laughed, chatted, and sang, declaring she had never passed a more pleasant time in her life." No blood was visible at any time. "This is so easy," she said, "I am going to do it all over again tomorrow night and three nights next week."[11]

While no one would claim that Minnock and Tardo inspired a trend of copycat crucifixions, there were others who followed in their footsteps.[12] In 1927, the bookers of the world-famous Palace Theatre in New York suffered through the audition of an unnamed Egyptian presenting an act called "The Crucifixion." Spikes were hammered through his palms, although "there was no blood. There also was no booking."[13] The 1931 Dreamland Circus Side Show in Coney Island featured "Mortado, the Sensation of Europe. The Only Living Man Captured by Savages and Actually Crucified." According to the impressive bannerline for the show, which featured a large number of freaks and novelty acts, Mortado's performance would constitute "A Realistic Reproduction of the Scene. See Him Nailed to a Tree. The Thrill of All Thrills." All this for one thin dime. Mortado was presented at "No Extra Charge."[14]

Mortado's technique was different from that used by Minnock or Tardo. He had "holes bored through his hands and feet to make it look like he had been crucified. Afterwards, he was forced to keep wooden plugs in the holes to keep them from growing together."[15] Mortado's self-imposed mutilation allowed him to "double" in another act called "The Human Fountain." While he sat in an elaborate specially prepared chair, water was seen to course through his four appendages simultaneously, as he evolved into a human geyser. Mortado soon lost his following, according to Daniel Mannix. "Shortly afterwards," he writes, "I read that a man had been found crucified to a wooden wall of an elevated train station in New York, but when the police investigated, they found it was a fraud; the man had crucified himself. As it is impossible to crucify yourself, I have often wondered if this was Mortado making his last bid for fame."[16]

Although I have been unable to confirm the details of Mortado's demise, history does afford us a report of the suicidal self-crucifixion of Matthew Lovat, a devout, leprosy-stricken, and mentally unbalanced Italian shoemaker. His initial brush with fame was a religious self-dismemberment (he cast the object of his excision into the street below his window) in July 1802. Constant ridicule forced Lovat from his home in the small village of Belluno, and he moved to Venice. Here he tried to impale himself on a cross constructed from his bed, which he had dragged into the street. He was restrained by passers-by just as he was driving a nail into his left foot. After a calmer interlude lasting several years, he succeeded in carrying out his plan. On July 19, 1805, having constructed a wooden apparatus attached to a net, he "proceeded to crown himself with thorns, two or three of which pierced the skin. With a white handkerchief, bound round his loins and thighs, he covered the place, formerly occupied by the parts of which he had deprived himself, leaving the rest of the body bare. Then passing his legs between the net and the cross, seating himself upon it, he took one of the nails destined for his hands and . . . drove it, by striking its head on the floor, until the half of it appeared through the back of the hand." He swung his weight forward until he and the cross were catapulted over the window frame, suspended in full view above the street. A surgeon was quickly summoned, who thwarted the suicide and rescued Lovat. He died in an asylum in April 1806.[17]

Some years later Faith Bacon, the nightclub stripper, appeared in a Billy Rose show performing a piece called "Sign of the Cross," in which she "hung nude from a crucifix and undulated to the strains of Ravel's *Bolero*." As impressive as this must have been, we should note that she was strapped rather than nailed to the large wooden cross. Even so, protesters soon forced her number to be withdrawn.[18] Years later, on September 26, 1956, the unfortunate Bacon committed suicide by jumping from a Chicago hotel window. *Variety*, in reporting the event, called her the "No. 1 Strip of the Gaudy-Bawdy Era." Although a stripper, not a zealot, Bacon had in common with Lovat a cross, a predilection for sharing her gender with the masses, and a dramatic defenestration.

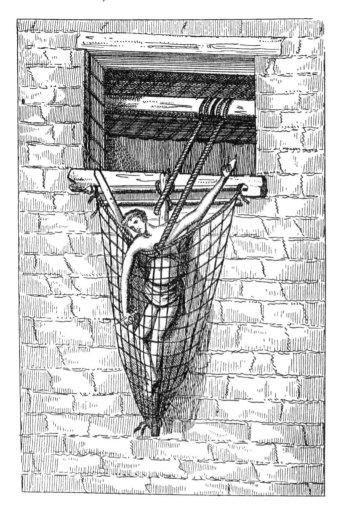

The resourceful Matthew Lovat

Colon, Michigan, is the felicitously named and self-styled "Magic Capital of the World," a dubious distinction based on three factors. From 1926 the town was the summer residence of Harry Blackstone, one of the most famous magicians in the world, and from 1934, the home of the transplanted Australian magician Percy Abbott and the Abbott Magic Company, one of the largest suppliers of conjuring illusions worldwide. Each year since 1935 (except when feuds between Abbott and local residents prevented it), the town has hosted a conclave of amateur and professional prestidigitators known as the Abbott Get-Together. Every August hundreds of enthusiasts descend on the small town to witness perfor-

mances, lectures, and dealer-demonstrations of the latest conjuring paraphernalia. The attendees cram into a high school auditorium (in years past a large tent sufficed) for the public shows featuring performers who run the gamut from hackneyed and intolerable to original and refreshing.[19] In an attempt to add novelty to the proceedings for a largely recidivist audience, the twentieth-anniversary edition of this extravaganza in 1955—held not in Colon but in neighboring Sturgis, Michigan—heralded the exotic South American Chami Kahn. *Tops*, the Abbott's house organ, announced:

Sensational News! After lengthy negotiations, arrangements have been completed to give you the most unusual act to ever appear at a Magic Get-Together. **Sensationalism Is Putting It Mildly!** This will be the first appearance in America of **CHAMI KAHN In a Spectacle of Fakirism.** Plane arrangements have been made to bring this attraction direct to STURGIS, MICH. We cannot go into the details of the act, but according to photos, data and reports, **CHAMI KAHN is a SENSATION!** As you know we comb the highways and byways to bring new acts, new faces to you. This is an American FIRST—An Abbott FIRST. ABBOTT'S 1955 MAGIC GET-TOGETHER **Headline Sensation![20]**

Kahn appeared on the Thursday evening show at Sturgis Auditorium. He was preceded by what was called in the parlance of vaudeville a "mixed bill." In this case the mix was literal. There were three top-notch performers: the affable Bob Lewis, who told homespun anecdotes while simultaneously presenting amusing magical effects or playing the banjo (well enough to be a frequent guest on *The Ed Sullivan Show*); Stanley Jaks, who had moved to America from his native Switzerland after performing his distinctive mentalism and mind-reading for European royalty; and Clarke "The Senator" Crandall, an irreverent and impressive wit who had delighted audiences in many personal appearances and on *The Garry Moore Show*. In contrast, there was Tom Rainey, who performed "Hippity-Hop Rabbits," a mechanical magic effect with wooden rodents, designed to produce squeals from easily amused youngsters; Valentine's Birds, an act with eight trained Australian cockatoos; "Smokini," who chewed up matches and cigarettes and discharged a seemingly endless amount of smoke from his mouth; and a sixteen-year-old girl named Ruth Ann Magee, who produced yet more lit cigarettes (no one seems to have found this peculiar or distasteful). Percy Abbott and family did a spot in which they filled the stage with a profusion of conjured objects, including a flock of live ducks; but my favorite act was an acrobatic turn by the Four Olympia Girls, a quartet of cheerleaders from the local high school (who could now add a most solemn and unusual credit to their permanent records). All this preceded the headliner Chami Kahn, who, no doubt observing the show-business adage that an act should be succinctly described, was nailed to a cross.

The lights were dimmed. Some introductory remarks were made by Percy Abbott: Chami Kahn, he announced, was a spiritual descendant of the Indian fakir tradition, a man who, because of the conviction of his faith, was able to withstand pain unbearable to the average human being. Next, the Rev. Don Bodley of Detroit, who was to lecture the next day on "Scripture magic," explained that the present demonstration had no religious connotations but was rather a demonstration of an ancient form of punishment. (Bodley was a member of a subset of those in attendance devoted to gospel magic, a branch of the art performed by "magi-ministers" who enlivened their pulpit sermons with conjuring object lessons based on biblical themes.) The audience was requested not to applaud.

The curtains then parted to reveal Chami Kahn, a thin, handsome, young Venezuelan. Although he sported a beard in his publicity photographs, he had been asked to shave before the event as his hirsute face was considered too Christlike. He disrobed and approached a massive cross that he mounted with assistance. The cross was elevated to allow for the nailing. Recil Bordner, Abbott's partner in the shop and the Get-Together, handed the long, thin silver spikes to a doctor, who drove them into Chami's hands and feet. Don Bodley, in the words of one spectator, "turned white as a ghost."[21] A reviewer for *Tops* magazine noticed that while Chami "steeled himself each time for the introduction of the spike, there was only a slight flinch as [it] was driven completely through the foot or hand into the wooden cross."[22]

To appreciate what the audience actually perceived as it watched the crucifixion of Chami Kahn in 1955, we need to go both backward and forward in time.

Kahn's performance in Michigan was of course being seen by an audience familiar with a long history of cross-escape illusions. (One such escape [pictured on page 25] was advertised by Ernst Basch in 1866.) Alexander Herrmann, the most heralded magician in America in the 1890s, Harry Houdini, and even Colon's own Harry Blackstone designed presentations in which they freed themselves from bonds that secured them to a cross. Blueprints for the effect were then available through magic emporiums such as Thayer's (who offered the plans for only one dollar).[23] Many of the spectators were anticipating a parody, or a switch of real nails for fake ones, or a secret release on the cross that would allow a surprise ending to take place. Only gradually did the guileless nature of the demonstration become apparent.

Two years later, in 1957, Chami was planning a crucifixion in his native Venezuela. He had received a permit to perform (using his real name, Ernesto Vilcher) in Maracaibo on January 31. After a ten-day fast to prepare for the event, he would be nailed to a cross and then hang suspended for ten days. On January 28 he was interviewed by the press. What, he was asked, was the most dangerous aspect of the test? "When they are hammering the nails through my hands and feet," he replied, apparently untroubled by the obviousness of his answer, and went on, "we Fakirs are ordinary men like everybody else. We only distinguish ourselves to mortal people when we enter the fasting phase and [the] crucifixion." Seven days after Chami mounted the cross, his experiment was terminated by the attending physician, Dr. Pedro Torres y Tovar, who believed his patient in grave danger. Chami, faint and hallucinating by turns, was lowered from the cross. "He did not seem to realize what happened to him, nor was he aware of his surroundings," reported the Maracaibo *Panorama* of February 7 in a front-page story accompanied by three photographs. His right hand and feet bled, and his back showed severe lacerations from his suspension, but "he did not complain or utter any cries of pain." Although he refused to be hospitalized, he was driven by ambulance to a clinic where he received massive doses of penicillin. Daniel Ferro, who identified himself as Chami's best friend, said the fakir, once home, requested a glass of cognac and then a glass of milk. Reporters wondered whether he would like a steak, fried chicken, or a pork chop when he resumed nourishment. In answer, "He smiled his first smile since being pulled down from the cross. 'No, I will just have a piece of buttered toast,' he said."[24] According to Ramon Cobo, the owner of the crucifixion site, "an inflammation of the hands and feet caused the test to be suspended." *Panorama* reported heavy losses for the performance: "The manner in which this spectacular show was presented failed miserably." Kahn regretted the sizable loss of money which the promotion had sustained. "But I am satisfied," he said, "to have broken the world record of 100 hours [on the cross] established in 1940 by the German, Harris, who died in Mexico."[25] Asked if he would repeat the test, Chami, the stricken trooper, said he was considering offers to appear in Hawaii or in a Las Vegas casino. "It depends on the contract they are offering," he concluded sensibly.[26]

In 1962 Chami was residing in Los Angeles, again preparing for a crucifixion. According to *Genii, the International Conjurer's Magazine*, Kahn's spectacular effect was accomplished by "mental control over the pain impulse and over bleeding....rigid self-discipline and self-hypnosis are the explanation, a branch of philosophy not too well known to the Western mind." It has been suggested that Chami's promotion in 1962 may have been arranged in conjunction with Gladys Abbott, who had also moved to Los Angeles, sometime after her husband Percy's death in 1960. Perhaps this seemingly incomprehensible partnership is best understood in light of a rumor that Chami and Gladys had been discovered *in flagrante delicto* by Percy Abbott himself.[27] This is the last report I have been able to locate on Mr. Kahn.

The magic journals of the day were remarkably respectful in their reportage of the 1955 crucifixion in Michigan. Those in attendance that day, however, have personally recounted a mass exodus from the auditorium. According to an old Colon saw, "first the kids, then the women, then the Catholics" departed, leaving only a handful of fun-seekers to witness the conclusion.

The late Robert Parrish, the wry and respected writer on events magical, candidly approached the subject in an unpublished novel. He described his account as "pretty much what took place." In the Parrish scenario, a few distinguished magicians were approached by a young man with a deck of cards, while Chami was on stage:

"For Christ sake," said an interloper, "they're nailing a guy to a cross and you're doing a card trick."

"Have they started?" Fisher said. He ducked under the side of the tent and was astonished to observe that half of the audience had left.

A tremendous wooden cross occupied the center of the stage, propped at a gentle slope against a couple of risers. On it reclined a muscular young man, bare to the waist and wearing brilliant blue satin trousers. His right knee was drawn up almost to his chest, and through the right foot protruded a gleaming silver spike. He lowered the leg slowly until the point of the spike touched the left instep, then he bent down and pushed gently on the spike, forcing it slowly through the lower foot. Then he motioned to a gentleman, ... Fisher, recognized to be a physician of considerable repute as a coin manipulator. The physician stepped forward with a hammer and drove the nail through the pinioned feet into the base of the cross. The entire operation was performed very slowly, to the accompaniment of soft organ music and a steady, quiet exodus of spectators from the tent....

In the wings, Fisher encountered the promoter of the conclave, staring transfixed at the almost deserted house. "This is terrible," he said, "terrible."

"He seems to be doing it very well," Fisher said.

"I didn't know it was going to be like this," the promoter said.

"The guy has no showmanship," said the master of ceremonies. "He needs a trained dove to fly down and light on his head."

"Shut up," said the promoter. "What am I going to do?"

More hammer blows rang out, the organ music stopped, and the man on the cross turned his head and said something in Spanish.

A young man who was serving as interpreter came over to the promoter and said, "He wants to have the cross lifted up and carried down through the audience."

"Close the curtain!" said the promoter. "Get him off of there," he said to the doctor.

When they pulled out the spikes, the blood spurted from each wound like a fountain."[28]

T he printed program for the 1955 Get-Together included the note: "Chami Kahn will appear other nights if announced." Additional performances were not required, but Chami, in a display of versatility, did apparently dress up like an American Indian and participate in yet another display of invulnerability—a new effect manufactured by Abbott's. It consisted of placing a rectangular box on a spectator's head and then penetrating the box, and seemingly the head, with arrows. When the part of the box covering the face was drawn aside, the arrows were visible but the head had apparently vanished. Ponder a discipline which exculpates the penetration of the human head; condones the bifurcation of daintily dressed assistants; underwrites new methods for the amputation of various and sundry appendages; and revels in acts of self-decapitation—yet loses fortitude when the tamest of these tortures turns out to be real.

Most reviewers of the magic press reacted to Kahn's crucifixion with textbook examples of denial.[29] Chami was described in these terms: "A very fine gentleman and a delightful individual to know"; "Another fine fellow was Chami Kahn, who was featured in the Inca tribal rite of Crucifixion"; and "One of the finest chaps ever to appear on a Get-Together show."[30] The noted magician Hen Fetch succinctly summed up this episode, one of the strangest in the annals of conjuring:

...to solemn organ music spikes were driven through Kahn's wrists and feet and he was nailed to the cross. It took about twenty minutes to complete the job.

Back to the showrooms for coffee and buns . . .[31]

NOTES

1. Thomas J. Minnock, "A Fakir's Exposé of Fakirs' Fakes," *The St. Louis Star*, September 4, 1904. Minnock's own articles, a series of four written for the *St. Louis Star,* are the chief source of information on him, and must of course be used with caution.

2. "After the Ball," by Chas. K. Harris, 1892. According to Ian Whitcomb, this song "was the first million seller to be conceived as a million seller, and marketed as a million seller" (*After the Ball* [New York, 1972], pp. 4–5).

3. Minnock's association with Charcot, which would be of great interest to historians of medicine, has not, to my knowledge, been confirmed. Loren Pankratz says that Charcot's will does not mention a legacy to Minnock ("Buried Alive: Digging up a Hoax," unpublished lecture, 1993, p. 7).

4. Occasionally, in a demonstration that might induce apoplexy in today's animal activists as well as the test subjects, some of the venom would be extracted from Tardo's arm and then injected into a rabbit that "would almost instantly go into convulsions and die in agony" (Houdini, *Miracle Mongers and Their Methods* [New York, 1920], p. 178).

5. Joseph Rinn, *Sixty Years of Psychical Research* (New York, 1950), p. 151.

6. Houdini, *Miracle Mongers*, p. 177.

7. Rinn, *Sixty Years*, p. 151.

8. Houdini, *Miracle Mongers*, p. 177.

9. See Herbert Asbury, *The Barbary Coast* (New York, 1933), pp. 133-36: "So far as journalistic or public knowledge went, Oofty Goofty had no other name than this singular appellation." He was so dubbed while enacting the role of a geek in a Market Street freak show, covered in tar to which horse hair tufts were liberally fastened, "lending him a savage and ferocious appearance." As he devoured raw meat he would occasionally rattle the bars of his cage and growl the words, "Oofty goofty! Oofty goofty!"

10. The *Chicago Chronicle*, February 6, 1898, and the *Chicago Journal*, February 7, 1898.

11. The *Chicago Chronicle*, February 11, 1898, p. 1, and the *New York Journal*, of the same date. Rinn quotes only the New York article and adds, "in the same issue…the Rev. R. H. P. Miles denounced Miss Tardo's exhibition in Chicago as blasphemy and a caricature of the crucifixion" (p. 154). I have been unable to locate the Miles article in that newspaper.

For material on religious crucifixion (out of the scope of this article) and the history of crucifixion see Antonio Gallonio, *Tortures & Torments of the Christian Martyrs*, with a special appendix, "On the Physical Death of Jesus" by William D. Edwards (n.p., n.d.). A remarkable account of pain (including resistance to fire, piercings, blows, and actual crucifixion) endured through supposedly religious inspiration is to be found in Eric Dingwall's *Some Human Oddities* (New Hyde Park, N.Y., 1962) in the chapter "The Deacon of Paris."

12. Performance artists, as well as artists working in the more conventional media of paint, sculpture, and photography, have often found crucifixion a viable subject for expression. Only limited space precludes the mention of some intriguing examples.

13. Joe Laurie, Jr., *Vaudeville: From the Honky Tonks to the Palace* (New York, 1953), p. 225.

14. Among the many identifiable sideshow attractions is the magician Al Flosso, "The Coney Island Fakir" (back row fifth from the left). There is speculation that the man with the hat in front of the Nedicks stand is Francis Carlyle, another wonderful conjurer.

15. Daniel P. Mannix, *Freaks: We Who Are Not Like Others* (San Francisco, 1990), pp. 119-20.

16. Ibid., p. 119.

17. This account is from the narrative of Doctor Cesar Ruggieri, published in *Kirby's Wonderful and Eccentric Museum* (London, 1820), vol. 5, pp. 274–87.

18. Stephen Nelson, *Only a Paper Moon: The Theatre of Billy Rose* (Ann Arbor, Mich., 1985), p. 51.

19. The source of much of the material about Abbott's and Colon is an eleven-page pamphlet, *The Magic Capital of the World* by Patrick M. West (Colon, Mich., 1976).

20. *Tops*, August 1955, p. 15.

21. Jim Alfredson, personal communication with the author.

22. Demon Rembrandt, *Tops*, October 1955, p. 10.

23. A half-sheet Erie lithograph announced, in the universal hyperbole-driven language of showmen:

Biggest Necromantic Exposition on Earth • Blackstone Colossal Combination • Greatest Magician The World Has Ever Known • The Epitome of Sensationalism • Burned at the Cross Blackstone falls into the Clutches of a Sinister Crew of Desert Bandits—lashed to a Cross, Stout hempen Cables Drawn by a giant camel and an Arabian Charger threaten to sever the unfortunate conjurer's body in twain, with murderous ingenuity the captors kindle their victim's funeral pyre—and then—

Blackstone was portrayed fastened to a log cross while imps tended the flames with pitchforks and bellows. The actual cross, a crude affair decorated with pseudo–American Indian symbols, bearing no resemblance to the one depicted, as well as the lithograph itself, is housed in the American Museum of Magic in Marshall, Michigan. A more famous Blackstone one-sheet flat by Erie known as "Oriental Nights" pictures the cross vignette on the far right of the poster. Here the cross has been transformed, perhaps by political pressure, into a simple log pillar. Blackstone, by the way, did not attend the 1955 Chami Kahn show because of his long-standing feud with Percy Abbott.

24. *El Universal,* January 29, 1957.

25. According to the September 29, 1943, *Variety,* a man named Harry Von Wieckede had been crucified for twenty-one days but died only four hours after leaving the hospital, where doctors had ordered the gold spikes removed from his hands. A heart attack was believed to be the cause of death. Little was known of the fakir, who was about thirty-five and was reported to be either German or Swiss. He had been crucified three times previously in South and Central America. Perhaps this was the man called "Harris" by Chami Kahn.

26. Contemporary unidentified newspaper clipping.

27. At least four different attendees of the conclave have mentioned this incident to the author in private communication. Also pertinent and peculiar is a letter from Gladys to Phil Calhoun dated September 14, 1955, in which she says: "Chami's act certainly was 'out of this world' and although sensational, we tried to convince him that there is really no market for it. There are so many angles to consider and in the final analysis it accomplishes nothing—and it is extremely dangerous. Whether we accomplished anything remains to be seen as our visits with him were only through an interpreter and thus very unsatisfactory."

28. Letter, and excerpt from the novel sent to the author, April 5, 1993. Another account of the Chami Kahn affair, as told by Frank Garcia to Harry Lorayne, riddled with errors, appears in the September 1978 issue of *Apocalypse.*

29. With the exception of the historian Milbourne Christopher, who had the protection of the *nom de théâtre* of Frank Joglar (*Hugard's Magic Monthly*, September 1955).

30. The first and third of these quotations appear in *Tops*; the second is from Gene Gordon (*Genii*, October 1955).

31. *M_U_M*, October 1955, p. 193. Magic aficionados may enjoy the remainder of the sentence and the subsequent one, "Back to the showroom for coffee and buns, demonstrations and gabfests. I had a card session with Marlo…"

ILLUSTRATIONS

Page 25. Linecut of *Wunderkreuz* from Bosch's *Le Cagliostro*, 1866.
Gatefold. Dreamland Circus Side Show photograph, 1931.
Page 28. Engraving of Matthew Lovat, published by Kirby, 1820.
Page 31. Color tip-in of Chami Kahn by Peter Kuper, 1994.
Page 33. Linecut of Eva Tardo from Chicago newspaper, 1898.

JAY'S JOURNAL OF ANOMALIES

Written by Ricky Jay and published four times a year by the author and W & V Dailey, Antiquarian Booksellers, 8216 Melrose Avenue, Los Angeles, California, 90046, (213)658-8515. Subscription $90 per annum. ¶ Printed letterpress by Patrick Reagh using Monotype Ehrhardt with Thorowgood heads on Rives Heavyweight paper. ¶ Designed by Mr. Reagh & Mr. Jay. ¶ The author wishes to thank Jim Alfredson, Greg Bordner, Jackie Flosso, Karrell Fox, Bob Lund, Ray Massecar, Jay Marshall, Gordon Miller, Loren Pankratz, Marcello Truzzi, Dan Waldron, and Susan Green for generous assistance in the preparation of this issue. ¶ Written and illustrative material, © Ricky Jay, 1995. Color illustration, © Peter Kuper 1994 ¶ All images are from the private collection of the author. Any subsequent use of any text or image is permissible only with the express written consent of Mr. Jay.

JAY'S JOURNAL of
ANOMALIES

VOLUME TWO, NUMBER ONE   SPRING, 1995   PUBLISHED QUARTERLY

The Smallest Show on Earth: or, Parasites for Sore Eyes

"THE EXTRAORDINARY EXHIBITION of the Industrious Fleas" debuted on Broadway in 1834. In contrast to today's multimillion-dollar musical extravaganzas, it was a modest venture in which the stars were unknown, unpaid, and almost unseen. It was no less fraught with disaster, however, than many a modern spectacle, and it closed almost immediately when some of its tiny stars caught cold and died.[1]

The brain of a fair-sized, well-adjusted flea, by my calculation, would weigh in at slightly more than one millionth of a pound—hardly enough to tip the scale; but, as history has shown, the insect is imbued with sufficient rationality to drive a chariot, impersonate Napoleon, or re-enact the siege of Antwerp. Culled from a gathering of playbills, broadsheets, and heralds is this epitome of flea performance: a death-defying dive from the top of a fountain pen, rope dancing, playing whist, riding toboggans, driving a hearse, jumping through hoops, shooting guns, reading newspapers, delivering the mail, fencing, mind reading, panning for gold, and demonstrating jujitsu.

Although the flea circus has become part of American culture, it inspires skepticism in a wide segment of the populace, for whom the mere notion of a trained, costumed insect-actor is incomprehensible. Their disbelief has been encouraged by specific deceptions: showmen have been known to exhibit preserved fleas cleverly affixed to apparatus or, indeed, to present shows with no fleas at all. In these performances, see-saws, carousels, and carriages move as if by flea strength but are actually empowered by subtly controlled mechanisms that drive the apparatus, with nary a live flea in sight. One especially clever such stunt is a high

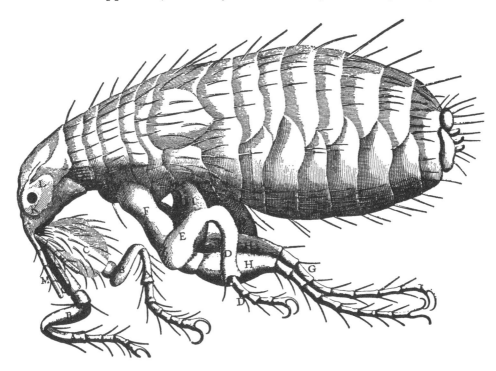

dive into a tank of water, attended by a splash as the imaginary flea-Louganis completes his dive. Not too long ago a British television producer was chagrined to discover that a circus he had with much anticipation transported from Canada to England for the show of a famous magician contained not a single flea. Although there is something deliciously deceptive about a flea circus with no fleas, the elaborate accounts of authentic parasitic performance may prove worthy of your approbation.[2]

Fleas are selected to perform according to natural proclivity, some trainers swearing that they have distinct personalities that allow them to accomplish specific feats in the repertoire. As the life span of these creatures is but a couple of months, a continual process of selection and training is required. When training begins, a hopeful artist is placed in a glass-enclosed tube or dome. Under the light the flea jumps with all his natural strength to the top of the enclosure and hits it with his head. This allows the trainer to analyze the strength of the flea and, more importantly, to introduce the flea to the concept of not jumping, which, to avoid hitting his head, the flea soon embraces with enthusiasm.

It is the harnessing of the flea that requires the greatest skill on the part of the trainer. The fastening of very fine wire around the insect, just enough to control it, not enough to endanger it, is critical. This is a task of such demanding delicacy that the director S. Jacobs, who played Brussels in 1885, offered a reward of five thousand francs, in gold, to any person who could attach a fine silk-thread collar (other trainers preferred to harness their actors with hair-thin gold or copper wires) around the neck of the flea. Jules Lemaître, the French literary and dramatic critic, observed, "it's as difficult to do this as to make double ballads with rich rhymes."[3]

The various acts performed by the insects were imaginatively devised extensions of their natural actions. Two fleas seen dueling with swords, for example, were in fact trying frantically to rid themselves of the tiny weapons affixed to their legs. A flea seen juggling or playing soccer was actually trying to kick away a very light ball coated with a chemical that the flea found repugnant. Getting rid of the ball created the illusion of superb athletic ability.

In the nineteenth century, the grand age of flea exhibition, the critters were advertised as impersonating famous performers: Léotard, who invented the flying trapeze; Antonio Diavolo, the famed acrobat; and Blondin, the first man to cross Niagara Falls on a tightrope. Political figures like Wellington and Kossuth, or literary characters like Don Quixote and Sancho Panza, were also mimicked by the tiny actors. According to promotion materials, hardy specimens of the species were able to pull a small streetcar twelve hundred times their own weight (some accounts say five thousand times, but one hundred fifty is probably accurate), operate a miniature Staten Island Ferry, juggle, waltz, or play musical instruments.

The David Merrick of his day was L. Bertolotto, often called the inventor of the flea circus. His book, *The History of the Flea;…Containing a Programme of the Extraordinary Exhibition of the Educated Fleas Witnessed by The Crowned Heads of Europe* (ca. 1833), considered the Bible in its field, presented amusing anecdotes along with some scientific discussion of the flea. Often reprinted, with some variations of title, the slim volume was successful in keeping Bertolotto's name before the public—and it established his connection with the art of flea exhibition in perpetuity.

According to Bertolotto, the Baroness Rothschild once accused him of presenting only flea-skins filled with tiny machinery. The showman protested, saying, "If I put one on your arm it will bite you." The baroness replied, "You are a great genius, and if you can make them walk, you can make them bite."

Although Bertolotto did enjoy royal patronage and perhaps more fame than any other flea showman, he was not, despite claims to the contrary, the first of his profession. The earliest reference I have so far uncovered concerns Mark Scaliot, a London blacksmith, who in 1578 made for exhibition a gold chain of forty-three links that fastened around the neck of a flea by a minute lock and key said to be easily pulled by the insect.[4] The chain, key, lock, and flea together weighed one and one-half grains. It may have inspired the following lines of verse, attributed to the seventeenth-century poet John Donne:

*One made a golden chain with lock and key
And four and twenty links drawn by a flea,
Which a countess kept in a box kept warm
And fed it daily on a milk-white arm.*[5]

Bertolotto

A sample of such engineering was preserved in that great seventeenth-century repository of curiosities, Tradescant's Museum, which in the catalog of 1656 listed "flea chains of silver and gold with 300 links a piece and yet but an inch long."[6]

Not the least remarkable aspect of flea exhibition was the opportunity it presented for great feats of engineering in small compass. In 1745, Londoners could witness, at Mr. Boverick's clock shop in The Strand, "A Landau, which opens and shuts by springs, hanging on braces, with four persons sitting therein; a crane-neck carriage, the wheels turning on their axles; a coachman's box, &c., of ivory; together with six horses and their furniture; a coachman on the box, a dog between his legs, the reins in one hand, and whip in the other; the footman behind, and a postilion on the leading-horses, in their proper liveries; — all so minute as to be drawn along by a flea. It has been shown to the Royal Society, and several of the nobility and gentry." An ivory four-wheeled chaise drawn by a flea, and "A Flea, chained by a chain of 200 links, with a padlock and key, curiously wrought; the chain and flea, padlock and key, weighing but one-third of a grain," were also on view.[7]

More than twenty years later, on July 20, 1767, a revival of the earlier exhibition was announced to the readers of the *London Gazetteer and New Daily Advertiser*. Shown were the ivory landau, the chaise, "and several other carriages drawn by fleas." Some of these pieces are mentioned with admiration by Mr. Henry Baker, Fellow of the Royal Society, in his book called *The Microscope Made Easy*: "N. B. The above curiosities have been shewn at the Courts of England, France, and Holland, and to the Professors of the Mathematics at Leyden; who have done the maker the honor to give testimonies of their approbation, under their hands, in French and Nether-Dutch; which may be seen by any person that desires it."

Mr. Baker, it should be noted, was not an impartial observer. "The flea," he waxed eloquent, elsewhere, "has two large beautiful black Eyes....Two Things in this Creature deserve our Consideration, to wit, its surprizing Agility, and its prodigious Strength, whereby it is enabled to leap above an hundred times its own Length: as has been proved by Experiments. What vigorous Muscles! what a Springiness of Fibres must here be! and how weak and sluggish, in Proportion to its own Bulk is the Horse, the Camel, or the Elephant, if compared with this puny Insect!"[8]

A Swiss clock maker named Heinrich Degeller used his precision skills to craft fine apparatus for his tiny wards during an exhibition of fleas in Stuttgart in 1812. In 1829 Londoners had the opportunity to observe a pair of fleas, "one drawing a kind of car, and the other a lock and chain, with the greatest of ease." In Nottingham the same year a competing pair of insect entertainers, fastened to gold chains, took to the stage: "one of them drew a carved cherry-stone, and the other a silver cannon."[9]

The fascination with these industrious insects was so extensive on the Continent that Victor Fournel once remarked, "The captive flea was one of the trendy objects of the seventeenth century."[10] Exhibitions were recorded by early naturalists, Lemery (who describes a flea that not only pulled a cannon but also, with military composure, stood unflinching as the ordnance was fired), Mouffet, and Hoock. Louis XIV, the story is told, was treated to a flea exhibition while a boy. When the Dauphin was shown a tiny flea pulling a chariot, he reportedly said to the Prince of Conti, "But my cousin,

DON'T BE SKEPTICAL
SEEING IS BELIEVING

DON'T FAIL TO VISIT

Fighting a Duel

PROF. WILLIAM FRICKE'S

Merry-Go-Round

Original = = Imperial

FLEA CIRCUS

THE ONLY SHOW OF ITS KIND IN THE WORLD

Genuine

European Novelty

Drawing Carriage

Direct from

Hamburg, Germany

300 PERFORMING FLEAS 300
Alive and Living - - - Not Mechanical

Using Only the Genuine European Human Fleas
in Various Performances

Juggling a Ball

Drawing Carriages, Juggling a Ball, Operating a Merry-Go-Round, Presenting Large Pantomime Ballet in Ladies Costume, Operating a Mill, Fighting a Duel, Operating a Swing, Walking a Tight Rope, Jumping Through a Hoop, and other Realistic Feats.

Dancing Ballet

An Exhibition showing what 41 Years of most tedious work has accomplished

EVERY ACT VISIBLE TO THE NAKED EYE!
EVERY FLEA HAS ITS OWN NAME!
THERE IS NO DANGER OF ANY DESERTION IN OUR FLEA FAMILY!

Walking Tight Rope

Riding a Bicycle

Jumping Through a Hoop

WITH the CARNIVAL

who has made the harness, some spider nearby?" Even the French Revolution couldn't kill this art, as a learned flea, it was reported, held the tricolor aloft in 1792. Walckenaër, in his history of insects, says he witnessed at the Bourse in 1825 fleas performing a military exercise of complicated maneuvers with pikes. Later, Hachet-Souplet referred to such exercises as "dreaming." Fleas wore black armbands on their coats at a re-enacted funeral of Napoleon in a nineteenth-century show presented by Ubini; and the newspaper *Temps*, in an issue of September 24, 1875, reported that a flea trainer was performing for a royal audience on the Continent when he noticed the Hercules of his troupe jump on a spectator. "Your highness," he said with embarrassment, "my student has taken refuge on your august person." Good-naturedly, the young princess went to an adjoining chamber and came back delicately holding the flea. With a quick glance at the insect, the trainer shook his head and, with all possible deference, announced that they would have to start over, because "the flea you have brought me is a savage flea."

These early flea exhibitions were a tribute to the craftsmen who constructed the apparatus. With the advent of Bertolotto, the emphasis finally shifts to the trainer of the fleas. He was able to overcome the intractability of the insect without cruelty, not only through the exercise of great patience but also by choosing performers selectively. The showman expressed a distinct gender preference, as he explained in the fifth revised edition of his book (New York, 1876): "The supporters of the women's rights movement will be delighted to know, that my performing troupe all consists of females, as I have found the males utterly worthless, excessively mulish, and altogether disinclined to work."

It was Bertolotto who popularized the flea circus in Europe and America, and competitors (some using pseudonyms as audacious as Bartoletti) tried to cash in on his name and reputation. I am aware of nineteenth- and twentieth-century attractions presented by such flea masters as Schmidt, Wagner, Kitichingman, Testo, Lidusdroph, Likonti, Reinham, Englaca, Ubini, Roloff, Fricke, Ruhl, Jacobs, Günther, Tomlin, and the widow Stenegry. This is a testament either to the popularity of their offerings or to a widespread starvation for diver-

sion. The repertoire of some of these showmen may be gleaned in detail from the accompanying playbills.

Flea shows became familiar enough to be parodied. Robert Ganthony's *Bunkum Entertainments* (London, 1895) suggested a sketch in which a few dots were to be drawn on cardboard to impersonate the fleas: "On this card you will perceive some ten or a dozen students. These I obtained from the orchestra of an east-end music hall (shows card) which I have by dint of enormous patience and assiduity taught a variety of musical instruments; they will now perform the Intermezzo from the opera 'Cavalleria Rusticana,' and I must ask for absolute silence, as it is such a strain on the insects' lungs to play while conversation or other fashionable accompaniment is in progress.... The fleas cannot get up and bow as they are fastened in their seats, but they would have appreciated your applause had you given them any."

FLEA PUBLICITY

Show-business publicists kept their collective tongues in tow while describing supposed flea antics in the attempt to garner press, favorable word-of-mouth, or column inches for their clients. The writer W. Buchanan-Taylor reproduced a classic bill in a memoir called *Shake It Again* (London, 1943):

£10 Reward

Missing

One of the principal performers of a Troupe of FLEA acrobats now appearing at REYNOLDS' EXHIBITION. It appears that his mind has been affected by nervous shock caused by a recent accident while essaying the daring act of Looping the Double Loop on a Motor, and he has lately been suffering from a certain malady* which has affected his naturally lively and energetic temperament, producing severe mental depression, and it is supposed, has caused him (to use a familiar phrase) to "Hop it." When last seen was wearing a gold collar and chain and he answers to the name of "Sunny Jim." The above Reward will be gladly paid to anyone who will restore him to his sorrowing friends.

* Phlebitis.

The May 21, 1927, issue of the Lewiston (Pennsylvania) *Sentinel* ran an article about a star turn in the flea circus of Professor Alexander, part of the "Johnny J. Jones Exposition," which was then appearing:

Gwendolyn is the bright particular star of the flea circus, and after her first performance she decided to add a thrill to her exhibition, and took one flying leap several feet into the air — and disappeared. Alexander was furious — it had taken him several weeks to train Gwendolyn, and she had become a star, but like other temperamental creatures who have suddenly been lifted to fame and fortune, the prima donna had become exceeding hard to control.

The hunt for the flea, although initially unsuccessful, had a happy ending. Considerably later that evening it was found asleep, "something hitherto unheard of in the flea world," on the arm of a woman spectator searched by the professor's wife: "Alexander rushed to the scene and when Gwendolyn looked up at her manager's face and saw the expression of joy upon his countenance, she burst into tears and said, in flea language: 'Mr. Alexander, I'll never leave you again.'"

The unnamed *Sentinel* reporter added with bemused candor, "If it had not been for the fact that 'Bill' Hilliar, Johnny J. Jones' publicity man, had been on the scene, this story in all probability would never have become public."[11]

Similar stories told in the trades are amusing but lack verisimilitude. According to *Variety,* for instance, the star of a small-time dog act died from a virulent attack of flea bites: "The trainer of the dog with the surviving fleas has started a flea circus and latest reports say he is doing better now than he did with the dog act."[12]

According to Bill Ballentine, "The Flea Circus has always enjoyed a good press, for almost every New York reporter and columnist worth his weight in copy paper has touched on Professor Heckler's [the flea master at Hubert's Museum in Times Square] spectacle." Except, he notes, Damon Runyon, who when he found out A. J. Liebling and George Jean Nathan had already turned their attention to the insects of industry, demurred.[13]

Ballentine also relates the story that George Cukor requested a flea for a scene in *Zaza*, starring Claudette Colbert, in which the insect was to insinuate itself in her blouse. Publicists concocted an elaborate story that involved shipping to California a flea trained not to bite.

Orson Welles filmed a flea-circus scene in *Mr. Arkadin*, in which Mischa Auer played the trainer. Fred Allen played Fred Floogle, a flea-circus owner, in *It's in the Bag*, although none of his tiny employees is actually shown. A Swiss feature called *Death of the Flea Circus Director*, starring François Simon, was a popular entry in European film festivals in 1974; and a number of newsreel features showing flea acts were shot by such companies as Gaumont, who produced "The International Flea Circus" at the Goose Fair Wonderland in 1934.

INSTITUTIONS like Barnum's American Museum catered to, and to some extent defined, the eclectic tastes of nineteenth-century patrons eager for knowledge, entertainment, and spectacle. These establishments fathered a more tawdry progeny of dime museums and penny arcades, closer to the carnival sideshow than to a scientific exhibition.

One of the last of these institutions was Hubert's Museum and Flea Circus, situated at Times Square on West Forty-second Street between Eighth Avenue and Broadway. Hubert's opened its doors in the 1920s, moved down the block in 1940, and continued to present live entertainment until 1965. Its presence was not highly lauded by the chroniclers of Broadway. Josh Alan Friedman, who describes it affectionately, still notes that it was "the forerunner of bad taste, signaling to some the downfall of Times Square." Brooks Atkinson at least gave the performing insects a backhanded compliment:

When the culture quotient of 42nd Street began to decline during the thirties the Flea Circus was blamed. It was rated as one step lower than the burlesque houses, which in turn were the poor farm of the theater....By the time 42nd Street had become the most depraved corner of the Broadway district, patrolled day and night by male and female prostitutes, Hubert's Museum was the ranking cultural institution. The trained fleas turned out to be the finest performers on the block.[14]

As a youngster already immersed in the mysteries of sleight of hand and other unusual entertainment, I was attracted to Hubert's, not for the beckoning arcade of pinball and Skee-ball machines, but for the mixed bill of variety entertainment. I saw Congo the Wild Man, Presto the Magician, Sealo the Seal-finned Boy, and Harold Smith ("Creator of Crystal Melodies") on musical glasses. I was initiated into the lore of the flea circus by the "outside talker":

"Ladies and Gentlemen, downstairs you'll meet Professor Roy Heckler's world-famous trained flea circus. Sixteen fleas, six principals and ten understudies, and they will perform six different acts. As act number one a flea will juggle a ball while lying on its back. As act number two, a flea will rotate a tiny miniature merry-go-round. As act number three, three fleas will be placed on chariots and the flea that hops the fastest will, of course, win the race. But the act, ladies and gentlemen, that most people talk about, the one they pay to see, three tiny fleas will be put in costumes and placed upon the ballroom floor and when the music is turned on those fleas will dance. I know that sounds hard to believe, but may I remind you that seeing is believing, and you'll see it all on the inside in Professor Roy Heckler's trained-flea circus."[15]

Professor Heckler, whose father, William, was the doyen of the American flea world and author of the classic tome *Pulicology* (1915), became the sole proprietor of the New York establishment in the 1930s. The elder Heckler's work, much like Bertolotto's pioneering effort, is filled with minutiae about the *Pulex irritans*, or human flea, the only one of the many varieties acceptable for training and exhibition (recently the near extinction of the human flea has necessitated the substitution of dog or cat fleas in the few remaining exhibitions of these insects). Heckler discusses size (approximately one-half grain), strength (it can jump more than three feet), and breeding habits (you don't want to know). As fleas differ considerably from country to country, showmen have argued about the virtues of, say, the Belgian or Russian natives, and a few dedicated impresarios have favored the Polish. Harnessing the flea is a matter of great importance, some trainers advocating a fine gold wire for that purpose. Heckler preferred a special copper wire obtainable only from John Roebling, the designer of the Brooklyn Bridge.

Heckler, the bald-pated, bow-tie-sporting charter member of "The Slow-talkers of America," enunciated every syllable of every word with the same deadpan delivery countless times a day for decades. In 1960,

Open on and after Friday, Dec. 26th, *1851*

THE GREATEST NOVELTY IN LONDON
FOR THE HOLIDAYS, AT
5, LEICESTER SQUARE,
Opposite the Entrance to Wyld's Model of the Earth.

HERR LIDUSDROPH'S

INDUSTRIOUS  RUSSIAN

AND

LEARNED FLEAS,

Whose extraordinary Performances have received the Distinguished Patron-age of the

EMPEROR NICHOLAS.

These surprising little creatures consist of a Troupe of
200 FLEAS OF ALL NATIONS,
who, after the most unwearied perseverance of the Proprietor for **five years,**
have been taught to go through a variety of Performances truly wonderful,
amongst which may be enumerated,

Russian Artillery Firing off Cannon,
STAGE COACH, COACHMAN AND GUARD,
DRAWN BY EIGHT FLEAS.
DOMESTIC FLEAS CARRYING PLATES, &c., &c.
**The Russian Hercules, 5 years old, carries 12 Fleas on
its back. Miniature Derby by 18 Fleas, &c.**

THE PATRIOT KOSSUTH.
Mounted on an Austrian Flee.

ADMISSION, - ONE SHILLING.
Feeding hour at 9 o'clock. **Open from 2 till 10.**
Powerful Microscopes are placed round the Platform.

J. W. PEEL's Steam Machine, 74, New Cut, Lambeth, Nine doors from Cornwall Road

Lenny Bruce, who not surprisingly loved Hubert's and Heckler, visited with his biographer Albert Goldman, who wrote:

The man seems so spaced, so indifferent to whether anyone is listening, you instinctively look to see if he has a malfunctioning hearing aid. "And now here's Napol-ee-on Bon-ee-part dragging his cannon. And here is Brutus pulling a chariot. Brutus is ahead. No, the winner is Napol-ee-on Bon-ee-part."

With his chin right on the table only a foot away from the fleas, Lenny watches barely visible little mites dressed in ballerina costumes, kicking soccer balls, turning carousels, lying in their cotton wool "flea hotel" and feeding greedily off the Professor's arm. . . . He even breaks up when the Professor cracks his one joke: "If a dog were to walk by, I'd lose my act."[16]

It was a sad day when the museum closed its doors for the last time. Now, in this era of splashy imported musicals and colorless revivals, I wish fervently for the flea's reprise. ◉

NOTES

1. George Odell, *Annals of the New York Stage* (New York, 1928), 4:43. The show took place in January at 187 Broadway. Later that year, Odell notes, the fleas were exhibited at P. T. Barnum's American Museum, the advertisement in the *New York Herald* claiming, "these fleas have been taught by a gentleman from Germany, and rendered so docile as to be harnessed to carriages and other vehicles of several times their own weight, which they will draw with as much precision as a cart-horse." Odell, long-suffering in the face of novelty entertainment that diverted attention from his beloved legitimate theater, mentions that Signor Blitz, the conjurer, was appearing at Barnum's at the same time as the fleas and "assuredly did nothing more astonishing than such feats of these tiny prodigies" (pp. 584–85). Bertolotto later showed his fleas at 39 Union Square (undated playbill, author's collection), and an imitator called Bartoletti exhibited at 659 Broadway in March 1859, according to a pair of hand-dated playbills at the Harvard Theater Collection. An uncorroborated case for an earlier show than Bertolotto's of 1834 is suggested by a cutting from the *Baltimore Sun* in a scrapbook kept by John Hill Hewitt, now on loan to the Peale Museum. Under the heading, "A Grandmother's Random Recollections from 1828–1830," the woman, possibly Flora Byrne, describes in some detail attending an exhibit of Industrious Fleas in her hometown around 1830. By contrast, the newest serious American flea impresario is Maria Fernanda Cardoso. She was the subject of an interview by Robert Enright in the Winter 1995 issue of *Border Crossings*.

2. Fleas have also been used to provide the hidden motive power for a spiritualistic illusion. Such an effect was described by Dr. Edward Saint in the *Phoenix* magazine and later used by William Lindsay Gresham in the novel *Nightmare Alley*, but it is outside the purview of this issue. Tom Palmer, in *The Famous Flea Act* (Chicago, 1975), describes a clever production and presentation of a non-flea circus, including the diving flea.

THE GREATEST NOVELTY IN LONDON FOR THE HOLIDAYS, AT 5, LEICESTER SQUARE, Opposite the Entrance to WYLD'S Model of the Earth. Herr LIDUSDROPH'S INDUSTRIOUS AND LEARNED RUSSIAN FLEAS, Whose extraordinary Performances have received the distinguished Patronage of the EMPEROR NICHOLAS. These surprising little creatures consist of a Troup of 200 Fleas of ALL NATIONS, who, after the most unwearied perseverance of the Proprietor for Five Years, have been taught to go through a variety of Performances truly Wonderful, amongst which may be enumerated—Russian Artillery Firing off Cannon, Stage Coach, Coachman and Guard, drawn by 8 Fleas, Domestic Fleas carrying Plates, &c., the Russian Hercules, 5 years old, carries 12 Fleas on its Back. Miniature Derby, by 18 Fleas, &c. The PATRIOT KOSSUTH, mounted on an Austrian Flea. COMPLIMENTARY TICKET TO ADMIT TWO PERSONS on Payment of Sixpence. Feeding Hour at Nine o'clock. Open from Two till Ten. Powerful Microscopes are placed round the Platform.

3. Quoted in Jacques Garnier, *Forains d'Hier & d'Aujourd'hui* (Orleans, France, 1968), p. 73. Jacobs also offered a post-show lecture on the feeding of fleas "with practical applications." He cautiously noted, "The public is guaranteed against any deserters." Playbill, hand-dated July 1885, author's collection.

4. William Howell, *Medulla Historiae Anglicane* (London, 1679), p. 419.

5. Quoted in Brendan Lehane, *The Compleat Flea* (London, 1969), p. 53.

6. *Musaeum Tradescantium* (London, 1656), quoted in Richard Altick, *The Shows of London* (Cambridge, Mass., and London, 1978), pp. 11-12.

7. *Wonders of Nature and Art* (London, Halifax, 1839), pp. 179-80.

8. *The Microscope Made Easy* (London, 1743), pp. 191, 195.

9. Degeller is mentioned in Gerhard Zapff, *Vom Flohzirkus zum Delphinarium* (Berlin, 1877), and quoted in Ruth Malhotra, *Manege*

ORIGINAL IMPERIAL FLEA CIRCUS From Hamburg, Germany PROFESSOR WILHELM FRICKE, DIRECTOR ADMIT ONE WELDON, WILLIAMS & LICK, FT. SMITH, ARK.

Frei (Dortmund, 1979), p. 142. The quotations on London and Nottingham are from *Wonders of Nature and Art*, p. 180.

10. *Le Vieux Paris* (Paris, 1877). This is the source for much of the material in this paragraph. See also Paul Heuze, *La Plaisanteries des Animaux Calculateurs* (Paris, 1928), Pierre Hachet-Souplet, *Les Animaux Savant* (Paris, 1897), and Jacques Garnier, *Forains d'Hier & d'Aujourd'hui*.

11. The publicist mentioned is almost certainly the magician, *Billboard* columnist, and founder of *The Sphinx* magazine, William J. Hilliar.

12. Quoted in John E. Di Meglio, *Vaudeville U.S.A.* (Bowling Green, Oh., 1973), pp. 30–31.

13. Bill Ballentine, *Wild Tigers and Tame Fleas* (New York and Toronto, 1958), p. 254. Ballentine failed to mention another great New York writer, Joseph Mitchell, who described Heckler feeding his fleas in *McSorley's Wonderful Saloon*, reprinted in *Up in the Old Hotel* (New York, 1992), pp. 91–92.

14. Quoted in Josh Alan Friedman, *Tales of Times Square* (New York, 1986), pp. 181–82.

15. I often watched Presto perform impressive coin manipulations while he was in the employ of Louis Tannen, founder of a local magic emporium that continues to this day. The musical glass impresario, I am sorry to report, was not the same Harold Smith whose remarkable collection of conjuring books now resides in the John Hay Library at Brown University. The outside talker was for a time T. A. Waters, the writer and authority on subjects mystical and magical, and sometimes it was Bobby Reynolds, who still operates carnival attractions in the face of ever-changing times.

16. Albert Goldman, *Ladies and Gentlemen, Lenny Bruce!* (New York, 1971); quoted in Friedman, *Tales of Times Square*, p. 183. See also Ballentine's *Wild Tigers and Tame Fleas* for a detailed description of Heckler. Like the flea, material on this subject grows exponentially in the author's archive; he has already addressed the topic in *Learned Pigs & Fireproof Women* (New York, 1986), the April 1989 issue of *Performing Arts*, and will revisit the little buggers again in the future.

ILLUSTRATIONS

Page 35. Engraving of flea from Johann Franz Griendel, *Micrographia nova*, Nuremberg, 1687.

Page 37. Frontispiece from Bertolotto's *History of the Flea*, New York, 1876.

Page 38. Undated playbill of Fricke's *Original-Imperial Flea Circus*.

Page 39. Playbill of Jacobs' *Cirque des Puces*, hand-dated Brussels, 1885.

Page 40. Engraving from Charles Frederick Holder, *A Frozen Dragon*, New York, 1888.

Page 42. Playbill of Lidusdroph's *Russian Fleas*, 1851.

Page 43. Ephemera: tickets of admission for the flea circuses of Lidusdroph and Fricke.

Page 44. Sketch and poem by Shel Silverstein.

I recently mentioned to Shel Silverstein that I was thinking of issuing a wee book on fleas and wondered if he might illustrate the volume. Ever gracious, he overlooked my presumption and remarked that he didn't even know what a flea looked like. He then lifted his pen and, without setting it down again, produced the following:

FOR RICKY

HERE IS A FLEA
IN A DERBY HAT
IT ISN'T TOO TALL
AND IT ISN'T TOO FAT
AND IT ISN'T THE GREATEST FLEA
EVER DONE
BUT IT IS A LOT BETTER
THAN RESEARCHING ONE.

JAY'S JOURNAL OF ANOMALIES
Written by Ricky Jay and published four times a year by the author and W & V Dailey, Antiquarian Booksellers, 8216 Melrose Avenue, Los Angeles, California, 90046, (213) 658-8515. Subscription $90 per annum. ¶ Printed letterpress by Patrick Reagh using Monotype Ehrhardt with Thorowgood heads on Rives Heavyweight paper. ¶ Designed by Mr. Reagh & Mr. Jay. ¶ The author wishes to thank Tim Tobin and Susan Green for generous assistance in the preparation of this issue. ¶ Comments and corrections to the text are welcome. ¶ Written and illustrative material, © Ricky Jay, 1995. ¶ All images are from the private collection of the author. Any subsequent use of text or image is permissible only with the express written consent of Mr. Jay.

JAY'S JOURNAL of
ANOMALIES

VOLUME TWO, NUMBER TWO   SUMMER, 1995   PUBLISHED QUARTERLY

Grinners, Gurners & Grimaciers

IN 1715 A YOUNG BOY was exhibited in London with the words *Deus meus* visible on his right eyeball and the same expression, in Hebrew, on his left. A century later in the same city Catherine Mewis, apparently blind, caused a small stir when her eyes miraculously became functional each Sabbath day. In the sixteenth century the artist Pieter Bruegel and the author Reginald Scot delineated apparatus for nose amputations, a conjuring illusion that would remain popular for hundreds of years. The use of yet another orifice for the pleasure of paying spectators can be traced to a pebble-eater of Prague in the year 1006, and more ambitious ingesters of stones, stoats, swords, and even airplanes (consumed, it might be noted, gradually) have followed his example. A later issue of this journal will explore the refined practice of "dental deception." This issue, however, eschews the particular features of eye, nose, and mouth to embrace the entire facial physiognomy.[1]

Although a serious advocate of specialization, I am willing to admit that on occasion the whole is indeed greater than the sum of its parts. Such was the case with Morimoto, a turn-of-the-century Japanese music hall artist. Although he had a discernible looseness of skin and a few profound wrinkles, nothing in the appearance of this performer presaged the remarkable flexibility of facial musculature that he displayed on stage. H.W. Otto, a leading German circus historian writing under the *nom de théâtre* of Signor Saltarino, described Morimoto's portrayal of the god of wealth, contented and angry by turns: "Bent under the burden of a half-full sack of gold he greedily leered and searched for new treasures in the womb of the earth. With a wooden hammer he knocked at the ground, eagerly, greedily listening to the sound, to determine the appropriate spot to harness wealth from the earth. As often as the sound revealed the location of gold, a broad, contented grin filled his wrinkled face and his eyes became beady and mischievous." When Morimoto portrayed the same god in anger, "The eyes turned trickily, suspiciously. Grooves

or wrinkles of deep disappointment appeared between the eyes at the root of the nose and forehead. His cheeks and chin muscles stretched unbelievably and pulled upward so the tip of the nose was covered by his mouth." Even more remarkable was his impersonation of the hermit god Daruma. Once again Morimoto stretched his lower lip over the tip of his nose, but while his earlier characterization allowed a hint of where the mouth had been, this portrait left not even a trace of that orifice: "The mouth is completely gone....the face gets buried in deep wrinkles, perhaps to portray the enormous abstinence of the hermit or loner god. The expression is completely different...[so] that you cannot see a resemblance to either his actual face or the god of wealth."

Although Otto took pains to attribute the captivating effects of Morimoto's performance to physical skill, he clearly thought the artist inspired: "Morimoto's transformation was effected by the most stunning sequential physiological changes. In each of his characterizations you not only saw a remarkable new face, but you felt a deep expression of the soul, something so powerful, so emotional, that you could not deny him his Art."[2]

Morimoto was a maker of faces—a profession not unlike conjuring in that its exegesis and appreciation is based on amateur rather than professional performance. The art of making faces is an innate human inclination. In those uncomfortable and mercifully rare moments when I have watched adults trying to amuse their progeny, I have invariably been witness to a primitive form of face-making—eye-crossing, grimacing, or the contortion of the lips—to win a child's favor. Charles Darwin was inspired to write *The Expression of Emotions in Man and Animals* (London, 1872) by the visage of his son; and your own mother warned that if you persisted in making a horrible face you would freeze that way— as did the protagonist's face (although for a different reason) in the Ray Russell story and subsequent William Castle film, *Mr. Sardonicus*.[3]

Over its long history, the art of making faces has been practiced by singular characters, distinguished by the slightly varying appellations of *grinners, gurners,* and *grimaciers*. The words *grin, gurn* (the spelling *girn* appears with equal frequency), and *grimace* were in common use in English by the sixteenth century. The tradition of

gurning in Japan is not easy to trace, but in the mid-nineteenth century the renowned artist Hokusai, in a series of cartoon drawings known as "manga," portrayed a half dozen men making funny faces and augmenting their performance with string and chopsticks ("Otona asobi no hyaku menso," or "Adult games making 100 faces"). He also caricatured the god Daruma in two ferocious grins that bear all the markings of a professional gurner ("Daruma no niramekko dai junihen," or "Daruma outstaring game").[4] In the West, professional grinning may have had its origins in the theater, where specific roles called for actors to paint their faces (usually with lees of wine) or to wear masks (as in the *commedia dell'arte* tradition). The gurning competitions in the British Isles or in America's Appalachian region confirm a long history of amateur amusement, as well.

Accounts of specific grinners can be found in seventeenth-century sources. Joseph Clark, the famous "posture master," or contortionist, was as well known for the elasticity of his face as the flexibility of his body. He was immortalized in two portraits by Marcellus Laroon in *The Cryes of the City of London* (1687; see illustration, opposite). His antics were recorded by the diarist John Evelyn in *Numismata*, by Joseph Addison in *The Guardian*, by James Caulfield in his *Memoirs of Remarkable Persons*, and by many later chroniclers of eccentrics. Clark's signature demonstration of his skill drove unsuspecting London tailors to distraction. He would have himself measured for a suit of clothes and return for the fitting having assumed an entirely different aspect. Clark's mastery of his muscles and joints came to the attention of *The Philosophical Transactions* in July 1698. Although a well-proportioned fellow, he could appear successively as "hunch-backed, pot-bellied, or sharp-breasted": "He turns his face into all shapes, so that by himself he acts all the uncouth, demure, odd faces of a quaker's meeting." Caulfield wrote, "This walking tumour puzzled all the workmen about town," and added, "The powers of his face were more extraordinary than the flexibility of his body." In their *Biographical Dictionary of Actors*, Highfill, Burnim, and Langhans relate that Clark's control over his facial muscles was such that he could "make himself unrecognizable" to people he had seen only moments before. They find no record that Clark exhibited his unusual skills for pay, or

indeed of any other employment. Thomas Frost, in *The Old Showmen and the Old London Fairs*, mentions that Clark, the son of a distiller in Shoe Lane, was to study medicine. Apparently he had an unappealing apprenticeship with an apothecary named John Coniers. He trained briefly as a mercer but this profession, too, was unsuitable. In 1678, Frost claims, he accompanied the Duke of Buckingham to Paris and there performed his comic postures. There is considerable disagreement about his demise. Evelyn suggests he died before 1667; Highfill, Burnim, and Langhans propose circa 1696; while Frost states that he passed away at his home in Pall Mall and was buried in the Church of St. Martin-in-the-Fields in 1690.[5]

Under the aegis of the impresario and conjurer David Cornwell (sometimes Cornwall), an attraction called "The Bold Grimace Spaniard" was exhibited in London in 1698. The youngster featured was supposedly a feral, or "wild," child. He had been discovered in the mountains where, it was said, he lived for fifteen years and was "reasonably suppos'd to have been taken out of his cradle an Infant, by some savage Beast, and wonderfully preserv'd." In what must have been a startling series of events for the boy, a group of traveling comedians espied him, perceived him as human, pursued him to his cave dwelling, and captured him in a net. "They found him wonderful in his Nature," and he accompanied the players on their engagements in Spain and Italy, where he was made to display his unusual physiognomy:

He performs the following surprising grimaces, viz., He lolls out his Tongue a foot long, turns his eyes in and out at the same time; contracts his Face as small as an Apple; extends his Mouth six inches, and turns it into the shape of a Bird's Beak, and his eyes like to an Owl's; turns his mouth into the Form of a Hat cock'd up three ways; and also frames it in the manner of a four-square Buckle; licks his Nose with his Tongue, like a Cow; rolls one Eyebrow two inches up, the other two down; changes his face to such an astonishing Degree, as to appear like a Corpse long bury'd. Altho' bred wild so long, yet by traveling with the aforesaid Comedians 18 years, he can sing wonderfully fine, and accompanies his voice with a thorow Bass on the Lute. His former natural Estrangement from human conversation oblig'd *Mr. Cornwell* to bring a Jackanapes over with him for his Companion, in whom he takes great Delight and Satisfaction.[6]

Ned Ward provides an unsavory take on the grinning craze in *The London Spy* (originally issued in parts from 1698 to 1703). On a visit to Bartholomew Fair, Ward had to contend with "the follies of the innumerable throng, whose impatient desires of seeing merry-andrew's grimaces had led them ankle deep into filth and crowded as close as a barrel of figs, or candles in a tallow-chandler's basket, sweating and melting with the heat of their own bodies. The unwholesome fumes of such a crowd mixed with the odoriferous effluvia that arose from the singeing of pigs, and burnt crackling of over-roasted pork, came so warm to our nostrils, that had it not been for the use of fragrant weed, tobacco, we had been in danger of being suffocated."[7]

At almost the same time we note the appearance in Oxford of a man called "Isaac the Grinner." He was, according to Caulfield, an uncomely man with the ability to make his face "still more disgusting," and he set himself up in "the trade of a public grinner." "Isaac," he explains, "was not the original inventor of this elegant art, but he brought it to more perfection than most of his predecessors or…successors."[8]

Scattered references to grinners can be found throughout the eighteenth century, but it is difficult to identify specific grimaciers because their names were often withheld from advertisements and playbills. In 1739 the comedy of *The Royal Chase, or Merlin's Cave* featured "the part of Pierrot played by 'Signor Arthurini,' who had a most surprising talent for grimace, and who, if he performed what the advertisements announced, introduced on this occasion upward of 50 whimsical, sorrowful, comical, Diverting faces."[9]

Mr. Romain, a multi-talented Italian performer—bandleader, violinist, singer, comedian, and theatrical manager—was also known for his droll grimaces. He appeared in London in the 1770s, sometimes on playbills headed by the well-known conjurer Philip Breslaw. For one such engagement at the Exhibition Room in Cockspur Street, Breslaw displayed his experiments with "Glasses, Letters, Cards, Numbers, Dice, Gold Medals, Silver Boxes, Caskets, Machinery, Silver Cup, Apparatus, &c. &c.," while Sieur Romain proffered "A New Comic Song, with Droll Grimaces in large Spectacles and Physicians Wig."[10] This description parallels an account in *Personnages Célèbres dans les Rues de Paris* (Paris, 1811), where J. B. Gouriet recounts "several amusing tableaus" that "dilated in my heart":

Look, see this Italian who hurries to receive me, with haste his peruke becomes all disheveled. It's the Grimacier, he stops, he strikes a pose: you admire his gestures, his poses, gesticulations, exclamations—could I possibly be received by someone more charming. He is in his grand outfit, silk stockings, knee breeches, long brocaded coat, and all of amplitude that proves his magnificence; the chignon of his long blond wig is his parchment purse ornamented with a long ribbon. On his nose are set immense cardboard eyeglasses. On his face large cardboard glasses [that his grimaces articulate]...already commence the movement of a pendulum, twenty shocking grimaces proceed in measure in accompaniment with the sound of his violin, he coughs, he has a hoarse tone, he sings "La belle Bourbonaise," he grimaces.

Gouriet's paean to grimaciers is offered in a Dantesque pastiche comparing the streets of Paris with the Elysian fields, moving from contemporary speculations on facial gymnastics to reflections on heaven and hell. He quotes liberally from a fifteenth-century tract on grinning. Although this work is likely a product of Gouriet's fancy, he cites from it the precepts of the grimacier's art. There are seven aspects that must be mastered:

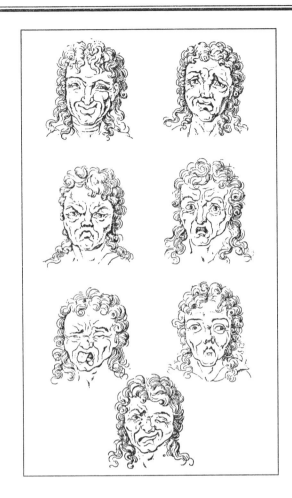

1. **The simple grimace.** Laughing and gracious expression, eyes rounded, features shrunken.
2. **The compound grimace.** Half laughing, half afflicted or even frightened; occasional cries are emitted.
3. **The laborious.** Sullen expression, nose swollen, trembling cheeks.
4. **The sad.** Eyes large and tearful, cheeks puffed out, lips trembling, some moaning.
5. **The boisterous,** or the **gregarious.** Eyes closed, mouth open, tongue protruding; shouts, laughter, and tears.
6. **The silent grimace.** Eyes staring, mouth pouting, cheeks drawn or hollow, a long face.
7. **The complex grimace.** The reunion of all the preceding: an indescribable laugh, a pain that nothing can assuage, cries that come without ceasing. Development of all the preceding methods only employed when the Bourbonaise woman of the song is at her deathbed.

Gouriet recommends caution to neophytes: "use wisely this method....to learn something without teachers and using only books, one risks bad habits."

Sieur Rea, another magician of the period, was like Breslaw a promoter of facial contortionists. At Bartholomew Fair he presented "Astonishing, Wonderful, Surprising and Unparalleled Deceptions and Recreations...To which will be subjoined, the Inimitable Gremaser who will hide his nose in his mouth, will also hold a Shilling between his nose and his chin and a wine glass full of Liquor in the same manner without the assistance of his hands, he challenges any person in the world to exhibit in the same manner."[11]

Philip Astley, the founder of the modern circus and also an occasional performer of conjuring illusions, presented in 1790 "The Famous Grimacier, Just arrived from Paris." According to an advertisement in the *Gazetteer* of July 26, 1790, his "Comic Expression of Countenance is entirely new in this Country, and allowed by the English Noblemen who have seen him in Paris to be the greatest Mimic ever beheld."[12] And for a performance at the Temple of Flora at Westminster Bridge, the *Morning Chronicle* of September 22, 1791, announced "Sig. Valsuani, the celebrated Grimacer, just arrived from Paris, whose inimitable comic expressions of countenance is truly beyond conception, and is allowed by the first Personages in the world to be the greatest Mimic ever beheld." Perhaps the similarity of these two cuttings resolves the identity of an Italian grinner lately arrived from Paris. One now ponders if this is the same grimacier here pictured from the famous "Bon Genre" series of engravings.[13]

Mr. Fitz-James, a well-known ventriloquist of the early nineteenth century, was also distinguished as a grimacier. According to an account from Nicholson's *Journal of Natural Philosophy, Chemistry, and the Arts*, Fitz-James, after an impressive display of his primary talent,

proceeded to show us specimens of his art as a mimic; and here the power he had acquired over the muscles of his face was full as strange as the modulations of his voice....while one side of his face expressed mirth and laughter, the other side appeared to be weeping....as he came from behind [a] screen [these facial expressions], together with the general habits and gait of the individual, totally altered him. In one instance he was tall, thin, and melancholy; and the instant afterwards with no greater interval of time than to pass round behind the screen, he appeared bloated with obesity and staggering with

fullness. The same man another time exhibited a face simple, unaffected, and void of character, and the next moment it was covered in wrinkles expressing slyness, mirth and whim of different descriptions.[14]

In his account of Isaac the Grinner, Caulfield mentions the custom of gurning contests as fairground attractions, particularly those held with the contestants' heads protruding through horse collars, "adding," he writes, "a whimsical frame to an ugly picture." The contestants were "stimulated to excel by the prize of a gold-laced hat, gloves, stockings, garters, or other articles of trifling value." On June 9, 1786, in "burlesque imitation of the Olympic Games," six contestants at the Whit-Tuesday celebration at Hendon, Middlesex, mounted a platform and extended their faces through horse collars. Over their heads was the legend:

> DETUR TETRIORI; OR
> THE UGLIEST GRINNER
> SHALL BE THE WINNER.

Competing for the prize of a gold-laced hat, "Each party grinned five minutes solus, and then all united in a grand chorus of distortion." The outcome, however, was tainted by the accusation that the victor, a vinegar merchant, had abetted his performance by rinsing his mouth with "verjuice."[15]

The dramatically named Framley Steelcroft offered an article entitled "Queer Competitions" in the August 1897 issue of *Strand Magazine*. Almost hidden among basket-carrying, grease-pole climbing, sheep-jointing, and perambulator races was the grinning contest:

Half-a-dozen typical East-end gentleman are seen making frightful grimaces through as many horse collars. The judge—an artist in diabolical leers—guards against undue haste in awarding the prize, which is probably a silver watch. He calls for many demonstrations in the way of facial contortion, awarding marks after every "round." Just before the final grin, the judge sums up, so to speak. He implores the men to brace themselves for a supreme effort, and the gallant fellows respond nobly to the call. The judge is sometimes assisted by five or six competent experts, and this interesting body holds consultations and deliberations with all the gravity of a committee of artists about to purchase a priceless work of art for the nation.

In recent years the flexibility of the face has become an important adjunct to the impersonations by comedians such as Frank Gorshin, David Frye, and, most recently, Jim Carrey. The amateur tradition continues in the gurning contests that are still a part of popular culture in Appalachia.[16] On October 2, 1995, I received a fax from Tracy Schlumpberger of the Minnesota State Fair. In response to my inquiry about gurning, Ms. Schlumpberger noted, "Some of the contests we offer include sugar-cube building, bubble-gum blowing, human bowling…and as we discussed, a children's funniest face competition."

NOTES

1. On the child with *Deus meus* on his eye, see *Coffee-House Keeper. By His Majesty's Authority. At Mr. Powell's Coffee-house, etc. Advertisement respecting a male child* (London, 1715). *A Faithful Account of Catherine Mewis* (Derby, 1810) contains more information on this account of religiously selective blindness. My *Learned Pigs & Fireproof Women* (New York, 1986) has much material on peculiar eaters, and I have undertaken research on nose amputations that will presently find its way into these pages.

2. Signor Saltarino, *Fahrend Volk* (Leipzig, 1895). *The Month at Goodspeed's Book Shop*, a publication of the well-known antiquarian book firm in Boston, featured a short piece on Morimoto that extolled his "tractable features and a fondness for sake" (vol. 1, no. 3, December 1929).

3. In Manila, according to an undated Associated Press story of the Sardonicus genre that appeared in the *Seattle Times* in the 1970s, a twenty-four-year-old carpenter was told a joke so amusing that he laughed until he collapsed, and he was then pronounced dead.

4. Yoshikazu Hayashi, et al., *Hokusai Manga to Shunga* (Tokyo, 1989), pp. 46–47. The renowned artists Utamaro and Thomas Rowlandson also illustrated grimaciers.

5. See Philip H. Highfill, Jr., Kalman A. Burnim, and Edward A. Langhans, *A Biographical Dictionary of Actors*, 16 vols. (Carbondale and Edwardsville, Ill., 1973–93). On Clark, see also *Learned Pigs & Fireproof Women*, p. 39.

6. The story of the Bold Grimace Spaniard is related by John Ashton in *Social Life in the Reign of Queen Anne*, new edition (London, 1897), pp. 209-10. See Henry Morley, *Memoirs of Bartholomew Fair* (London, 1859), pp. 322, 323; Thomas Frost, *The Old Showmen and the Old London Fairs* (London, 1875), pp. 61–62; and Sydney Clark, *The Annals of Conjuring*, serialized in *The Magic Wand* (London, 1924-28), and republished (New York, 1983), p. 57. Frost, whose text is quoted here (there are some variations, probably of transcription), provides the date of 1698. There is extensive material on the subject of feral children, but I can find no reference to the Bold Grimace Spaniard in that literature.

7. Arthur Hayward, ed., *The London Spy* (New York, n.d.), p. 177.

8. *Memoirs of Remarkable Persons* (London, 1820), vol. 1, pp. 115–17.

9. Handwritten notice, 1739, Bartholomew Fair Scrapbook, author's collection. "Arthurini" was probably John Arthur (1708?–72), the actor, inventor of mechanical stage effects, and manager, who was known, often to his detriment, for the flexibility of his face. The critic of *A Letter to a Certain Patentee* (1748) found him an inferior actor who had a "comical Screw of his Face," and the *Theatrical Review* noted that "he had a face adaptable to a variety of ludicrous expressions which made laughter irresistible." Highfill, et al., in *A Biographical Dictionary of Actors,* comment on the pejorative connotation of gurning (similar to the dismissal by some modern stand-up comedians of fellow performers who rely on the use of props to garner laughter).

10. Undated playbill, private collection, c. 1775–77. Romain is briefly discussed in *A Biographical Dictionary of Actors.*

11. Undated playbill, post-1792, private collection. I have seen a fair number of Rea playbills and cuttings dated between 1774 and the early 1790s, but this is the only mention of him as the presenter of the "Gremaser." More recently, the French conjurer Félicien Trewey (1848–1920) was known for his remarkable grinning skills. According to the great Dutch magician Okito, "No one has ever approached him in chapeaugraphy—the art of creating characterizations with the aid of a simple band of felt twisted to form various hats. His facial expressions were so masterly that he was able to create the most astonishing range of impersonations." Quoted in *Okito on Magic,* by Theodore Bamberg with Robert Parrish (Chicago, 1952), p. 28.

12. Caulfield, in his piece on Isaac the Grinner, mentions the appearance of this performer at Astley's Circus in 1790 but identifies him as "an Italian buffoon who appeared under the title of the celebrated grimacier, and distorted his face into thirty different characters, totally dissimilar one with another; the salary of this man was ten pounds a week."

13. Another likeness of this man appears among the many characters in the folding frontispiece, the work of George Cruikshank, to *The Englishman's Mentor. The Picture of the Palais Royal* (London, 1819), but I can find no mention of him in the text.

14. *The Portfolio,* Philadelphia (October, 1809), pp. 315–16.

15. Edward Fillingham King, ed., *Ten Thousand Wonderful Things:*

Comprising Whatever Is Marvelous and Rare, Curious, Eccentric, and Extraordinary in all Ages and Nations (London, n.d.), p. 13.

16. For a number of years "The Tonight Show" featured finalists in gurning competitions. Gary Owens, the announcer of the popular "Laugh-In" program, was briefly involved in a gurning group. A recent publication, *Dear Mr. Ripley* (Boston, Toronto, and New York, 1993), features a number of photographs of accomplished gurners from the files of Robert Ripley's "Believe It Or Not."

ILLUSTRATIONS

JAY'S JOURNAL OF ANOMALIES

Written by Ricky Jay and published four times a year by the author and W & V Dailey, Antiquarian Booksellers, 8216 Melrose Avenue, Los Angeles, California, 90046, (213) 658-8515. Subscription $90 per annum. ¶ Typeset & printed letterpress by Patrick Reagh using Monotype Ehrhardt with Thorowgood heads on Rives Heavyweight paper. ¶ Designed by Mr. Reagh & Mr. Jay. ¶ The author wishes to thank Andrew Cahan, Susan Green, Russ Johanson, John Solt, Angela Freytag, and Tim Tobin for their generous assistance in the preparation of this issue. ¶ Comments and corrections to the text are welcomed. ¶ Written and illustrative material, © Ricky Jay, 1995. ¶ All images are from the private collection of the author. Any subsequent use of text or image is permissible only with the express written consent of Mr. Jay.

JAY'S JOURNAL of
ANOMALIES

VOLUME TWO, NUMBER THREE   FALL, 1995   PUBLISHED QUARTERLY

Isaac Fawkes: Surprizing Dexterity of Hand

IN 1726 A WIDELY CIRCULATED ANNOUNCEMENT proclaimed that the conjurer Isaac Fawkes would take loyal patrons on a journey to the moon. This must have eclipsed what had heretofore been considered his most miraculous illusion—the production of hens' eggs from a small black bag.

The lunar voyage was of course never undertaken. So well known was Fawkes that magical hyperbole was regularly attributed to him in the popular press. His notoriety was enhanced by accounts of his wealth and well doing. His coffers were filled and his praises were sung by gentry and commoners alike. In his own day his success was the benchmark for other performers.

The scarcity of information about Fawkes (sometimes "Fawks," "Fauks," or "Faux"—even his first name, "Isaac," was unknown until Harry Houdini discovered it in 1904) is therefore as remarkable as it is frustrating.[1] Since Edwin Dawes published his important monograph *Isaac Fawkes Fame and Fable*, almost twenty years ago, I have gathered some new data about the great conjurer through contemporary references in newspapers, playbills, and a lone broadside, without being able to answer a number of basic questions. Where was Fawkes born? How did he become interested in conjuring? What was the configuration of his fair booth? His theater? How large was his audience? How long was his show?[2]

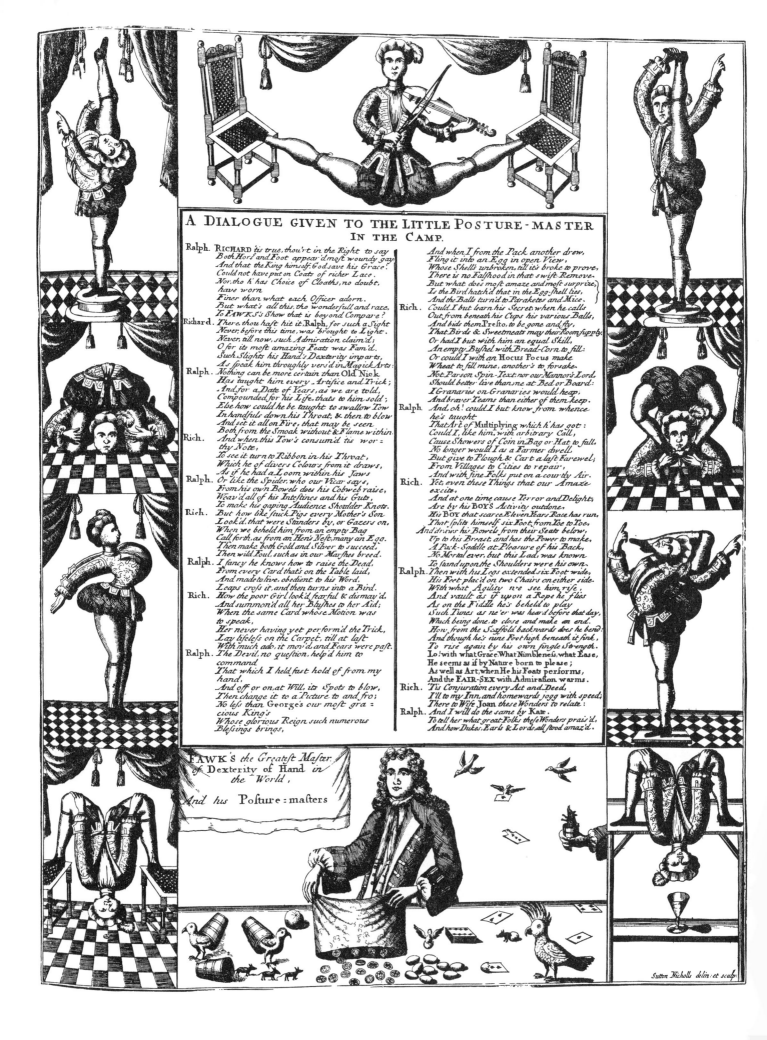

The earliest newspaper account I have seen that mentions Fawkes by name appeared in 1722, and his name comes up frequently from that point forward.[3] As early as 1711, Fawkes may have been the subject of a brief article that appeared in the *Daily Courant* of October 4. At the Duke of Marlborough's Head in Fleet Street was the "famous Posture-Master of Europe, who far exceeds the deceased Posture-Masters Clarke and Higgins.... the Famous English Artist ... turns his Balls into living Birds; and takes an empty Bag, which after being turn'd, trod, and stampt on, produces some hundreds of Eggs, and at last a living Hen." The presentation of sleight of hand in conjunction with the escapades of a contortionist was favored by Fawkes throughout his career, and the magic effects described above are signature pieces from his repertoire.[4]

Numerous references have been made by historians to a portrait of Fawkes by Sutton Nicholls, long thought lost or a bibliographical ghost. Some years ago I discovered it on a broadside at the Huntington Library in San Marino, California. It is uncharacteristically large and elaborately illustrated, and the depiction of Fawkes seems to have inspired all subsequent portraits.[5] The extensive text, although cast in the most conventional doggerel, is a fascinating take on Fawkes's performance. Two supposed spectators recount the details of Fawkes's show, including one effect not mentioned anywhere else, in which he produced large quantities of varicolored ribbon from his mouth, "as if he had a Loom within his Jaws":

A DIALOGUE GIVEN TO THE LITTLE
POSTURE-MASTER IN THE CAMP.

Ralph. RICHARD 'tis true, thou'rt in the right to say
Both Horse and Foot appear'd most woundy gay:
And that the King himself, God save his Grace!
Could not have put on Coats of richer Lace.
Nor, tho h' has Choice of Cloaths, no doubt, have worn
Finer than what each Officer adorn.
But what's all this, tho wonderfull and rare,
To FAWKS's Show that is beyond Compare?

Richard. There, thou hast hit it, *Ralph*, for such a Sight
Never, before this time, was brought to Light.
Never, till now, such Admiration claim'd;
O for its most amazing Feats was Fam'd.
Such Slights his Hand's Dexterity imparts,
As speak him throughly vers'd in Magick Arts:

Ralph. Nothing can be more certain than *Old Nick*
Has taught him every Artifice and Trick;
And, for a Date of Years, as we are told,
Compounded for his Life, thats to him sold;
Else how could he be taught to swallow Tow
In handfuls down his Throat, & then to blow
And set it all on Fire, that may be seen
Both from the Smoak without & Flame within.

Rich. And when this Tow's consum'd 'tis wor = thy Note,
To see it turn to Ribbon in his Throat,
Which he of divers Colours from it draws,
As if he had a Loom within his Jaws

Ralph. Or like the Spider, who our Vicar says,
From his own Bowels does his Cobweb raise,
Weav'd all of his Intestines and his Guts,
To make his gaping Audience Shoulder Knots.

Rich. But how like stuck Pigs every Mother's Son
Look'd, that were Standers by, or Gazers on,
When we beheld him from an empty Bag
Call forth, as from an Hen's Nest, many an Egg.
Then make both Gold and Silver to succeed,
Then wild Foul, such as in our Marshes breed.

Ralph. I fancy he knows how to raise the Dead,
From every Card that's on the Table laid,
And made to live, obedient to his Word,
Leaps cross it, and then turns into a Bird.

Rich. How the poor Girl look'd fearful & dismay'd,
And summon'd all her Blushes to her Aid;
When the same Card whose Motion was to speak,
Her never having yet perform'd the Trick,
Lay lifeless on the Carpet, till at last
With much ado, it mov'd, and Fears were past.

Ralph. The Devil, no question, help'd him to command
That which I held fast hold of from my hand,
And off or on, at Will, its Spots to blow,
Than change it to a Picture to and fro;
No less than *George's* our most gra= cious King's
Whose glorious Reign such numerous Blessings brings,
And when I from the Pack another drew,
Fling it into an Egg in open View,
Whose Shell's unbroken, till it's broke to prove,
There is no Falshood in that swift Remove.
But what does most amaze and most surprize, ⎫
Is the Bird hatch'd that in the Egg-shell lies, ⎬
And the Balls turn'd to Paraketes and Mice. ⎭

Rich. Could I but learn his Secret, when he calls
Out from beneath his Cups his various Balls,
And bids them, *Presto*, to be gone and fly,
That Birds & Sweetmeats may their Room supply.

Or had I but with him an equal Skill,
an empty Bushel with Bread-Corn to fill:
Or could I with an *Hocus Pocus* make
Wheat to fill mine, another's to forsake.
Not Parson Spin-Text, nor our Mannor's Lord,
Should better live than me at Bed or Board:
I Granaries on Granaries would heap,
And braver Teams than either of them keep.

Ralph. And, oh! could I but know from whence
he's taught
That Art of *Multiplying* which h' has got:
Could I, like him, with arbitrary Call,
Cause Showers of Coin in Bag or Hat to fall,
No longer would I as a Farmer dwell,
But give to Plough & Cart a last Farewel;
From Villages to Cities to repair,
And with fine folks put on a courtly Air.

Rich. Yet, even these Things that our Amaze
excite,
And at one time cause Terror and Delight,
Are by his BOY's Activity outdone,
His BOY that scarce Eleven Years Race has run,
That splits himself six Foot from Toe to Toe,
And draws his Bowels from their Seats below,
Up to his Breast, and has the Power to make,
A Pack-Saddle at Pleasure of his Back,
No Mortal ever, but this Lad, was known
To stand upon the Shoulders were his own.

Ralph. Then with his Legs extended six Foot wide,
His Feet plac'd on two Chairs on either side.
With what Agility we see him rise,
And vault as if upon a Rope he flies.
As on the fiddle he's beheld to play
Such Tunes as ne'er was heard before that day,
Which being done, to close and make an end.
How from the Scaffold backwards does he bend:
And though he's nine Foot high beneath it sink,
To rise again by his own single Strength.
Lo! with what Grace, What Nimbleness, what Ease,
He seems as if by Nature born to please;
As well as Art, when he his Feats performs,
And the FAIR-SEX *with Admiration warms.*

Rich. 'Tis Conjuration every Act and Deed,
I'll to my Inn, and homewards jogg with speed;
There to Wife *Joan* these Wonders to relate:

Ralph. And I will do the same by *Kate.*
To tell her what great Folks these Wonders prais'd,
And how Dukes, Earls & Lords, all stood amaz'd.

The thought of these charmed spectators running home to tell their wives about the show is fetching, if slightly incredible.

Tracing Fawkes's early career from other newspaper cuttings, we find him in August 1722 in his booth at Smithfield near Hosier-Lane End at Bartholomew Fair, and in October at the Great Booth at Southwark Fair.[6] Eggs were mysteriously produced from an empty bag; cards thrown in the air became live birds; and live animals appeared on the table. He changed the spots and pictures on cards seemingly by magic. He presented a posture-master, a French boy about eleven years of age who did "one hundred surprizing actions," including many featured on the Sutton Nicholls broadside. By December he was at the foreroom of the French Theatre in the Haymarket. Here he presented "the most surprizing Tricks by Dexterity of Hand, with his Cards, Eggs, Corn, Mice, curious India Birds, and Money." On the bill was the "surprising Activity of body" by "his Little Boy" of twelve (this was likely his own son, who was to succeed him as a conjurer and fairground producer). In broad outline, this was evidently the pattern of his career: he moved from formal fair dates to his own produced shows.

Cuttings from 1723 show that Fawkes rapidly became the toast of all the world, courted by its crowned heads sacred and secular. According to an item hand-dated January 5, 1723, "very strenuous applications are making to him by the Friends of *Rome,* in order to bring him into the bosom of the Church; for his encouragement they offer to make him *Miracle Worker General* but how far he may be Proof against such proposals we are in the Dark to know." On January 19, 1723, a celebrity-laden audience was described in *Mist's Journal,* with a royal command show said to be imminent. Not surprisingly, four days later *Mist's Journal* reported that the prince and several noblemen visited Fawkes at the Haymarket, and "were extremely well pleased with his extraordinary Performance." But Fawkes worked hard for success: in April he appeared at Upper Moorfields doing three shows a day at three, five, and seven o'clock. Houdini claimed that Fawkes became, at a later point in his career, the first two-a-day performer, but he sometimes did as many as six shows a day. A playbill for Fawkes's show at his French Theatre in the Haymarket is the earliest known poster for his show and, indeed, one of the earliest known playbills for any performance of magic (see page 57).

Did Fawkes's repertoire expand to deserve this universal applause? The claim of novelty appeared in some newspapers, but the degree to which he was innovative

By His Majesty's Permission.
(*Note*, That besides their usual Peuformances, the little Posture-Master performs every Night a great many curious · Fancies by Dexterity of Hand before his Master begins, being different from his Master's Tricks.)

IN the FORE-ROOM in the FRENCH THEATRE in the Hay-Market, is to be seen the Famous *FAWKeS's* Dexterity of Hand, together with his little *French* BOY the Posture Master. First, his Dexterity with his Cards: He lays a Pack of Cards on the Table, and while you are earnestly looking on them. he causes them to be alive, and any of them to follow him leaping along the Table, without being near them; he turns the Cards into living Birds flying about the Room; he commands a Card out of any Persons Hand; he blows the Spots of the Cards off or on, and changes them to any Pictures; he causes a Card to jump into an Egg after any Person has drawn it out of the Pack; he conveys living Creatures into any Persons Hand, without their knowing of it; he causes several sorts of living Beasts and Birds to appear upon the Table, no Person shall know how or which way they came. He lays his little Bag upon the Table, and shows you that it is empty; first, He commands a great many Eggs out of it, then several Showers of real Gold and Silver; then you perceive the Bag begin to swell, and several sorts of curious *Indian* Birds run out of it alive, as Cockatoos, Parakeets, Virginia Nightingales, and others, which no Person in *Europe* shows but himself, the Birds alone giving an entire Satisfaction to those that are curious, besides the Performance.

Likewise the surprizing Activity of Body performed by his Boy about Twelve Years of Age. He splits himself six Foot from toe to toe, he draws all the Bowels of his Body up into his breast, and makes a Pack Saddle of his Back, he stands upon his own Shoulders, he makes a Seat of his own Head, and sits as proper upon his Head as any Person can upon a Chair, he contracts his whole Body upon the bottom of a drinking Glass, he folds his Body three or four double like a piece of Cloth, he stands on a Scaffold nine Foot high, and bends backward, till his Body comes below his Feet, and rises again without any help of his hands, he splits himself two Yards betwixt two Chairs, and vaults betwixt the Chairs as if he was upon a slack Rope, with variety of tumbling and dancing, he performs such prodigious Actions, as surpasses Human Faith to believe without Seeing, he gives great Satisfaction to those that are very curious, and for his wonderfull Performance has received great Rewards from most of the Nobility of this Kingdom.

Beginning every Evening at 5 o'Clock, and again at 7. Vivat Rex.

cannot easily be established. In July 1723 Fawkes moved from the French Theatre to the Great Booth in Upper Moorfields, adding a second posture-master, this one only nine, who performed "a great many lofty postures, all different from what his own Boy performs." In August 1723 his repertoire at Bartholomew Fair consisted of "several curious fancies different from what has been performed before, being all entirely new." What these new creations were is not specified. Also on the bill were the little boy of twelve and an exhibition of supposedly novel vaulting and throwing postures on the slack wire.

Many newspaper items proclaimed Fawkes's wealth. A cutting in the Harvard Theatre Collection hand-dated August 1723 dares any of his colleagues to put the sum of seven hundred pounds into the bank, evidently the amount of Fawkes's proceeds from the Bartholomew

and Southwark fairs. And indeed, he had so much money that he no longer required the income from performance. He began to taunt his audience with threats of retirement. In the *London Post* of February 7, 1724, Fawkes made a formal announcement that he would retire at the end of the season. A physical problem, a "Mortification in one of his Legs," is mentioned on February 18, but neither death nor retirement eventuated, as he was performing once more at Queen Anne's Tavern in September of that year.

In July 1724, *Mist's Journal* noted his plans to leave London for Bristol (then the second-largest city in England but only one-seventeenth the size of the capital). This notice is the first I have seen of Fawkes's use of a viewing machine, an apparatus that became a feature of his shows: "he has lately, for the greater Diversion of the Publick, purchas'd a most curious and amazing Machine, in which is heard a fine Consort of Music on various Instruments, as the Organ, Bass-Viol, Trumpet, French Horn, and all other Wind Music. With a fine moving Picture, shewing the proper Motions of each Person performing on the several instruments."[7] This device was said to be capable not only of charming kings and princes but also of inducing patrons of all ranks to feel that they had safely traveled a long distance, without leaving the spot.

> Here Roger may come, without Danger or Fear,
> And the lofty Gibralter both view and draw near;
> Nor need Cicely, his Darling, e'er doubt but he'll be
> As safe as tho' clasp'd on the Arms of dear she
> Therefore all bie away to the fam'd Bristol Fair,
> And the conjuring Fawkes you'll be sure to find there.

An item from *Mist's Journal* of December 25 announced Fawkes's partnership with Martin Powell, the famous puppet showman, who was to combine his figures and machines and exhibit with Fawkes at the Old Tennis Court, "where any credulous persons may be satisfied he is not left this World, if they please to believe their Hands, though they can't believe their Eyes." At about this time, Fawkes's name was invoked in what may be the first reference in print to the most familiar motto of magic, "The hand is quicker than the eye." The anonymous author of *The Whole Art and Mystery of Modern Gaming* (1726) noted that "when you first saw the famous Fawkes perform his Dexterity of Hand, I doubt not but it appear'd wonderful, that a Man's

Actions should be quicker than your Eyes, and yet…you will soon become Master of these seeming Mysteries" (p. 46). In January 1726, Powell and Fawkes presented their combined attraction, "Concluding with an extraordinary Piece of Machinery, after the Italian Manner, representing the splendid Palace of Diana; breaking into Double and Triple Prospects with all the Changes of Scenes and Decorations belonging to the Play."[8]

Whether or not Fawkes actually performed in Bristol I am unable to say, but by August he was at his familiar site at Bartholomew Fair. He presented his posture-master, sleight of hand, a musical clock, and, in a significant departure, "a Miracle in Nature, being a Woman with a Horn on the back part of her Head ten Inches long; who is allow'd by Sir Hans Sloan[e] and the Royal Society, to be a surprizing Curiosity.…We show the Woman with the Horn and the Musical Clock all Day without loss of Time.…At 6 & 8 all four were shown, with ladies and gentleman, as usual, given a private show with one hour's notice."[9]

The "Horned Woman" was Elizabeth French, one of a select but hardly unique group of citizens sporting an excrescence (in her case excrescences) described, particularly by the showmen exhibiting such persons, as a horn. French was witnessed and chronicled by James Paris du Plessis in his wonderful manuscript on anomalies, *A Short History of Human Prodigies and Monstrous Births, of Dwarfs, Sleepers, Giants, Strong Men, Hermaphrodites, Numerous Births and Extreme Old Age:* "She was born at Tenderden, in the Weald of Kent: she had growing at the back part of her head, a horn 10 inches long, and solid, form'd and coloured like a ram's horn of a yellowish colour something like a roll of ising-glass, as hard as any horn whatsoever; it grows out of a bunch like a 'Ven' about the bigness of a common walnut; she has several like bunches on her head, which is thought will produce in time such like horns upon each of them. It is to be observed, that the said horn is not fastened to the skull as it is with beasts, but moveth to and about by them that touch it, and when it is touched a little violently she suffers pain: the bunches on the other part of the head are five or six in number." Plessis then explains: "The famous Mr. Fauks, hired her for a certain number of years for a great sum of money, which he paid her before hand: but a little while after, she accidentally fell down one pair of stairs, and broke her horn off her head,

which horn is said to have been bought by Sir Hans Sloane, Doctor of Physic and Physician in Ordinary to his British Majesty George the Second."

Not only the horn but the manuscript as well were acquired by the insatiable Sloane, founder of the Royal Society and the British Museum (where the manuscript now reposes: Sloane MS. 5246; p. 101). The purchase, for one guinea, was consummated when Plessis, once the servant of Samuel Pepys, became destitute in old age. The exhibition of French was in a time-honored tradition in which conjurers presented other novel attractions, often with less than satisfying results.[10]

Fawkes's fame was neither achieved nor manipulated only by self-promotion. So quintessentially associated with the theater was he that his persona was invoked by other artists; he became a sort of character indispensable in visual and verbal portraits of the world of the theater. In the depiction of Burlington Gate in Hogarth's *Masquerades and Operas* (1724), the engraving shows the "Long room. Fawk's dexterity of hand." In one state of the print are verses suggesting that

Fawkes, if he did not satisfy the standards of all reviewers, had become the benchmark for popular success:

> O how refin'd how elegant we're grown!
> What noble Entertainments Charm the Town!
> Whether to hear the Dragon's roar we go.
> Or gaze surpriz'd on Fawk's matchless Show.

Fawkes was invoked in this manner even after his death. He was featured (or perhaps it was his son) in Hogarth's famous engraving of Southwark Fair, published in 1734.[11]

In *The British Stage; or, the Exploits of Harlequin: a Farce*, performed in London in 1724, the character of Punch enters with some puppets: "What pity 'tis I must quit my acting Station, and that the glorious Hero should be the Droll of a Puppet-Shew?—But so it is, and I've been a whole half Year in learning to dance and cut capers; I can jig it with a *Shaw* or a *Thurmond*, dance upon my Hands, and play a Violin standing on my Head: For I find there's nothing to be done without a Dance and a Posture; and if we don't excel the immortal *Fawks*, we are ruin'd and undone."[12] So pleased was Fawkes by this comparison to the Patent theaters of Lincolns Inn Fields and Drury Lane that he referred to it in his own advertising in *Mist's Journal*.

Inevitably, some allusions to Fawkes were pejorative, but these too reveal the extent of Fawkes's reputation.[13] In 1728, his feats were dismissed, along with performers having too few limbs and cows having too many, as "mere bagatelles."[14] Thomas Woolston, in a *Fifth Discourse on the Miracles of our Savior*, was careful to distinguish the magical from the miraculous, and it was Fawkes who stood for all of the unscrupulous purveyors of the former, who fool "the ignorant and the credulous, whom a much less Juggler than Mr. Fawkes could have easily impos'd on."[15]

On May 2, 1726, a startling announcement appeared in a paper called *The Country Gentleman*:

ADVERTISEMENT.
The famous Planetarian Caravan, which I spoke of before, being now entirely finish'd and render'd convenient for all such Persons, who have any desire to visit the Moon, Venus, Mercury, or any other of the Planets, is remov'd from Mr. Deard's Toy-shop in Fleet-Street, to Mr. Fawkes's great Booth in the Tennis-Court, near the Hay-Market; where Passengers may be accommodated with every Thing proper for so long a Journey. This Machine sets out from thence to the Moon very soon (only waiting at present to introduce the famous Faustina, who is to make her Entry into the Opera, at the Roof of the Theatre, over the Heads of all the rest of the Singers.)

Any Person who intends to go this Way, or send any of their Friends, must send their Names before the first Day of June next, and likewise must deposite their Earnest-Money, in the Hands of the said Mr. Fawkes, which being one Half of the fare to the Moon, will come to a Hundred and Twenty-five Pounds. The Machinist contents himself with this moderate rate Price, (being only one Farthing a Mile) purely to serve his Country, and facilitate the Means of Transportation, having long observ'd, how useful this Project has been to the Inhabitants of this Island.

In the same Place also, may be seen the Planetary Carricule, which is a Vehicle prepar'd only for two Persons, being a lighter Carriage, and very fit for a Couple of Lovers, who have a Mind to spend their Honey-Moon in Venus, and perhaps should take a Fancy to come back again in Haste.

Apparently not a description of any scheme originated by Fawkes, this piece of social satire was representative of a genre involving moon travel. This example was composed by one Erasmus Philipps, who in 1726 began a series of political and social reflections called *The Country Gentleman;* it appeared in eighty-four issues. These pieces reappeared in various other papers, including the *Edinburgh Evening Courant* of August 23 to 25, 1726, and the collected papers were reissued early in the 1750s in *Miscellaneous Works, consisting of Essays Political and Moral.*[16]

On August 5, 1727, according to a hand-dated cutting, Fawkes was to perform at Bartholomew Fair with "The Temple of the Arts and the two Moving Pictures." The advertisement states: "This wonderful Machine was invented and is but just Finish'd by Mr. Pinchbeck, Musical Clock-maker in Fleet street; the Landskip [i.e., landscape] and Figures by Mr. Joshua Ross and the Sea and Shipping by Mr. Peter Monamy."[17]

Fawkes also announced in 1727 a benefit performance for William Phillips, the famous posture-master: "And besides their usual Performances, Mr. Fawkes and Mr. Phillips will perform several Curiosities never shewn in London before. According to W. R. Chetwood, Phillips, born in 1699, "was taught tumbling and sleight-of-hand 'by that great Master of Art, the stupendous Mr. Faux' but he outdid his master in some tricks."[18] Remarkably, this Phillips is the same character prevalent in the Bottle Conjurer hoax. In 1749 it was announced that an unnamed magician would for an undisclosed sum insinuate himself in a quart bottle on the stage of the

Haymarket Theatre. The venue was filled to capacity with high-paying customers who waited for a long time before some wag, realizing that the performer would not be forthcoming, yelled that he would, for twice the price, enter a pint bottle. The spectators rioted and damaged the theater substantially. It was Phillips who spoofed the bottle conjurer on stage in the productions of *The Royal Chase* and *Apollo and Daphne* in 1749, and he is the subject of the most famous representation of this episode, the harlequin in the funnel in the print *An Apology to the Town, for HIMSELF and the BOTTLE* (London, 1749).[19]

The audiences at Fawkes's Theatre in James Street saw in 1727 "several Curiosities of the Kind entirely New. In particular, he throws the Cards up, and causes any of them to stick against the Ceiling, and the rest to fall down. Likewise he causes the whole Pack to stick to the Ceiling, and calls them down by their Names one by one." This effect became a staple of Fawkes's repertoire and was one way in which he daunted foreign nobility, including a visiting court of Indian princes in 1730. On September 30 of that year the *Gloucester Journal* reported their visit to Fawkes's booth at Smithfield. Praising his sleight of hand, and particularly the effect where the conjurer made playing cards animate by command, "The King and Prince declared, that they had never yet been so agreeably diverted, and desired to see it over again: but, above all they were surprized at the calling of the cards down one by one; and when the King had viewed one of the cards, and saw nothing fastened to it, he was amazed: and all of them went away with a generous acknowledgment of the pleasure they had received."

He also presented at Fawkes's Theatre a puppet play called *The False Lover; or, The Bachelor's Last Shift*, and a "curious Piece of Machinery, representing King George with the most illustrious House of Lords as they sit in Parliament." The viewing machine was later expanded in its scope from Parliament to the entire globe of earth. In December of 1729, with business as usual, the *Journal* reported that Fawkes was concerned with a new machine: "We are credibly inform'd that the curious Piece of Workmanship brought from High Germany, call'd the Artificial View of the World, which for a few Weeks was shown at Fawkes's Theatre in James-street

near the Haymarket and gave great Satisfaction, is now purchased by Mr. Fawkes, and large Amendments made to the Work." In addition to sleight of hand and the customary posture-master, this new machine was shown at his theater near the Haymarket in January of 1730. It was not quite a voyage to the moon, but the perspective was cosmic:

The Artificial View of the World. In this curious Piece is seen the FIRMAMENT spangled with a multitude of STARS: the Moon's Increase and Decrease; the Dawn of DAY; the SUN diffusing his Light at his Rising, the beautiful Redness of the Horizon at his Setting, as in a fine Summer's Evening.

The OCEAN is also represented with Ships under Sail, as tho' at several Miles Distance, others so near that their Shadow is seen in the Water; and as they pass by any Fort, Castle, or fortified Town, they salute each other with their GUNS, the Report and Echo of which is as plainly heard as tho' from the real Places they appear to be.

This performance offered views of Windsor Castle, Gibraltar, the City of Stralsun[d] in Pomerania, and Venice. In subsequent weeks one could see Cairo, Algiers, Oxford, Hamburg, and London.

As his fame grew Fawkes continued performing on his regular circuit. A representative program from about 1729 appears on the back cover of this issue.

Fawkes's success spawned unscrupulous emulators, or so it was given out in the popular press. On May 10, 1729, *Fog's Journal* reported: "We hear that last Week, a foreign Gentleman, who went to see Mr. Fawkes, was so vastly delighted with his Performances, that he offer'd him 400 Guineas for his Musical Clock, or 600 for his Venetian Machine; but Mr. Fawkes not being willing to part with those curious Pieces, the said Gentleman proposed to give 1000 £ to go abroad with him one Year, to show his Dexterity of Hand along with those Machines, to which Mr. Fawkes has agreed." This also allowed Fawkes to suggest that his English audiences had been disloyal of late: "We have so many *Tricksters* besides him, that his Country may spare him for a little Time." By June, however, the relationship had been severed, and *Fog's Journal* reported that his foreign hosts "only wanted to learn his mysterious Art, and (as the Phrase has it) *Bite the Old-one*: And having likewise some Staggering in his Faith, whether he should find the whole Sum agreed for the same Stamp and Standard at the Earnest; he has left them to conjure by themselves, and play the

D-v-l in their own Country Way; and has now taken a fair Leap from the *Old-Tennis Court* into *Moor Fields*, where he will, for a short time, continue to divert and surprize People of all Degrees from the Highest to the Lowest; being resolv'd still to remain his own Master."

On December 30, 1730, the *Daily Post* announced an important addition to the magician's repertoire: "First, His diverting and Incomparable Dexterity of Hand, in which he performs several Things entirely new. N. B. In particular he causes a Tree to grow up in a Flower-Pot upon a Table, which will blow and bear ripe Fruit in a Minute's Time." This was the first notice of a magical effect that was to capture the attention of conjurers and their audiences until the present day.[20] In February of 1731 both the *Gentleman's Magazine* and *The Craftsman* mentioned Fawkes performing his miraculous new illusion for the Algerian ambassador and his entourage. Appropriately, for this show he presented a prospect of the city of Algiers, but it was the fruit trees, bearing ripe apples in less than a minute's time, that caused the greatest sensation. So dumbstruck were they, it was reported, that "none of the Algerines would touch any Thing belonging to Mr. Fawkes." Despite this demur, the ambassador gave Fawkes's little posture-master a piece of gold.

Although there was no mention of any illness in the press, on May 25, 1731, Fawkes died. A clipping from May 28 notes, "he had honestly acquired a fortune of above ten thousand pounds, being no more than he honestly deserved for his great ingenuity, by which he surpassed all that ever pretended to that art."[21] He was interred in St. Martin's Church "in a very handsome manner," according to *Fog's Journal*, on May 29. The *Gazetteer* of June 3 and the *Gentleman's Magazine* also mentioned the figure of £10,000 as Fawkes's net worth.[22] On June 5 *Fog's Journal* published the following:

> Epitaph on the famous Mr. Fawkes
> Two strove each other to outvie,
> Both dext'rous to deceive the Eye;
> *Fawkes* was *the only Man i'th' World*,
> But on his Back the Man is hurl'd;
> Old Raw-bones envy'd, and in Rage,
> Unseen, he tripp'd him off the Stage.
> Reader, believe me, here he lies,
> Lifeless, and stripp'd of all Disguise,
> Or you could not believe your Eyes.

In *Round About Our Coal Fire or, Christmas Entertainments*, published at about the time of Fawkes's death,[23] there are two references to the magician, both alluding to his great wealth. The first suggested that he was the only modern performer whose remuneration rivaled that of ancient conjurers, "except Mr. *Lun*" (as played by John Rich, the famous Harlequin and theater impresario). In the second reference, the author, sometimes listed with the nom de plume of Dick Merryman, summarizes Fawkes's act and attributes his financial success to his popular appeal, to his "Sense of the People":[24]

These are the old Heroes in Magick; and next to them I place Mr. *Fawkes*, one of our modern Conjurers, who, after having anointed himself with the Sense of the People, became so great a Conjurer, that he amassed several Thousand Pounds to himself: He was so celebrated a Magician, that either by the Force of his Hocus-Pocus Powder, or by the Influence of his Conjuring Wand, he could presently assemble a multitude of People together, to admire the Phantoms he raised before them, *viz.* Trees to bear Fruit in an instant, Fowls of all sorts, change Cards into Birds, give us Prospects of fine Places out of nothing, and a merry Jig without either a Fidler or a Piper; and moreover, to shew that Money was but a Trifle to him, with a Conjuring-Bag that he had, would every now and then shower down a Peck or two of Gold and Silver upon his Table; and that this Money should not die with him, he has conjured up a son who can do the same things; so that one may say his Conjuration is hereditary.

Fawkes's son inherited the mantle of magic, and his family, in conjunction with the Pinchbeck dynasty, provided entertainment for another generation of bemused spectators. A tenet of fame is that a son rarely outdoes his father. We read about the elder Fawkes for years after his death but rarely encounter a comment about his progeny unless the father is also mentioned. But other laws governing Fawkes's fame remain mysterious: Why does Isaac Fawkes, out of myriad fairground magicians of his generation, emerge as the great showman of his age? He was not particularly innovative; his program did not change very much over his long career and more than half his repertoire consisted of effects that had already been explained in sixteenth- and early-seventeenth-century books of tricks.[25]

Perhaps it is a tenet of magical fame in particular that there is room for only one great magician in the collective imagination at a time. Hence Robert-Houdin in mid-nineteenth-century France; Dr. Hofzinser at the same time in Vienna; and, in succession, Herrmann, Kellar, Thurston, and Blackstone in America. Houdini, although he died in 1926, still eclipses the recognition of any current performer. Perhaps the very notion of more than one great magician is unmagical. How could a performer defy the law of nature, create miracles, do the unfathomable—while another magician defies the laws of nature, creates miracles, does the unfathomable.

Perhaps Fawkes, in all the aspects of performance lost to history—the skill with which he excuted familiar material, the presentation and combination of effects, his personality—was simply unsurpassed. History does attest the universal appeal of this performer, who was equally at ease with royalty and commoners, foreign dignitaries and provincial farmers. ◉

NOTES

1. In 1904 Harry Houdini and the clerk at St. Martin's church, R. Bennett, uncovered the Fawkes will, which is kept at Somerset House. This important document contains the first mention of the given name Isaac and lists his wife Alice as sole executrix. There is no mention of his son, who was to succeed him, and no one's age is indicated.

2. The historians of magic Harry Houdini, Sydney Clarke, Jay Marshall, and the antiquaries Thomas Frost, Henry Morley, George Daniel, and John Ashton have led the way. Dawes's *Isaac Fawkes Fame and Fable* was published in Hull in 1979. In preparation for this piece, I have sketched a chronology of Fawkes's life that is almost twenty thousand words long. One senses that this, too, only scratches the surface.

3. Although I am pleased to offer a number of periodical citations that I think are new to the magic fraternity, I do so with caution despite my best efforts at corroboration. One must take into account that newspaper cuttings often appear loose or in scrapbooks, detached from the original publications. The identification of the periodical and the date of issue are typically provided by hand and sometimes not at all. Cuttings presented here are from the Harvard Theatre Collection, the Harry Price Library at the University of London, the Lysons scrapbooks in the British Library, the American Museum of Magic in Marshall, Michigan, and the author's collection.

4. Sydney Clarke speculates on the identity of the unnamed conjurer in his *Annals of Conjuring* (reprint, New York, 1983), p. 63. Newspaper accounts provide the principal source of biographical information about performers in the early eighteenth century. Daily periodicals were just emerging as a source of information, and there is no reason to assume that their reportage is strictly accurate. But public notices of performances, "mini-reviews," as well as accounts of the comings and goings of celebrities did appear, and perform-

ers began to use newspapers for advertisements, which sometimes appeared in supplements or as separate prints. The Fawkes playbills and broadside are reproduced here for the first time.

5. Among the many portraits of Fawkes based on the Nicholls broadside is the engraving in James Caulfield, *Memoirs of Remarkable Persons* (London, 1820). The famous fan of Bartholomew Fair, published by Setchel in 1824, was based on a painting by Thomas Loggan, the dwarf fan painter of Tunbridge Wells. The original is housed in the British Library. See Dawes, *Fawkes*, pp. 5-8.

6. Bartholomew Fair was established by Henry I in 1123 and continued until 1855. It commenced on August 24, St. Bartholomew's Day, and usually ran for fourteen days. Southwark Fair, also known as Lady Fair, began in 1462 and was held on September 7, 8, and 9.

7. Christopher Pinchbeck (c. 1670–1732) was the leading builder of automata in his day. He often exhibited his creations in connections with Fawkes, who predeceased him by only a year. Pinchbeck was succeeded by his sons Christopher Jr. and Edward, who continued in partnership with Fawkes's son. Alice Fawkes, the widow of Isaac, married Edward.

8. See Philip H. Highfill, et al., *A Biographical Dictionary of Actors* (Carbondale and Edwardsville, Ill., 1987): "in 1726 Fawkes and Powell produced a puppet show at the James Street Playhouse, which for a while was called 'Fawkes's Theater'" (5:207).

9. A hand-dated cutting of 1725 in the Harvard Theatre Collection mentions the horned woman, as does a hand-dated cutting of August 11, 1725.

10. See, for example, the account of the Bold Grimace Spaniard in *Jay's Journal*, vol. 2, no. 2.

11. This posthumous reference is mentioned by both Dawes and Highfill.

12. *British Stage*, p. 10. See also M. Wilson Disher, *Clowns and Pantomimes* (London, 1925), p. 252.

13. Ronald Paulson, *Hogarth*, vol. 1: *The Modern Moral Subject* (New Brunswick and London, 1991), pp. 77-80.

14. James Ralph, *The Touchstone, or Historical Critical Political and Philosophical Essays on the reigning Diversions of the Town* (London, 1728).

15. Woolston quoted in Dawes, *Fawkes*, p. 4.

16. The *Courant* issues were made available to me by the late Leslie Cole. *ESTC* lists the date for the collection as 1751. Brian Lake conjectures that Philipps was not Sir Erasmus Philipps, to whom the work is attributed in the *DNB* and *ESTC*, as he died in 1743 and our Philipps was still writing in 1749.

17. These viewing machines became popular in the late seventeenth century. According to Clarke, *Annals*, "in spite of the grandiloquent descriptions, the 'motions' were only painted backgrounds, with moving figures, painted on card or wood, crossing in the middle distance and foreground. Pinchbeck's machines were elaborations of these earlier exhibits, and may be described as a mixture of a glorified peepshow, a musical box, and a diorama, actuated by clockwork" (pp. 65-66). The Temple of the Arts, the Pantheon, and the Panopticon appear in various forms into the later eighteenth century.

18. Highfill, *Biographical Dictionary*, 11:293-99.

19. The Bottle Conjurer will be the subject of a subsequent issue of this Journal.

20. Robert-Houdin's mid-nineteenth-century version required borrowing a handkerchief from a woman spectator. Her keepsake was burned and the smoke allowed to waft into the branches of a small mechanical orange tree. The tree began to flower and bloom. Oranges next appeared on the tree. These were plucked and tossed to the audience, who were surprised to discover real fruit. The topmost orange, which was mechanical, split apart on command and two metal butterflies flew out, each fluttering upward while holding a corner of the woman's handkerchief.

21. Highfill, *Biographical Dictionary*, 5:207.

22. This figure has been questioned by some historians but, as I think these citations show, without cause.

23. Toole-Stott and the British Library date the first edition of this book as c. 1730, but the text mentions Fawkes's death and thus could not have appeared before the end of May 1731.

24. Quoted by Dawes, *Fawkes*, p. 4.

25. I have been able to trace in earlier printed sources the card on the ceiling, the card moving across the table, the card changing into a bird, commanding a card from a person's hand, the egg bag, the production of ribbons from the mouth, and the cups and balls.

N.B.: Italic type in some quoted material has been set in roman.

ILLUSTRATIONS

JAY'S JOURNAL OF ANOMALIES

Written by Ricky Jay and published four times a year by the author and W & V Dailey, Antiquarian Booksellers, 8216 Melrose Avenue, Los Angeles, California, 90046, (213) 658-8515. Subscription $90 per annum. ¶ Printed letterpress by Patrick Reagh using Monotype Ehrhardt with Thorowgood heads on Rives Heavyweight paper. ¶ Designed by Mr. Reagh & Mr. Jay. ¶ The author wishes to thank Susan Green and Larry Vigon for generous assistance in the preparation of this issue. ¶ Comments and corrections to the text are welcomed. ¶ Written and illustrative material, © Ricky Jay, 1995. ¶ All images are from the private collection of the author with the exception of the Sutton Nicholls broadside, which is reproduced with the kind permission of the Henry E. Huntington Library, San Marino, California. Any subsequent use of text or image is permissible only with the express written consent of Mr. Jay.

FAWKES At his Theatre, In *James-street,* G R near the Hay- Market;

Performs the following Entertainments.

First, HIS Surprizing and Incomparable DEXTERITY of HAND, in which he will perform several intirely new Curiosities, that far surpasseth any thing of that kind ever seen before. *Second,* a curious MUSICAL-CLOCK, that he lately purchas'd of Mr. *Pinchbeck,* Clock-Maker in *Fleet-street,* that plays several fine Tunes on most Instruments of Musick, and imitates the Melodious Notes of various kinds of Birds, as real Life: Also Ships sailing, with a number of curious and humorous Figures, representing divers Motions as tho' Alive. *Third,* another fine CLOCK or MACHINE, call'd Arts Masterpiece, or the *Venetian* Lady's Invention, which she Employ'd Workmen to make, that were Seventeen Years contriving; the like of which was never yet Made or Shewn, in any other part of the World, for variety of moving Pictures, and other Curiosities. There is also the said Lady's Picture very finely Painted on the Machine that moves by Clock-work, like Life.

Besides his inimitable *Posture-Master,* who is vastly Improv'd in his Performances, he has a little CHILD of five Years of Age, who shews such wonderful *Turns of Body,* that it is impossible to believe without seeing.

N. B. During our short stay, we shall begin every Evening precisely at 7 o' Clock. This is the last Week of Performing here.

JAY'S JOURNAL *of* ANOMALIES

VOLUME TWO, NUMBER FOUR   WINTER, 1996   PUBLISHED QUARTERLY

Dancing on the Ceiling

VERSATILITY WAS THE TRADEMARK of an early-nineteenth-century performer named Sanches (sometimes Sanchies, Sanchias, or Sanchez). He warbled imitations of the nightingale, thrush, canary, and skylark, danced on the tightrope – occasionally flaunting his strength by lifting a pony or a passel of stage hands while so balanced – and accompanied himself on guitar. He mimicked various instruments and whistled full overtures. He was known for vaulting onto the curtain and swinging out over the stage and the orchestra, the drapery clasped only between his feet. He was also an accomplished magician (and a tutor of Billy Purvis, the beloved Newcastle Conjurer).[1] Posterity, however, should recognize him principally for creating an act that became a theatrical convention: walking upside down while suspended from the ceiling.

An eyewitness account of Sanches's first attempt at the stunt survives in a British Library manuscript. The author, one John Cawes, mentions the ceiling walk as only part of Sanches's repertoire: "Herr Michailloto Sanchies the Rope dancer appeared at Sadler's Wells the Easter Monday – 1806 – and was engaged in addition to his rope dancing to perform some other feats such as walking on the ceiling of the

stage – which was done by iron shoes which fitted in grooves [slots] in a board fastened to the top of the stage." This attempt to explain the apparatus or technology of the exhibition set a trend followed by many later chroniclers of this peculiar category of performance art.[2]

I can find no evidence that Sanches offered the stunt again until 1812. The response of the audience may have had something to do with the hiatus. Cawes had noted: "This Part of his Performance the audience did not like – so it was not repeated – but his rope dancing was original & to those who had not seen the same thing done at the Dutch Fairs – was extraordinary."[3] Perhaps Sanches's versatility allowed him the luxury of withdrawing the ceiling walk until he had improved his technique: in his initial attempt he had managed to take only three steps in the upside-down position.[4]

The reprise met with considerable success. Billed as the Wonderful Antipodean in the *Morning Post* of March 31, 1812, Sanches reappeared at the Regency Theatre on Tottenham Court Road: "The frequent enquiries after the above astonishing performer has induced the proprietor, though at very great expense, to re-engage him for a short time, being anxious to gratify public curiosity to its full extent." Even though this newspaper cutting claimed Sanches would soon depart the kingdom, in August he was performing the ceiling walk at the Surrey Theatre as "the most extraordinary Feat never executed by any other Person." Almost a year later, on separate benefit nights for Mrs. Bishop (August 3, 1813) and Mrs. Douglas (August 9, 1813), he declined the walk and performed only vocal imitations and slack rope evolutions. In October 1813, however, he featured his antipodean turn at the Theatre-Royal in Chester (at this engagement he also introduced a new musical instrument of his own invention called the Egyptian harmonic lyre).

An illustrated playbill in the Harvard Theatre Collection mentions his success on the Continent, "particularly at Constantinople, and before the Imperial Russian Court, at Petersburgh and Moscow." The conclusion of this advertisement augurs his improved technique, promising that his performance will excite "the strongest sensations of pleasure derived from the confident security of the performer." Subsequent imitators, it will be noted, often failed specifically in this

respect. The British Library holds a similarly illustrated Sanches playbill from the Regency Theatre in Bristol: "This surprising Performer will Walk against the Ceiling with his Head downwards, Exhibiting in various forms a Flag in each hand [an attractive woodcut displays this pose], and when at the extremity of his Walk, will suspend himself by one Leg; he will also turn around and Walk back again, as composed by the rest of the World upon Terra-Firma, no part of which was ever performed by any Man but himself."

It was a woman, however, who was one of the first to duplicate his stunt (and his advertising cut) for an appearance in Nuremberg in May 1828. This unnamed Spanish performer walked a beam with flags in her hands, "free like a fly," and "danced a polonaise to the beat of the music." With more modesty than one expects amid such puffery, it was announced that "as this piece has never been shown here and as she is the only one to have performed it in the outmost cities with much applause, the young artist hopes to surprise the spectators with the boldness of this experiment." (See illustration, page 67.) Ching Lau Lauro performed the walk in England the same year.

A short time later the stunt was featured in America by a Mr. Peters, who demonstrated it at the Salem Theatre in Massachusetts in August 1829. The Peters family offered rope dancing and Indian balancing, after much-heralded performances in Lisbon, London, and Madrid. Peters himself presented "the wonderful exhibition called the Antipode, which is walking on the ceiling of the theatre head downwards."[5]

Sanches's method involved acrobatic skill and great courage, but little in the way of sophisticated technology: just as Cawes explained after watching his first performance, he placed his reinforced boots into iron staples that protruded from a plank about twelve feet long that was fastened to the ceiling. As late as the 1860s Olmar performed at the Alhambra by hooking his feet into large rings (although some ninety feet in the air!). A twelve-year-old girl called Little Corelli used a similar method, but her rigging was much closer to the ground. The naturalist Francis Buckland observed that she walked in such "a cautious perfunctory way that it was painful to watch."[6]

In his *Letters on Natural Magic* (1832) the famous

scientist David Brewster described two methods for ceiling walking, both far more complex than anything employed by Sanches. He approached the topic in a spirit at once helpful and critical: how could performers improve the effect and make it look more natural? In the first technique, the walkers were to be attached to the ceiling by rope or wire and held there by others standing above:

Two parallel grooves or openings were made in the ceiling at the same distance as the foot-tracks of a person walking in the sand. These grooves were narrower than the human foot, so as to permit a rope or chain or strong wire, attached to the feet of the performer, to pass through the ceiling, where they were held by two or more persons above it

But this would at best produce a sliding or shuffling like "walking in the dark," he noted. "A more regular motion," he recommended,

might be produced by a contrivance for attaching the rope or chain to the sole of the foot, at each step, and subsequently detaching it. In this way, when the performer is pulled against the ceiling by his left foot, he would lift his right foot, and having made a step with it, and planted it against the grooves, the rope would be attached to it, and when the rope was detached from the left foot, it would make a similar step, while the right foot was being pulled against the ceiling.

Although plausible, this method could not have generated the pace of even a leisurely postprandial stroll.

The second method recommended by Brewster seems truly fanciful:

A more scientific method of walking on the ceiling is suggested by those beautiful pneumatic contrivances by which insects, fishes, and even some lizards are enabled to support the weight of their bodies against the force of gravity.[7]

Perhaps a more accurate analogy would have been the suction apparatus of the octopus. But this description proved prophetic in terms of actual practice, for indeed, performers were using such suction devices later in the century.

A revival of interest in ceiling walking in the 1850s was in large part owing to the compelling figure of Richard Sands. He was a versatile and effective circus performer and impresario who performed the stunt both in his native America and in England. In the *Illustrated London News* of April 2, 1853, Sands was said to have "received the secret from a scientific man" (elsewhere he is identified as Professor Hunt), and to have first performed the stunt in Auburn on May 29 of that year. This article, "The Air Walker at Drury Lane," goes on to compare Sands's method with that of Sieur Sanches at the Surrey Theatre years earlier (ironically Sands was soon to perform his stunt at the Surrey as well), praising the current performance as "altogether of another class." A temporary ceiling was erected, about twenty feet long and twenty feet into the air. It was supported by a sturdy timber framework. At each end of the apparatus was a bench suspended from ropes, designated "a slung seat." Sands climbed up a ladder and lay down on one of the benches, and he was then pulled to the ceiling feet first. He detached himself and commenced a journey across the platform, occasionally lifting one leg for effect, until he reached the second bench and descended down a second ladder. A net was stretched below the entire affair as a precaution, Sands reminding the *Illustrated News* reporter that he had taken a fall in a performance at Penn Yan, New York, the previous July. Overzealous reporters had gone so far as to announce his death on a number of occasions. In his *London Labour and the London Poor* (London, 1861), Henry Mayhew interviewed a strongman who did the ceiling walk:

of course I darn't do it in the Professor Sands' style, for mine was a dodge. Professor Sands used an air-exhausting boot, on the model

of a fly's foot, and it was a legitimate performance indeed; he and another man, to whom he gave the secret of his boots, are the only two who ever did it. The chap that came over here wasn't the real Sands. The fact is well known to the profession, that Sands killed himself on his benefit night in America. After walking on the marble slab in the Circus, somebody bet him he couldn't do it on any ceiling, and he for a wager went to a Town-hall, and done it, and broke his neck. The chap that came over here was Sands' attendant, and he took the name and the boots, and came over as Professor Sands. (Vol. 3, p. 103)

Another apocryphal account of Sands's demise is listed in John Turner's *Victorian Arena* (Formby, England, 1995): "Killed in 1861 when challenged to ceiling walk outside the circus, he used a ceiling in a civic building at Melrose, Massachusetts, and a whole section of the plaster came away." As the official record has it, Sands died from yellow fever in Havana, Cuba, February 24, 1861.

Sands's pedal extremities were augmented with a pair of sandals that were placed over his boots, and to these were attached brass loops; "these were connected by springs, with a pair of platter-like soles, in which lay the secret as they were brought to the theatre in a locked box, and conveyed away with similar caution at the close of the performance." The reporter from the *Illustrated London News* concluded his piece: "It is surmised that the support is occasioned by the hollow soles being exhausted of air, upon the same principle as that by which a fly walks upon the ceiling – the performer's feet being detached by the pressure of a valve, which readmits the air. The performance has been throughout very neatly executed."

Two other well-known circus owners also tried the act. The highly regarded equestrian and clown Big Jim Meyers did the ceiling walk at Joseph Cushing's New York Circus at the National Theater in Boston in 1856. On a bill that featured the famous clown Dan Rice, Meyers offered "The First Exposition of the Scientific Feat of Reversed Pedestrianism ... the Wonder of the Age."[8] (See illustration, page 65.)

Gilbert N. Eldred, who broke into the circus as a clown in 1834 and was an accomplished comic rider who performed with John Robinson, offered a ceiling walk in the 1850s. According to Stuart Thayer, it is possible that he purchased Sands's equipment, and certain that he used Sands's advertising cuts.[9] A Mr. Lenton hung from the ceiling at the Old Broadway theater in New York on February 7, 1856.[10]

But Sands's major competitor was John McCormick, whose billing as "The Great Philosophical Antipodean Pedestrian from Ohio" cannot fail to delight subscribers to this journal. He seems to have preceded Sands by some ten months and at the same venue, the Bowery Amphitheatre in New York City, on February 16, 1852. Sands was willing to discuss the suction method openly (without, of course, revealing the specific modus operandi); McCormick attempted to deny it. Sands gave credit to others for the invention, and on one occasion even sanctioned a performer in his employ to use his apparatus and to claim the invention as his own.[11]

McCormick insisted on being credited as the "Original Inventor Of The Miraculous Antipodean Feat Of Walking Against Gravity On The Under Surface Of A Highly-Polished Slab Of Marble," and perhaps he was the first to use the impressive marble surface. He stuck by his claim of innovation, and for a show in London at "The People's Cheap Concert Hall," he threw down the gauntlet to science:

This astounding feat is considered by men of science to be the most wonderful discovery of the present age and must be seen to be believed and understood, as the general impression seems that this marvelous feat is accomplished by the aid of SUCKERS, to prove how utterly in error this idea is, the advertiser will give a REWARD OF £20 to any person who will produce a sucker that will hold a man 12 stone weight [168 pounds] up to the marble for the space of 5 minutes."[12]

The scientific debate was addressed more formally by Albert Hopkins, the editor of *Scientific American*,

BORO' MUSIC HALL,
UNION STREET, BORO.'
THE PEOPLE'S
CHEAP CONCERT HALL,
Having lately undergone
VERY EXTENSIVE ALTERATIONS!
Is now capable of comfortably
SEATING 1000 PERSONS,
Beautifully Decorated, brilliantly Lighted, thoroughly
Ventilated, and for diversity of Entertainments is not to be
surpassed in London!
PROFESSOR McCORMICK
The original Inventor of the Miraculous
Antipodean Feat of Walking against Gravity
ON THE UNDER SURFACE OF A
HIGHLY-POLISHED SLAB of MARBLE

This astounding Feat is considered by men of science to be the most wonderful disco-
very of the present age, and must be seen to be believed and understood, as the gene-
ral impression seems that this Marvellous Feat is accomplished by the aid of SUCK-
ERS; to prove how utterly in error this idea is, the advertiser will give a
REWARD OF £20
To any person who will produce a Sucker that will hold a
Man 12 stone weight up to the Marble for the space of 5 minutes
Miss JULIA WESTON
The Genius of Fun and Folly.
Mrs. GEORGE WARE
Comic Character Singer and Dancer.
Miss Theresa WOODMAN
Contralto and Serio-Comic.

who in 1897 revealed perhaps more than anyone would want to know about the pneumatic shoes worn by M'lle Aimée, a popular ceiling walker of the 1880s and '90s who apparently executed the stunt with singular grace and ease. Attached to her shoe was

an india-rubber sucker with cup-shaped adhering surface. To its center a stud is attached, which is perforated near the end. This stud enters a socket fastened to the sole of the shoe. The socket is also perforated transversely. A pin is secured through the apertures, securing the hold between socket and disk. The socket is under the instep and is attached to the shank of the shoe sole.

A wire loop that extends forward under the toe of the shoe is pivoted on two studs....A short piece of string is secured to the india rubber and passes through a hole in the extension, or rearwardly projecting arm, of the loop. The disk when pressed against a smooth surface is held fast by the pressure of the atmosphere. If now the loop is pressed toward the surface to which it adheres, the string will be drawn tight and will pull the edge of the india rubber away from the board. Air will rush in, and the adhesion will cease. As each new step is taken, one disk is made to adhere by pressure, and the other is detached by the action just described. (See masthead illustration.)

He then presented an elaborate calculation to demonstrate that the device could easily support the weight of a performer weighing up to 240 pounds—thereby rebutting McCormick's claim.[13]

On May 14, 1884, in Wilton, Massachusetts, a Signor Pedanto proffered a long-winded announcement consistent with his cognomen:

PEDANTO The Aerial Gymnast, The Man Fly (formerly teacher of the Young Men's Christian Association Gymnasium.) Introducing the Greatest of all Sensations, his ANTIPODEAN SPECIALTY, that of WALKING THE CEILING OF THE HALL – which gave him such a reputation in Europe and South America. An act performed by no other person. As a Gymnast Pedanto stands at the front. He has had under his control the largest Gymnastic Schools in America. He has taken advantage of the opportunities offered to invent and practice new feats in Gymnastics. He will positively appear each evening in a variety of Gymnastic Performances.[14]

As antipodean performance proliferated, new methods of operation were invented and a spate of patents were issued. On June 16, 1885, C. H. Newman and W. Berrigan were granted a patent for "an electrical device to allow showmen to walk on the ceiling." The apparatus consisted of boots of soft plate-iron and a plank made of electromagnets placed in strategic positions, each strong enough to support the acrobat's full weight. The performer would disengage the magnet that held him firm by means of a walking stick. As the magnets were switched on and off, he could proceed along the track. A novel variation was patented by C. H. Cox in Great Britain in 1898. In this version brass balls were suspended from the ceiling at intervals about a pace apart. The performer, again with iron-soled boots, moved from sphere to sphere. An ammeter was arranged in circuit so that as the one magnet was de-energized the next would be energized, allowing the acrobat to move along without a cane or any other apparatus to disengage the current.

Ernest George of Manlius, New York, patented a similar invention by which a performer could roller-skate across the ceiling. This too relied on electromagnets, but here the sequential energizing was entrusted to an assistant on the ground.

In something of a scientific throwback, a vacuum invention was credited to J. W. Frakes in 1912. An entire line of cylindrical cups was suspended from a plank-like apparatus that contained an air-suction pump to regulate atmospheric pressure. The performer was able to move from cup to cup by means of a circular metal plate that was larger than the circumference of the protruding cylinder. This plate had the effect of creating a vacuum as it closed each successive cup. As late as 1931 a new device that allowed actors to walk and even dance on the ceiling was patented by J. L. Brierley and Roy Lankton. Their system called for a hanging track and carriage combination, with complex harnesses and supporting cables. The performers were allowed considerable movement within their restraints while the carriage secretly moved above them, giving a strong illusion that they were walking on the surface of the ceiling.[15]

After a brief efflorescence at the turn of the century, these high-risk acrobats walked the ceiling with decreasing frequency. But if the phenomenon declined in the theaters and circuses, it became an increasingly popular image in our imaginations. Film in particular proved a powerful means of capturing this appeal. The most famous of all ceiling walks is Fred Astaire's marvelous dance sequence in *Royal Wedding* (1951), directed by Stanley Donen (whose biography was entitled *Dancing on the Ceiling*). Stanley Kubrick used a ceiling walk most effectively in *2001: A Space Odyssey*, and

Ingmar Bergman presented a startling image of suspension in *Hour of the Wolf*.[16] In the world of performance art, Trisha Brown has effectively choreographed ceiling walks, and more recently Mathew Barney has had himself rigged into the appropriate position. An Australian dance troupe, Chunky Move, has in suitable attire thrown itself against Velcro walls, a precursor, or perhaps successor, to David Letterman's somewhat less artistic attempts at the same effect.

The Moscow Circus featured an extraordinary version of the effect in the 1960s. An acrobat walked upside down over an open cage of tigers at the same time that a tiger walked on the beam above him. The tiger's footsteps actually triggered loops that successively appeared and retracted, allowing the performer to walk across the board safely. Unless the man and beast matched their steps perfectly, however, the human performer would tumble to the ground.[17]

In the 1980s, I was entranced by a wonderful comic turn in Australia's Circus Oz when an equilibrist, Tim Coldwell, enjoyed an upside-down dinner on the ceiling of the building. As the audience responded warmly to the novelty of this presentation and the brilliance of execution, I recalled a predecessor who had enjoyed his suspended repast a hundred and sixty years earlier:

The Great and Extraordinary Marche Ærienne or, Antipodean Walk! Mons. Davoust will climb up a Cord, by the Strength of his Wrists, from the Stage to the top of the House, where he will Walk with his Feet against the Proscenium, his Head Downwards! Cross the Proscenium from End to End; directing his Walk slowly so that spectators may follow his Steps! And Play with Hoops to prove He Is Not Held By Any Wire, &c. [and they will] Take a Table up to him, where he will Eat and Drink, as easily as on the Ground![18]

For those who have a friend with the inclination but not the skill to embark upon reversed pedestrianism, may I suggest the following stunt. Prepare a room "where all the furnishings, drapes, pictures, fireplace are upside down. The rugs and the furniture are fastened to the ceiling while the floor contains a single object—an elaborate chandelier thrust upward in the center." Invite your aspiring acrobatic friend to your home and wait for him to imbibe an improbable amount of intoxicating brew. When he passes out, carry him to the upside-down room. When he awakens share with him the joys of his newfound prowess.[19]

NOTES

1. Accounts of Sanches's role as tutor of the conjurer appear in all three nineteenth-century biographies of Purvis, those by Robson (1849), Bowman (1879), and Arthur (1879); in *Hocas*, ed. Peter Lane, vol. 1, no. 1 (London, 1982); and in Allen Berlinski, *Purvis, the Newcastle Conjuror* (1981).

2. Just as in the case of magic illusions, one should be wary of public exposures. Seldom does the revelation of a secret provide the complete explanation or account for an entertainer's success.

3. Raymond Toole-Stott quotes the British Library manuscript in his bibliography, *Circus and Allied Arts* (Derby, 1962), 3:336.

4. George Spaeight, *A History of the Circus* (London, San Diego, and New York, 1980), p. 77, quoting Charles Dibdin's *Professional and Literary Memoirs* (1956), which Spaeight edited.

5. *Salem Gazette*, August 25, 1829. According to the *Boston Advertiser*, Peters performed in that city from August to October 1829. Stuart Thayer, in *Annals of the American Circus* (Seattle, 1992), cites part of the program (3:59). I was recently excited by the discovery of an 1801 reference to the "Antipodean Whirligig" at the Hay-Market Theatre in Boston, which I had hoped might be the earliest recorded reference to the ceiling walk. I was chagrined but amused to find that the act was instead a precursor of break dancing, featuring a Mr. Robinson, "who with his head on the top of a common table goes round at the rate of 60 to 100 times minute, without the assistance of his hands."

6. Buckland, *Curiosities of Natural History*, quoted in Spaeight, *History of the Circus*, p. 77.

7. Brewster, *Letters on Natural Magic* (London, 1832), pp. 234–35.

8. Playbill, author's collection. Both Meyers and Sands apprenticed to the venerable circus showman Aaron Turner.

9. Stuart Thayer, *Bandwagon* (Jan.–Feb. 1991), p. 45.

10. Brown, *A History of the New York Stage* (New York, 1903), 1:404.

11. In 1857 Signor Bliss used Sands's apparatus for a ceiling walk on a unit of the Sands, Nathans & Co. show that year; Sands last performed the effect in 1856 (Thayer, *Annals of the American Circus*, 3:95). George Chindahl, in *A History of the Circus in America* (Caldwell, Idaho, 1959), quoting from *White Tops*, April–May 1939, p. 12, col. 3, says there was a lithographed poster of Bliss proclaiming him to be "the inventor and original experimentor of this wonderful performance" (pp. 49–50).

12. Playbill, London c. 185?, author's collection. See Brown, *A History of the New York Stage*, 1:237; and Thayer, *Annals of the American Circus*, 3:59.

13. Hopkins, *Magic* (New York, 1897), pp. 144–45. A very similar account and illustration appeared in German in Signor Saltarino's [W. H. Otto], *Fahrend Volk* (Leipzig, 1895), and in French in Brignogan's *La Sorcellerie Amusante* (Paris, c. 1898). According to the *New York Clipper* of December 19, 1885, M'lle Aimée was born in London and first appeared in the famous Circus Rentz in Berlin while still a child. She was taught the ceiling act by R. G. Austin and toured with it on the Continent as far east as Russia and in Mexico, America, and Australia. She was also accomplished on the trapeze. Many other women did versions of the act; two are pictured here: A contemporary of Aimée's, "Miss Silvia, the Skandenavian Ceiling Walker," is featured on page 72, and Anna Merkel, who later performed with various American circuses, is on page 74.

14. Playbill, author's collection.

15. The patent for Mr. Cox's brass-ball device can be found in Terrence Fees and David Wilmore, *British Theatrical Patents 1801–1900* (London, 1996), pp. 138–39. The others are from the United States Patent Office.

16. A patent to "accomplish the seemingly impossible feat of walking around the interior of a vertically positioned circular frame or track" was awarded to John Fitzpatrick in 1912. It featured a rotating corset-like body support allowing a maximum of movement, while the track itself revolved in a circular motion. This was far more intricate than the methods used in film, where one had the option of revolving the camera. Ceiling walks have been featured in many films, and I have singled out only a few of the most striking examples.

17. Conversation with the designer of the act, Alexander Okun.

18. Playbill, June 4, 6, 7, and 9, 1821. See j. B. Findlay, *Eighth*

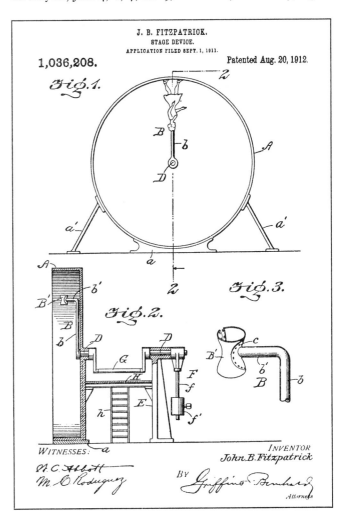

Collectors Annual International Guide to Posters & Playbills (Shanklin, Isle of Wight, 1972), p. 23. Findlay also lists a bill featuring Micaleto Sanches in Breslau, c. 1840, but it is not reproduced.
19. This account of the room is from H. Allen Smith's *The Compleat Practical Joker* (New York, 1953), p. 207.

ILLUSTRATIONS

Page 65. Meyers playbill, London, 1856.
Page 67. German playbill, Nuremberg, 1828.
Page 68. Sands engraving from *Illustrated London News*, April 2, 1853.
Page 69. Sands playbill, Surrey Theatre, London, 185?
Page 70. McCormick playbill, London, 185?
Page 72. Silvia, color lithograph, Friedlander, Hamburg, [1891].
Page 73. United States Patent Office illustration, 1912.
Page 74. Anna Merkel, color lithograph, Erie Litho (Penn), n.d.

JAY'S JOURNAL OF ANOMALIES

Written by Ricky Jay and published four times a year by the author and W & V Dailey, Antiquarian Booksellers, 8216 Melrose Avenue, Los Angeles, California, 90046, (213) 658-8515. Subscription $90 per annum. ¶ Printed letterpress by Patrick Reagh using Monotype Ehrhardt with Thorowgood heads on Rives Heavyweight paper. ¶ Designed by Mr. Reagh & Mr. Jay. ¶ The author wishes to thank Susan Green, Larry Vigon, Laurence Senelick, John Turner, Jim Steinmeyer and John McKinven for generous assistance in the preparation of this issue. ¶ Comments and corrections to the text are welcomed. ¶ Written and illustrative material, © Ricky Jay, 1996. ¶ All images are from the private collection of the author. Any subsequent use of text or image is permissible only with the express written consent of Mr. Jay.

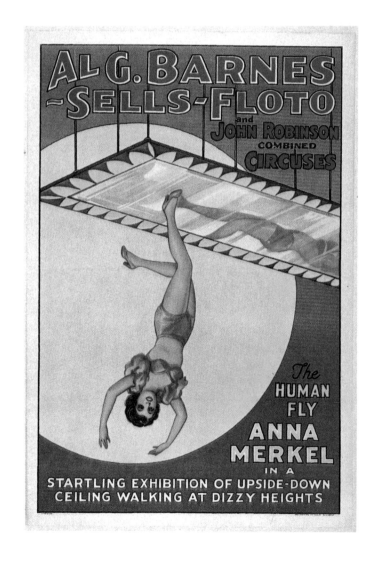

JAY'S JOURNAL of
ANOMALIES

VOLUME THREE   NUMBER ONE   1997

Magical Mayhem: or, The Celebrated Nose Amputation

I N CONJURING, THE THEATRICAL PROFESSION whose oldest recorded performance is the effect of decapitation, it is not surprising to note the enduring popularity of severing from the head its most protuberant organ – the nose.

The decapitation illusion was performed for Cheops, the builder of the Great Pyramid. The magician, one Dedi of Dedsneferu, severed the head of a goose and placed it at one end of a great hall, far away from the animal's body. After the appropriate words were uttered, the head and body moved toward one another, in a funky pre-Rufus Thomas waddle, until they were united and the beast "cackled with joy." Dedi repeated his stunt with a pelican and eventually an ox but, unlike scores of his successors, declined to decapitate members of his own species. Many centuries later, when the invention of movable type in the West encouraged the chronicling of magicians' exploits, we find the cutting and restoring of human heads and limbs in accounts of illusionists in many cultures and countries.

The "Decollation of John the Baptist" is one of the most important effects introduced in the first significant study of conjuring in the English language, Reginald Scot's *Discoverie of Witchcraft* (London, 1584). It was performed by a conjurer called Kingsfield at Bartholomew Fair. Scot also records a more manageable illusion, a trick bodkin or dagger, that allowed one "to cut half your nose asunder and to heal it again presentlie without any salve." (See illustration, page 77.) Scot described another piece of nose necro-

mancy that was to become popular in the conjuring repertoire: an effect called "the bridle," in which a cord was apparently pulled back and forth through the nasal cavity.[1] The conspicuous image of a monkey, its nose impaled with a knife as described by Scot, had appeared some twenty years earlier in a copper engraving by Pieter Bruegel the Elder, "The Fall of the Wizard Hermogenes."[2] *The Disobedient Child*, an Elizabethan interlude attributed to Thomas Ingelend, refers to the illusion in the following verse:

> What juggling was there upon the boards!
> what thrusting of knives thro' many a nose!
> What bearynge of formes! what holdings of swordes!
> what puttying of bodtkyns through leege and hose![3]

To accomplish the effect, an ordinary knife was shown and then covertly switched for another knife with a half-moon shape cut away from the blade. The cut-out portion allowed the knife to rest over the bridge of the victim's nose, giving the illusion that the blade had cut deeply into the flesh. But why, one might ask, would so simple a trick become a staple effect in the repertoire of conjurers for the next four hundred years? Certainly the ease of performance and the modest expenditure for props must have been appealing and, in the parlance of the trade, "it packed flat"– or at least flatter than the two employees that assisted the magician in the performance of decapitation.

It is difficult to underestimate the importance of noses in the sixteenth century. In his classic work *De Curtorium Chirurgia per Insitionem* (Venice, 1597), Gasparo Tagliacozzi (1546–99) gave the first detailed account of the surgical restoration of noses to appear in the West. He had a number of predecessors in the East, where nose amputation had long been the punishment of choice for adultery.[4]

Tagliacozzi's description of the medical operation called rhinoplasty came too late to help Tycho Brahe, the astronomer whose highly accurate observations of planetary motions paved the way for Kepler. Manderup Parsbjerg, an instructor at the University of Rostock, took such offense at a mathematical principle proposed by Tycho Brahe that he challenged the astronomer to a duel and cut off his nose. Tycho Brahe purchased a nose made of gold and silver, in appearance much like the one sported by Lee Marvin in *Cat Ballou*, and carried with

him always a little box containing special salve that he applied whenever the nose became wobbly.

As a penalty for adultery, nose amputation – a sly variant on "an eye for an eye"– is no less appropriate when one realizes that the loss of the nasal organ often accompanied severe cases of syphilis. Such indeed was the fate of the playwright Will Davenant, often said to be the godson or illegitimate son of William Shakespeare, whose encounter with a "black handsome wench" cost him his nose and a fortune in ineffective medical treatments. Shortly after Davenant was named England's Poet Laureate, Sir John Suckling authored the following doggerel:

> Will Davenant ashamed of a foolish mischance
> that he had got lately traveling in France
> modestly hoped the handsomeness of the muse
> might any deformity about him excuse.
> And surely the company would have been content
> if they could have found any precedent.
> But in all their chords either in verse or in prose
> there was not one laureate without a nose.

Let us stop for a moment and consider why someone would want to cut a nose asunder. The most obvious answer is, of course, "to spite a face." The nose has long been an object of figurative elaboration as well as magical diminution. We are told to follow our nose, or to pay through it. We can lead by a nose and then win by it. We can see as plainly as the nose on our face, or turn up our nose in contempt. More contemptuously, we can brownnose or, more currently, consume nose candy. More cryptic is a usage recorded by George Mastell, retired New York chief of police, in his *Vocabulum, or the Rogues Lexicon* (New York, 1859): "His pal nosed and the bene cove was pulled for a crack"– that is, his partner informed against him and the good fellow was arrested for burglary.

Slang and satire were often partners. At the beginning of the eighteenth century Ned Ward created his fictional "No Nose Club," at which unfortunates deprived of their olfactory organs were persuaded to meet, eat, and drink their cares away with punning declamation in the company of like souls.[5] The theme "a long nose is to a lady's liking" had its greatest champion in that unlikely hero, a lanky English parson named Laurence Sterne, who within a few months of the publication of *Tristram Shandy* (London, 1759) may have be-

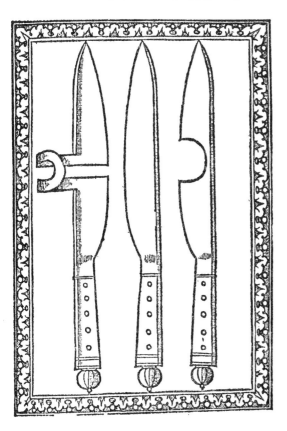

come the most famous man in England. (Pinocchio achieved even greater fame by enacting the variant, "A liar is to a lady's liking.") Sterne's rollicking, quirky novel, with its remarkable play on noses, preceded by 150 years the appearance of the most prominent nose-play ever penned, Edmond Rostand's *Cyrano de Bergerac*.[6]

Beneath such verbal pyrotechnics there is a profound link between conjuring and rhinoplasty that is rooted in the legends of sympathetic magic. After a graft from the arm to the nose, for instance, when the arm is injured the nose falls to the ground. A number of versions of this apparently popular conceit are discussed in Lynn Thorndike's *History of Magic and Experimental Science*, in eight volumes (New York, 1923–58): Francis Bacon tells of men with large and ugly noses who have cut off the excess flesh and then healed the wounds by making a gash in their arms and holding their noses there for a time, "which, if it be true, shows plainly the consent of flesh and flesh." On the same theme is the story of a reconstructed nose that putrefied when the donor of the flesh died. Caspar Schott, who doubted this often told tale, nonetheless credited the restoration of a nose achieved by putting it in cold water or snow (quoting Daniel Schwenter's *Deliciæ physico-mathematicæ* [Nuremberg, 1636]). In *Hudibras*, Samuel Butler was not above having some fun with this superstition – and even more fun with the notion of supplying the new organ from a volunteer's bottom.

> So learned Taliacotius from
>   The brawny part of a porter's bum
> Cut supplemental noses, which,
>   Would last as long as the patient's breech,
> But when the date of Nock was out
>   Off dropt the sympathetic snout.

Both Schott and Schwenter, well known for their contributions to the literature of performance magic, waxed poetic on wobbly noses. Schott propounded (although he later rejected the theory) that demons could produce "some animals from putrid matter and that if a murderer approached his victim, the corpse would bleed. (This superstition is linked specifically to the nose in Humphrey Wanley's *Wonders of the Little World* [London, 1678], where it is reported that in 1632 a man had murdered his very pregnant wife, whose child was then laid out beside her. When the husband viewed the corpses, the baby's began to bleed from the nose – thereby implicating the husband.) However, Schott did question the tale of the nose that putrefied when its donor died. Stories from many primitive cultures, in which demons, devils, and dybbuks enter the body through the nostrils, are recounted in Doctor Harold Holden's *Noses* (Cleveland and New York, 1950).[7]

Allusions to nose magic are found in many works on conjuring of the eighteenth and nineteenth centuries. One fetching example is articulated in the charming rarity, *Round About Our Coal Fire* (first ed., London, c. 1731), which mentions that Dr. Faustus would "change men's noses into grapes or grapes into noses which was the same thing." In 1764 George Alexander Stevens, a mediocre actor and writer, had a resounding success with his *Lecture on Heads*. Displaying a papier-mâché wig block, Stevens satirized the leading characters and conventions of his day. This parody bore progeny in a number of similarly themed productions, the most apt of which, for our purposes, is the *Dissertation on Noses*, first published with *A Satyrical Lecture on*

Hearts by Doctor James Solas Dodd in 1767. Dodd claimed that his work was not influenced by Stevens, and as unlikely as this seems, there is another worthy nasal precedent. According to *Fog's Weekly Journal*, October 19, 1728:

This day is published, A Dissertation on Noses, viz. On the Long High Roman Nose (as was in fashion in K. William's Day). On the large Bottle Nose. On the Snub, the Flat Nose. On the little contemptuous Grinning Turn'd up Nose. On the Short Cocking Nose. On the thin Pinch'd-in Nose. On the Red Nose. And on those who have Lost Their Nose…With all these several sorts of Noses finely engraved. This Book is Given gratis Up One Pair of Stairs at the Sign of the Anodyne Necklace, Approved of by Dr. Chamberlen for Children's Teeth, and Fits, over-against Devreux-Court, without Temple-Bar.

Stevens's lecture featured as a subject for parody the famous eighteenth-century magician Jonas, therein described as "The Card Playing, Conjuring Jew."[8] The portrait of the conjurer holding some playing cards – however crude – is the only likeness known to survive. Much less widely known is that Philip Breslaw, also a renowned prestidigitator, was featured in the *Lecture on Heads* when Jonas's fame was no longer. Jonas was the victim of mayhem at the hands – or rather the teeth – of his own learned dog, gone mad, who attacked his exhibitor and so disfigured his face as to have a profoundly deleterious effect on their performing careers.[9]

The *Dissertation on Noses* featured a magician as performer rather than subject of parody when it was included in the act of Richard Potter. A mulatto – and the first native-born American magician celebrated in his own country – Potter exhibited a varied repertoire: experiments with playing cards, eggs, resistance to fire, and the *Dissertation on Noses*. In the latter, he was fond of "personating different characters of the wearers." Introducing his monologue he announced that his presentation "satirically lashes thieves and follies of man-kind, and forms a source of rational and elegant amusement."[10]

Nineteenth-century nose magic reached a pinnacle in homage to one Thomas Wadhouse, or Wedders, a Yorkshire citizen who was recorded as having a nose seven and one-half inches long.[11] By midcentury, magicians were wont to attack the nasal organ with alarming frequency. A generic performance of the popular stunt was

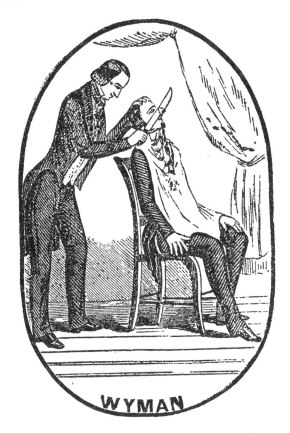

described by Edward William Lane in his *An Account of the Manners and Customs of the Modern Egyptians* (London, 1836 [2:105–6]). A kind of sleight-of-hand performer called a "Hha'wee" was frequently featured in Cairo. His repertoire might consist of snake charming, along with a number of magic effects in the minor mutilation category. Locking a padlock through a boy's cheek, thrusting a spike into his throat, and "placing the boy on the ground, he puts the edge of the knife upon his nose, and knocks the blade until half its width seems to have entered."[12]

In America, the presentation of the same effect has varied greatly in tone. In 1855, the playbill of a Punch-and-Judy man and conjurer, A. Walker, promised "the whole to conclude with the celebrated nose amputation, large noses preferred."[13] Almost that exact phrasing reappears on the bill of two of Mr. Walker's more prominent brethren. Professor Young at Lyceum Hall, Milford, Massachusetts, at least had the delicacy to reduce the size of the type from thirty-six points to twelve. Macallister, a well-known performer of Scottish ancestry, featured a garish woodcut of two flying imps wield-

ing a blood-dripping giant knife that has severed the organ of a horrified spectator. His copy read, "a great Surgical operation. Macalister [so spelled] will cut off the Nose of any gentleman present, and again restore it, by virtue of the Balsam of Farabus"– whatever that was– before noting, "large noses preferred."[14] (See figure, page 78.)

Of Americans who favored the trick in this period, none made a more elaborate spectacle of it than the impressive Professor Wyman, a very successful showman who counted President Lincoln among his admirers. Some of his playbills featured an audience member sitting in a barber chair bedizened with a long smock (no doubt to catch the blood) as Wyman ominously commenced surgery. That such operations were humorous rather than frightening is confirmed by the notices of the day, and the verse that appeared in a poetic description of Wyman's show.

> Now bank notes next are shot in to candles
> and then a sharp knife he readily handles
> which to the audience strangely exposes
> queer looking geniuses without any NOSES.[15]

The amputation was further described in conjuring chapbooks such as Sieur Blismondi's *Hand Book of Magic*. These cheap pamphlets, usually sold at the shows of itinerant performers, depicted the simple knife used to accomplish the decapitation but offered little description to help the would-be conjurer.

By the 1890s a noticeable improvement on the effect was chronicled. A prop knife was constructed with two blades; one had the half-moon cut away, the other was ordinary. After the regular blade was displayed, a spring device caused it to rotate into the knife handle while cleverly sending the trick blade into the proper position. This explanation, accompanied by a wonderful illustration of a startled woman-subject, appeared in the turn-of-the-century Italian magic magazine, *Il Prestigiatore Moderno*.[16] The popularity of the effect – perhaps sharing the limelight with *Cyrano de Bergerac*, which first appeared in 1897 – now manifested itself in illustrations in the leading magic trade catalogs of the day.

In the 1930s a well-known New York thug, who went by the moniker "Bob the Nose-Biter," made the etymologically inclined recall the textbook definition of the

NOSE AMPUTATING
KNIFE.

With this magical piece of cutlery one-half of your friend's nose may be cut off, and it then falls to the floor. Mark, we do not say whether it is the nose or the knife that falls. You must try the knife to know that. We will say, however, that your friend will not suffer any during the operation.

Price.... $1.50.

word "mayhem" (to bite off the nose or ears) when he used his teeth to defile the noses of those silly enough to disagree with him. His notoriety, say some, sparked renewed interest in the amputation effect, which was reflected in product advertisements in such publications as the popular Johnson-Smith catalog from Racine, Wisconsin. Fortunately this magical reliance on nose amputation, which led the entire profession into decline in the 1940s and '50s, was not seriously resurrected – not even by the melodic Martin Mull hit, "Noses Run In My Family," or by the considerable success of Steve Martin's wonderfully sanguine update of *Cyrano*, the film *Roxanne*. Nor was it helped by the sanguinary nosecutting scene in Roman Polanski's *Chinatown*, or Hannibal Lector's enactment of mayhem in *The Silence of the Lambs*. There are, however, uncorroborated reports of its resurgence in the repertoires of conjurers whose labors are primarily featured between ice cream and party favors at children's birthday fêtes. ◉

NOTES

1. This device, later called "magic cord pillars," makes one think – all right, makes *me* think – of Amy in Louisa May Alcott's *Little Women,* who sported a clothespin on her nose "to uplift the offending creature." It is curious that by 1900, although the device remained the same, the effect had changed; the nose was mysteriously expurgated from all but the illustration (see illustration and description, page 82). Yet another effect, "The Extraordinary Broken Nose," was featured in a Hamley's magic catalogue in the 1890s. A performer bends his assistant's nose between his fingers until "there is heard a loud crack" and the nose is twisted out of joint. The process is repeated in the opposite direction, "when again there is heard a loud crack of the nose going back into joint. This trick causes a great amount of amusement and loud laughter, and can be performed at any time and on any person. Price one shilling."

2. Probably printed in 1564, this engraving included many contemporary conjuring props such as cups and balls, cards, dice, the padlock through the cheek, and the decollation effects described by Scot.

3. *A Pretie and Mery new enterlude: called the Disobedient Child, compiled by Thomas Ingelend late student of Cambridge,* the work is a morality play about a wealthy father and his profligate son, during the course of which a servant describes a drunken gathering with "What leaping, what jumping about that I wondered their braynes dyd not fall out." See also Sidney Clarke, *The Annals of Conjuring,* reprint edition (New York, 1983), p. 37.

4. The first published account of the Hindu method of rhinoplasty to appear in the West was published in London in *The Gentleman's Magazine* (October 1794) under the heading of "Curious Chirurgical Operation." The first successful rhinoplasty performed in England is described in the surgeon Joseph Constantine Carpue's *An Account of Two Successful Operations for Restoring a Lost Nose* (London, 1816). On a more peculiar relationship between medicine and the nose see *The Complete Letters of Sigmund Freud to Wilhelm Fliess, 1887–1904,* ed. J.M. Masson (Cambridge, Mass., 1985), which includes a bizarre, apparently homoerotic, exchange on the sexuality of the nose and the treatment of nasal disorders with cocaine.

5. A nineteenth-century version of the club might have included Kovatsov, the nose-losing civil servant in Nicholas Gogol's *The Nose.*

6. Sterne was also the subject of parodies such as *A Treatise on the Custom of Counting Noses* (London, 1779). Though political in intent, the work hearkens back to the manner of Sterne's Slawkenbergius and mentions in homage Dr. Johnson's definition of the nose: "The prominence on the face, which is the organ of scent, and the emunctory of the brain." A possible precursor of *Tristram Shandy* is *Rinology: A description of the Nose, and Particularly of that Part of it, call'd the Bridge. Wherein is shewn, that the Bridge is the proper support of the Nose; that it is Essential to it; that a Nose Don't deserve its Name without it…to which are subjoin'd several Accounts of Persons who had high Noses, and some who had none at all…By Timothy Bridgeabout, formerly Fellow of St. Patrick's College, and Operator for the Nose to the Great Mogul* (Dublin; reprint, London, 1736).

7. Also mentioned in Thorndike is the account from Sylvester Rattray's *Aditus novus* (Glasgow, 1658) on the antipathy and sympathy of vegetables, animals, and minerals: If the arm from which a nose has been made rots, the nose will also rot (see *History of Magic and Experimental Science,* 8:18). The same idea is discussed in *The Mathematical Lexicon of Hieronymus Vitalis* by Theatine of Capua (Paris, 1668). With admirable skepticism, Christian Friedrich Garmann (1640–1708) discounted this theory in his *De miraculis mortuorum libri* (published posthumously by his son in 1709), but he was uncertain if baptism took away the stench of Jews; if Egyptians ever grew bald; if Muscovites ate the hearts of infants; and if it was excessive sexual intercourse that so often impaired the eyesight of Italians.

8. Jonas was probably introduced by Stevens at the Haymarket Theatre in 1765. See Gerald Kahan's important study *George Alexander Stevens & The Lecture on Heads* (Athens, Ga., 1984).

9. Undated cutting, c. 1807, reproduced in *Magicol* of October 1960 (Oak Park, Ill.), p. 8. In *Punch and Judy*, Mr. Punch often suffers at the teeth of his dog Toby, who bites his prominent proboscis in many versions of the famous puppet play.

10. Richard Potter playbill (c. 1820), reprinted by Robert Olson at Old Sturbridge Village. In his reenactment of Potter, Olson performs a *Dissertation on Noses* based on the text of a Dr. Valentine, published in the 1850s. A playbill in the British Library shows that before the close of the eighteenth century, a lesser-known conjurer, Mr. Barns, was performing the "Dissertation" during his evening's entertainment.

11. Martin Howard, *Victorian Grotesques* (London, 1977), p. 74. Wedders is depicted to the left of the masthead on page 75.

12. The sequel must remain a mystery. Mr. Lane concludes, "Several indecent tricks which he performs with the boy I must abstain from describing: some of them are abominably disgusting."

13. Playbill, author's collection. Punch himself can hardly be ignored in the annals of nasal innuendo. The nose of the famous puppet figure has long been considered a symbol of concupiscence.

14. The Young playbill is in the collection of the Theater Arts Library of the Harry Ransom Humanities Research Center, University of Texas at Austin; quoted in James Hagy, *The One Young* (Shaker Heights, Ohio, 1986), p. 42. The Macallister playbill is from the author's collection.

15. Undated playbill in the scrapbook of Wyman the Wizard, Mulholland Collection, in the International Museum and Library of the Conjuring Arts.

16. *Il Prestigiatore Moderno* (Rome, 1894), pp. 1, 26.

ILLUSTRATIONS

Page 75. Woodcut on the left from Hamley Brothers, *Illustrated Catalogue of Conjuring Tricks, Illusions, &c.*, 189? On the right is a detail from an engraving in *Il Prestigiatore Moderno*.

Page 76. Detail from the engraving *The Fall of the Wizard Hermogenes*, c. 1564.

Page 77. Engraving from Scot's *Discoverie of Witchcraft*, 1584.

Page 78. Woodcut from playbill of Macallister, 1854.

Page 79. Detail from undated playbill of Wyman the Wizard.

Page 80. Woodcut from undated Peck & Snyder catalog.

Page 82. Woodcut from Martinka & Co. catalog, c. 1900.

JAY'S JOURNAL OF ANOMALIES

Written by Ricky Jay and published four times a year by the author and W & V Dailey, Antiquarian Booksellers, 8216 Melrose Avenue, Los Angeles, California, 90046, (213) 658-8515. Subscription $90 per annum. ¶ Printed letterpress by Patrick Reagh and typeset in Monotype Ehrhardt with Thorowgood heads on Rives Heavyweight paper. ¶ Designed by Mr. Reagh & Mr. Jay. ¶ The author wishes to thank Susan Green, Russ Johanson and Michael Weber for generous assistance in the preparation of this issue. ¶ Comments and corrections to the text are welcomed. ¶ Written and illustrative material, © Ricky Jay, 1997. ¶ All images are from the private collection of the author. Any subsequent use of text or image is permissible only with the express written consent of Mr. Jay.

23. Magic Cord Pillars.

A string is shown threaded through two pillars; a knife is taken and passed through, and the string is shown cut, when simply by breathing on it, it is joined again. Very mysterious, still quite easy to perform, and may be repeated as often as desired................Price, **15c**

JAY'S JOURNAL *of*
ANOMALIES

VOLUME THREE   NUMBER TWO   1997

The Wizard of the North and the Aztec Lilliputians

JOHN HENRY ANDERSON, the most famous magician in the English-speaking world, was received at Buckingham Palace on July 4, 1853. In his profonde that day was not "The Inexhaustible Bottle," "The Cards of Cadmus," or "The Speaking Half Crowns," but rather, a pair of diminutive children. For a bemused Queen Victoria he introduced a boy and girl who, he claimed, were the only surviving descendants of an ancient caste of sacerdotal Aztec priests. Even though this was not a traditional conjuring performance, it was, as we will see, a presentation worthy of an eminent trickster.

It is difficult to imagine a nineteenth-century public life more public than John Henry Anderson's. He was born in Scotland in 1814 and was performing professionally by the early 1830s as the "Caledonian Conjurer" and the "Wizard of the North."[1] Anderson arguably plied his trade for more people than any other conjurer of his day. He built the largest theater in Scotland, acted on stage, produced shows other than his own, and exposed the methods of gamblers and fraudulent mediums. His misfortunes as well as his triumphs were avidly chronicled in the periodical press.

Anderson's performances were patronized in numbers that would be impressive to Broadway producers today. Anderson flooded cities in which he was appearing with written accounts of his life – stories of his family, anecdotes of his triumphs, and travails of his travels. He papered whole towns with lithographs and playbills. His likeness appeared on sheet music covers, and was even impressed into pats of butter. Houdini, who would inherit his title as the preeminent magical publicist, pronounced him the "greatest advertiser" the world of magic had ever known, and acknowledged that Anderson "left nothing undone that might boom the attendance at his performances."[2]

In such a newsworthy life, the neglect of even a brief interlude would be surprising, but Anderson's involvement with the Aztec children occasioned a large gap. Anderson's biographers abruptly break off their accounts after his first American tour, in 1853, resuming more than a year later; it was during this interval that Anderson was promoting the Aztec children in London and the provinces. Although he manipulated the story of the Aztecs to promote the act, as we will see, he invariably downplayed his own involvement. I have examined more than half a dozen posters or playbills for the Lilliputians in which Anderson is conspicuous but not identified. Why this panjandrum of publicity, pasha of the press release, caliph of conundrums, nabob of neologism, and Aladdin of alliteration should have chosen not to celebrate his role in the presentation of the Aztec children is, to say the least, puzzling.[3]

It is thus not to Anderson that one can turn to shed light, however dim, on the saga of his diminutive wards. There were fortunately a number of contemporary accounts of the "Aztec Lilliputians," as they were later known, the two extraordinary children said to have been discovered deep within the Yucatán in 1849. By a circuitous route, the two children reached New York in December of that year, and subsequently were introduced to a curious world by a number of entertaining if far-fetched pamphlets describing their capture or rescue – depending on one's point of view. The first of these was entitled *Memoir of an Eventful Expedition in Central America; Resulting In the Discovery of the Idolatrous City of Iximaya in An Unexplored Region; and the Possession of Two Remarkable Aztec Children, Descendants and Specimens of the Sacerdotal Caste (now nearly extinct) of the Ancient Aztec Founders of the Ruined Temples of that Country Described by John L. Stevens [sic], Esq., and other travelers. Translated from the Spanish of Pedro Velasquez, of San Salvador.*[4]

This story of intrepid adventure, unknown kingdoms, archaeological ruins, and daring rescues – all crammed into less than forty pages of surprisingly stylish prose – purports to be a firsthand account of the journey to Iximaya undertaken by Señor Huertis, a well-traveled young man from a wealthy Cuban family that had settled in Baltimore; and Mr. Hammond, a civil engineer from Canada. Their guide, Pedro Velasquez, the narrator and supposed author of the work, was a man of some education and a wealthy trader in indigo. Hammond and Huertis were inspired to undertake the journey to Iximaya by Stephens's *Incidents of Travel in Central America, Chiapas, and Yucatan*, published by Harper in 1841, a ground-breaking work on the Mayans

that became a best seller and is still in print. A sophisticated and articulate mixture of archaeology and adventure, it recounted the tale of the unknown city of Iximaya as narrated to Stephens by the Padre of Santa Cruz del Quiche. This protected community, having heard tales of the Spanish conquest and horrible carnage in the surrounding areas, lived in fear of discovery. Apparently, no white man had ever reached its borders. The city was said to be inhabited by Mayan-speaking natives who used no currency, and were so secretive that they "kept the cocks underground to prevent their crowing from being heard." Unable to contain their enthusiasm, Hammond and Huertis prepared to journey to Iximaya, and they gathered supplies and sailed from New Orleans for Belize in the fall of 1848. There they met Velasquez, an experienced traveler and ex-soldier, who offered to lead the party. The story I retell here is based on his narrative.

On the first leg of the difficult journey, from Vera Pax to Santa Cruz del Quiche, they survived an attack by hostile Indians, but Hammond was wounded. Once in Quiche they happened upon the very padre who had told Stephens of the great unknown city. With spirits restored by this encounter, the group made their way past magnificent Mayan ruins and lush forests to Iximaya. Along the way they heard tales of priests said to sacrifice (and eat) white men, but they remained resolute. Velasquez, meanwhile, learned some of the local Mayan dialect, which proved most helpful in later encounters. As they neared their destination, they crossed paths with two horsemen in bright blue and yellow tunics, bedizened with turbans sporting three large plumes of the quetzal. They were leading "a long retinue of athletic Indians…in brilliant red tunics" (hardly prudent duds, it seems, for rooster-hiding natives). Armed and accompanied by a brace of fine bloodhounds, this patrol party protected the city by hunting down any foreigner that came within twelve leagues of its borders; they soon departed for reinforcements. Even in larger numbers the natives were no match for the explorers, who were armed with repeating rifles. The brightly dressed Iximayans had never seen such weapons and were of course immediately subdued. Even more surprising must have been the wish expressed by the explorers to enter the city, despite the clear warning that they would not be allowed to leave.

Side by side the travelers and Indians marched to the unknown city, past flat-roofed dwellings with overhanging eaves and spiral flutings, past men clad in light blue tunics and reticulated buckskins. When they reached the city, they crossed over a drawbridge and then down a wide avenue between columns of tall trees interspersed with stone statues forty feet high. They soon arrived at the palace and were immediately presented to the king. Attended by his councilors, he was apprised of the recent skirmish outside the city. The visitors were allowed to remain, unguarded but in effect imprisoned – forbidden to leave this city of 8,500 inhabitants.

Huertis eagerly began his scientific explorations while Hammond rested, hoping to recover from his wounds. Velasquez befriended a priest named Vaalpeor who was responsible for the care of two orphaned children, Maximo and Bartola – the principal players in the drama. Of diminutive stature and rudimentary intelligence, these children were, nevertheless, "held in high veneration and affection by the Iximayan community." Their strangely shaped skulls, bearing striking similarity to the sculptured monuments among the ancient ruins, were taken as a sign of their special ancestry.

Hammond soon died from his wounds. Meanwhile, Velasquez plotted to escape from the city with Vaalpeor and the Aztec children. Unfortunately, Huertis disclosed the plan to an Iximayan woman, who betrayed him (tempting though it may have been, Velasquez avoided editorializing). The resulting ritual sacrifice of Huertis on the Altar of the Sun considerably accelerated Velasquez's departure. With Vaalpeor, the children, and fifteen of his original guards, Velasquez swam the moat that surrounded the city. The Iximayans followed in hot pursuit. After fourteen perilous days, the Velasquez party reached the city of Ocosingo and safety.

Vaalpeor died "from the unaccustomed toil and deprivations of the journey" and Velasquez took charge of the children. With them, he reached San Salvador in February of 1849. Persuaded that they would be of great interest to the scientific world as well as the curious public, he exhibited them first in Grenada and then, under the direction of temporary guardians, in Jamaica and New York. The young Aztec children took New York and the rest of the country by storm. Velasquez's pamphlet – which concluded with the remark that they were "specimens of an *absolutely unique* and nearly extinct race

of mankind"–was sold on site. Appended to it were illustrations, redrawn from the Stephens book, of figures carved in the ancient Aztec ruins–figures that, with their small pointy skulls and radically sloped foreheads, bore remarkable similarity to the youngsters. Also included were likenesses of Assyrians taken from Austen Layard's work *Nineveh*, which, it was evident, resembled the peculiar physiognomy of the children – supposedly confirming the Iximayan claim that the children were descended from these Middle Eastern peoples.

Once the Aztecs reached New York, the scientific community attacked them with calipers, scales, and a barrage of questions. Throughout this ordeal, the children displayed a universally admired equanimity and amiability. Extensive testing was conducted by Dr. J. Mason Warren, whose findings were then read to the Boston Society of Natural History on January 1, 1851, and published in the *Journal of Medical Science* in April of the same year. Warren concluded that the Aztecs were possessed of only rudimentary mental ability, that they had likely been born to mixed Indian parents, and that they did not belong to a race of dwarfs. This might have done much to preempt both popular and scientific interest in the children but, paraded about in ridiculous pseudo-Aztec regalia provided by their exhibitors, they attracted large audiences everywhere.

The promoters were gratified when a committee of less prudent investigators, Mr. William Fosdick, Dr. Tom Edwards, and Dr. Jerome Mudd, issued rather different findings. Although the children were "deprived of the power of conversation," they nevertheless exhibited "considerable aptitude and readiness of understanding":

...so far from considering these children idiotic, we look on them as being possessed of uncommon sprightliness of mind.... They are not dwarfs or *lusus naturae*, but are diminutive specimens of the Mestitze inhabitants of Central America. We offer this opinion without pretending to account the causes which may have produced these strange beings – such as intermarriage, physical restriction, confinement or compression, the exclusive habits or peculiarities of a specific caste or order, or other hypotheses. We readily pronounce them the most remarkable and curious phenomena of the genus Homo we have ever seen, and so far from being revolting or offensive to the beholder, they are strikingly interesting and agreeable.[5]

W. Byrd Parnell, "late Professor of Cerebral Physiology and Medical Geology in the Memphis Medical Institute and member of the Société Française of Statistique Universelle of Paris," and a Dr. William Marsden confirmed this view, stating that the children "are the offsprings of human beings of a nearly worn out race of pagans and of the sacerdotal order or caste."

Phrenologists found much of interest in these oddly shaped heads. Professor Joseph R. Buchanan, whose "system...differs somewhat from the prevalent school," allowed his chart and findings to be affixed to a pamphlet about the Aztecs. Using Warren's measurements, he ascertained that the brain of the boy was twice as large proportionately as it would be for an adult American, but, confusingly enough, cautioned that the brains of children were proportionately larger than those of adults. He was able to discover a great deal about the boy's ancestry and character by examining his head:

The height of the head indicates amiable dispositions, the moral organs being very well developed except in the regions of conscientiousness, industry, temperament, and self-control or restraint. For want of these organs he cannot be expected to exhibit any strict moral principle. His tendencies will be toward the vices of a heedless, indolent, sensual but rather good-natured character. It is obvious therefore that he has descended from an ancestry of ignorant, indolent, and reckless character, but not of any ferocious or bloodthirsty habits.

The church, pleased to learn that Velasquez had the children baptized Catholics, naming them Maximo and Bartola Velasquez, acknowledged their special status. The *Christian Advertiser and Journal*, the *Churchman*, and the *Christian Observer* were unanimous in their observations that the children were not dwarfs but rather some strange specimens of humanity. "No intelligent man can look on them without novel and profound emotions," said the *Observer*. "We are not easily humbugged," added the *Advertiser*, in pronouncing their justifiable interest in the children.

But even more mainstream periodicals, like *The Express*, heralded the Aztecs as "a wonder and delight from which none could come away disappointed." N. P. Willis exclaimed in the *Home Journal*:

An entirely new type – a kind of human being which had never before been seen – with physiognomies formed by descent through ages of thought and association of which we had no knowledge – moving, observing, gesticulating differently from all other children – and, somehow, with an unexplainable look of authenticity and conscious priority, as if *they* were of the "old family" of human nature, and *we* were the mushrooms of today.

ROYAL AQUARIUM

In announcing the discovery of "a new race of human beings…of historical as well as critical importance," the *Journal of Fine Arts* credulously related that when a small stone image, found in Chapultepec, Mexico, was shown to the children, "they caress and fondle it in a manner which plainly indicates that they have seen something of the kind before. When it was first shown by the lady who presented it to Mr. Knox [then the Aztec's manager], the boy, Maximo, danced with delight, and when it was taken away from him, he wept and mourned most piteously."[6]

Armed with these endorsements, a Mr. Know and a Mr. Morris, both then being listed as proprietors, presented the Aztecs. They did a brisk business and achieved significant celebrity when the children were shown to members of the U.S. Senate and even to President Millard Fillmore at the White House.

The response of the respected newspaperman Horace Greeley may offer a partial key to the enthusiasm that issued from all quarters of American society. Greeley was distinctly not a gawker or appreciator of freaks: "I hate monstrosities, however remarkable, and

am rather repelled than attracted by the idea of their truthfulness." But he, too, extolled the Aztecs. Precisely because their authenticity was uncertain, they were perceived as charmingly exotic rather than genuinely monstrous. Because their true nature was so widely debated, it was possible not only for unscrupulous promoters but also for the curious public, not only for quacks but also for serious scientists, to project widely varying notions of the nature of the human upon them. Ten years before the publication of *The Origin of Species*, the Aztec children reveal something about the midcentury boundaries between the disciplines of archaeology and anthropology, and what was about to become evolutionary biology. Cultural forces were at work, too: for an America trying desperately to seek an identity independent from Europe, the discovery of a fabulous people in their own hemisphere, in their own backyard, was doubtless wildly appealing.

Arriving on American shores in August 1851, John Henry Anderson portrayed himself much as a modern international star would, as a figure of vast and deserved celebrity destined to delight his admiring over-seas public. In its turn, America was primed to receive him: the nation seemed ready for the kind of "good, clean" entertainment that he offered, and ready to welcome, as it still does, a charming foreign celebrity. Anderson's repertoire consisted of very strong and apparently original material (although much of it was purloined from other conjurers who had not visited these shores). He had a fine physical appearance and an impressive stage presence that compensated for his tech-nical limitations as a magician and, according to review-ers, his even more severe limitations as an actor. Add to this mix his opportunism, and the stage is set for his association with the survivors of Iximaya.

Anderson's debut in New York was an unqualified success. After a long run, he moved to Philadelphia, where he performed at Musical Fund Hall from mid-October to the end of November. The Aztecs were scheduled to appear in the same building a few weeks later. The scenario of their meeting in Philadelphia, or elsewhere on the eastern seaboard, is a likely one, as both attractions toured and generated considerable publicity.

In March, Anderson toured New Orleans, and then Mobile, Memphis, St. Louis, and Louisville before heading back to New York. In September he played Boston, and by the end of the year he had returned south for engagements in Charleston and Savannah. He returned again to New York, where he gave a series of farewell performances before embarking for Britain in June 1853.[7]

A few weeks later, Prince Albert, the Prince of Wales, the Prince and Princess of Prussia, Prince Hohenloe, the Duke and Duchess of Saxe-Coburg, and Queen Victoria herself welcomed the Aztecs to Buckingham Palace. "So interested was her majesty, that she remained with the 'Aztecs' for nearly an hour and previous to their depar-ture expressed herself much gratified with their visit," reported the *Illustrated London News* of July 9, 1853, adding that "the children were accompanied and pre-sented by Prof. Anderson."

Promising as was this royal acknowledgment, it should be stressed that the queen had a predilection for such business. It is impolite but not unfair to character-ize her as a "groupie" of unusual entertainment. She attended exhibitions of Ojibbeway Indians, the Happy Family (a mixed menagerie of rats, owls, monkeys,

hawks, ferrets, and kittens in a single cage), an assort-ment of freaks and physical anomalies like Tom Thumb, and three times visited the famous American lion tamer Isaac Van Amburg.[8]

Royal patronage insured that the opening of the Aztecs at the Hanover Square Rooms on July 11 would be momentous, as attested by the price of a seat: five shillings, reserved; two and sixpence, second seats. By July 23, Anderson was advertising that ten thousand spectators had already viewed the unique attraction.

While emphatic New York notices had declared the children an "absolutely and nearly extinct race of mankind," under Anderson's management they were apotheosized almost to immortality:

HERE THEY ARE! LIVING! and open to public view and examina-tion – not merely imaginary creatures like the strange men of Africa mentioned by Herodotus, the phoenix, or the mermaid. Not a fictitious people like the fauns and dryads of the Arcadian vales – not the moonlight fairies; the little gray men of the Norse legends – not nymph, sprite, nor elf – but human beings, of flesh and blood – the remnant of a strange and wonderful race – the greatest mar-vel of the land of wonders, and of the nineteenth century– more strange than the vast skeletons of the Mastodon, which have been exhumed in the same region; but, like the black swan of New Holland formerly regarded as a myth, now a well-established exis-tence. In short, as curious and well substantiated as the singular sightless fish of the mammoth cave in Kentucky.

Such hyperbole surpassed even showman's rodo-montade, and a backlash soon followed in the press. Professor Richard Owen, the famous comparative anatomist, examined the Aztecs and concluded that "these alleged representatives of a 'lost' race were noth-ing more glamorous than a pair of severely retarded chil-dren belonging to a contemporary people." (His wife, however, wrote admiringly of them in her diary.) Writers in the *Times* of London and the *Athenaeum* attacked the veracity as well as the morality of the Velasquez story of Iximaya, and criticized his capture of the children. The naturalist Charles Waterton fumed, "I really cannot stomach the account given by Velasquez de San Salvador," and questioned why, if the children could understand language, they could not speak. A phrenol-ogist, Mr. C. Donovan, offered that the term "Lilli-putian" was inapplicable (although outside of eigh-teenth-century fiction, it is hard to imagine what it might designate appropriately). They were not, he said, "educable in the ordinary sense of the word. They may be taught to perform some slight feats or utter a few words in a parrot-like manner, but beyond this, advancement is denied them." Donovan called them "the zero of moral and intellectual inferiority." The damaging account of the American doctor J. Mason Warren was now published in the London press.

Anderson rebutted these attacks in a paid column in the *Times*, but he had little to fear, as the controversy seemed only to boost attendance. Whatever their genus or origins, Maximo and Bartola, cute and affectionate, had a genuine and almost indefatigable ability to charm and interest the public. Within a month of their opening, Anderson claimed that fifty thousand of the "elite of the metropolis" had paid to see them.

Shortly after the London opening, a broadside published by J. Fairburn gave a less hyperbolic, but still celebratory and detailed, account of the act and its principals. Anderson is depicted in it but is again unnamed:

The exhibition of the children is prefaced by a lecture, briefly detailing the circumstance of Velasquez's narrative. When the children are put upon the platform, we see a couple of active, diminutive beings, with countenances decidedly Jewish, who run and roll and jump and leap about in the most abundant enjoyment of animal spirits, and expressing in their arts and looks a relish for fun and frolic. [Other descriptions of the children variously describe them as Assyrian, Indian or Hindu.] In their conduct towards each other, and to strangers who show them kindness, they are affectionate and loving. The boy is generous and disinterested and will readily bestow on the girl a part or the whole of any delicacy he receives, but she is less so. He is easy tempered; she, irritable and soon incensed, but as soon pacified.

The first impression of the spectator is that they are dwarfs – an impression which is banished, however, by a second glance. The head of the dwarf is invariably larger in proportion than the body – the heads of these children are smaller, and both together are less than that of the renowned Tom Thumb. Their mode of sitting down is peculiar; when seated on the ground they turn the soles of their feet outward. The hypothesis of their being a new race is, at least, countenanced by some unaccountable differences in physical conformation. When they bite their food, they do it with their side teeth, because their front teeth do not meet, but those of the lower jaw strike against their palate; but the ears of both these children are not in the place where the ear is found upon the head of other races. In them, the ear is in fact elevated its whole length above the usual position – the lower portion of it being upon a level, not with the base of the nose, as it is with us, but with the center of the eyes, and the top of it upon a level, or nearly so, with the crown of the head. The forms of both are in perfect proportion, their actions are in all respects natural and graceful.

But by far the most remarkable circumstance in connection with these human phenomena is, their *silence*. Here are two human beings, of the ages of eleven and seventeen years, possessing the organs of speech in perfection, yet utterly unacquainted with a language, even the most simple or fragmentary. Three years ago, when they first came under the control of their present guardian, neither of them could articulate a word of any language; since which time they have learned a few English words, which they pronounce with tolerable accuracy. They laugh loudly at times; and if one, in their frolics, happens to strike the other, the hurt is immediately compensated, after the manner of infants, by a kiss. Considering their want of speech, they exhibit a most pleasing degree of intelligence, and appear to understand whatever is spoken to them by their guardian. They fetch any article for which they are sent, evidently remembering, though they cannot utter, the names of things. They will eat nothing they receive from the hands of strangers until their guardian permits them to do so.

In mid-August, having tapped the beau monde of its easy money, the Aztecs moved to the Marionette Theatre in Adelaide Street where, at the more modest price of one shilling, members of the working class could attend. Thousands paid homage before the Aztecs departed for a tour of the provinces on September 17.

For performances at the Britannia Theatre in Hoxton, posters featured the tiniest representation of the Aztecs yet. One scene featured the Pagan Temple of Iximaya with the children high on pedestals and priests kneeling at their feet. Other vignettes displayed Anderson holding a drum that Maximo strikes with a stick; a visit from Queen Victoria and the royal family; and Maximo playing a violin almost as large as his entire body (a fiddle appears in at least three posters of the Aztecs, yet not one review mentions that they played the instrument). In the three days at the Liverpool Zoo, a playbill announced, 18,109 persons had paid to see them; and at the Rotunda in Dublin, they did a brisk trade. "For the accommodation of the elite of Limerick and the District," a playbill announced the appearance of the Aztecs with the refreshingly "tell-it-like-it-is" banner line, "Extraordinary Cheap Exhibition of Living People with Heads Like Birds."[9]

For another playbill, Anderson reproduced *in toto* a mixed review from *Freeman's Journal* of October 3, appending the preposterous claim that the exhibition had been witnessed by two million spectators. On another bill, their arrival was hailed: "WONDERFUL, WONDERFUL, WONDERFUL, WONDERFUL, are thy ways, oh, providence. How wonderful are thy works."

Returning to London for the Christmas season, the Aztecs were shocked to find another pygmy attraction, the Erdemänne or Earthmen, ensconced in the metropolis. The name had been coined by early Dutch settlers of South Africa for natives that they likened to ground squirrels. The Earth People supposedly used their hands and feet in an approximation of a rodent burying food, but this, in view of their delicate appendages, seemed highly unlikely. They were a boy of sixteen and a girl of fourteen, three and a half feet tall, said to subsist on insects and plants. In a dig at the Aztecs, their advertising stated that they were "perfect in their kind," offering "a happy contrast to the little Central Americans arrested in their growth." The managers of these opposing

anomalies reached a truce by combining their attractions on the same platform. To avoid the inevitable loss of revenue, they hatched a double-booking scheme, appearing at the Queen's Concert Rooms in the late morning for a two-shilling crowd, and then rushing off to Linwood Gallery, Leicester Square, where general admission was only sixpence, for afternoon and evening shows. Eventually, a vocal and instrumental concert was added to the proceedings at no extra charge.

By 1854, one could see a wax effigy of the Aztecs, in the company of five hundred other figures, at Reimer's Anatomical and Ethnological Museum at Saville House, for sixpence.[10] By 1855, however, the interest in the Aztecs waned at last, and Anderson resumed his career as a magician (with its usual ups and downs). He seems to have had no further involvement with the children.

The Aztecs continued to surface periodically for the next *half century*. P. T. Barnum, not one to ignore such appeal, hired them for his American Museum in New York in 1860 and subsequently. A sham wedding between the children garnered much publicity for the act in London in 1867.[11] Under the names of Señor Maximo Valdez Núñez and Señora Bartola Velasquez, the Aztecs were "joined in matrimony" in the registrar's office on January 7. Their wedding breakfast was given at Willis' Rooms under the directorship of Mr. Morris. No expense was spared. Edward Wood covered the event as if it was a society wedding:

The bridegroom wore evening dress, with a white waistcoat, a red camellia in his button hole, and a strip of crimson ribbon denoting his claim to a foreign order. He had a stooping, jerky gait; and so had his bride, although not in so noticeable a degree. She wore a white satin dress, cut low, and liberally adorned with brilliants, a wreath of orange-blossoms, and a lace veil, which caused her a great deal of trouble.[12]

The gown was said to have cost two thousand pounds.

Toward the end of the century, Maximo and Bartola spawned a passel of imitators: "Estics," "The Wild Girl of Yucatan," "The Wild Mexican Boy," "The Ancient Aztecs," "Gora and Ara," "The Original Aztec Indian Midgets From Old Mexico," "Maggie, the Last of the Aztecs," and "Tik Tak the Aztec Pinhead," to name a few. They all capitalized on the elaborate mythology of the originals, who were still promoted at the Crystal Palace in 1870 and on the Barnum and Bailey Circus shows of 1888, 1889, and 1890.[13] Other references can be found from 1901, and even as late as 1905 an appearance was mentioned in a newspaper column by Harry Houdini: "The Aztecs that were once a feature with Barnum and Bailey's side show" were exhibited by "Herr Fritz Geissler, who is known as the German Barnum."[14] The "Original Aztecs" were advertised in France that same year.[15]

In the world of mendacious showmen who would embellish, manipulate, and massage the truth for their own ends, the saga of the Aztecs is hardly surprising. What is surprising is the enduring appeal of the act, not undermined by investigation or exposure, and the success of the Velasquez narrative in attracting attention to it. A particularly clear-eyed explanation of the nature and origin of the children was published in 1857, when Dr. Carl Scherzer wrote, in his *Travels in the Free States of Central America:*

The two mulatto children...are nothing more than two remarkably underdeveloped individuals of this mixed descent [Indian and Negro], the twin children of two persons named Innocent and Marina Burgos, who are still living in the village of Decora, in the department of San Miguel. A Spanish trader, of the name of Ramón Selva, got them from the mother, to whom they were very burdensome on account of their helpless awkwardness, under pretense of having them educated in the United States; but instead of that, he made a show of them, and afterwards sold them to a person named Morris, who is at present, I believe, parading them about in the best company of Europe.[16]

But the Velasquez account not only achieved universal popularity, it also transcended veracity. Through its imaginative and timely combination of folklore, mythology, and psychology, the pamphlet prepared the way for the hugely enthusiastic American reception of the act. Whoever wrote the short volume had formidable linguistic and narrative skills, and it captured the attention of rich and poor, educated and uneducated alike. In its compelling appeal and its ability to withstand exposure, it demands comparison with the writings of Carlos Castaneda, whose works on the magical Mexican Indian hero Don Juan were best sellers in the 1960s and '70s, and are still being published.[17]

The sweet and charming Maximo and Bartola were mentally retarded microcephalics or, in carnival jargon, "pinheads." The Aztec Lilliputians, neither Aztec nor Lilliputian, were the subjects of an extraordinary hoax — reason enough, one supposes, for a master of deception like John Henry Anderson to become involved in their phenomenal career. ◎

NOTES

1. Anderson claimed that this title was bestowed by the literary Wizard of the North, Sir Walter Scott, but this was just one example of his showman's license.

2. Harry Houdini, *The Unmasking of Robert-Houdin* (New York, 1908), p. 147. Says E. P. Hingston in an authorized biography of our subject: "Other men have sought to entrap fame by dint of large type and bold pictures, but they are bunglers in comparison with Professor Anderson. The invention, the variety, the fancy of his posting-bills, entitle him to the praise of being uncontested head of the mural literature and art of this metropolis" (E. P. H., *Biography of John Henry Anderson* [Birmingham, 1858], pp. 22–23).

3. This description of Anderson appears in Ricky Jay, *The Magic Magic Book* (New York, 1994 [1995]), p. 42. I presented a talk, "The Wizard of the North and the Aztec Lilliputians," at the first "Conference on Magic History," held in Los Angeles, November 2–4, 1989. The major sources for biographical information on Anderson are Sidney W. Clarke, *The Annals of Conjuring*, reprint ed. (New York, 1983); Charles Pecor, *The Magician on the American Stage* (Washington, D.C., 1977); and Edwin Dawes, *The Great Illusionists* (Secaucus, N.J., 1979); Milbourne Christopher, *The Illustrated History of Magic* (New York, 1973); E. P. H., *Biography of John Henry Anderson;* Anon., *The Wizard of the North: Life Story of John Henry Anderson* (printed serially, Glasgow, 1901); John Mulholland, *The Sphinx* (March 1944); Thomas Frost, *Lives of the Conjurors* (London, 1876); J. B. Findlay, *Professor Anderson and His Theatre* (Shanklin, Isle of Wight, 1967); and the recent but unreliable full-length biography by Constance Pole Bayer, *The Great*

Wizard of the North (Watertown, Mass., 1990). None of these mentions Anderson's involvement with the Aztecs.

4. There seems to be no way to establish priority between the Bell and Applegate editions, both printed in New York and dated 1850. A subsequent edition, imprinted Bell, 1850, contains four prefatory pages rebutting criticism of the Aztecs. I have seen more than a half dozen variations, printed in the U.S. and Great Britain, that appeared before the end of the decade. Occasionally the titles would change, for instance, *Pagan Rites and Ceremonies of the Mayaboon Indians in the City of Iximaya in Central America*, but the text would remain almost identical. Most of these, including later versions, such as *Life of the Living Aztec Children Now Exhibiting at Barnum's American Museum* (1860), were clearly designed to be sold at the exhibition.

5. This report and those quoted below are reproduced in a pamphlet entitled *The Aztecs' Last Week in Philadelphia* (New York, 1852).

6. The newspaper articles quoted here are reproduced in *The Aztecs' Last Week in Philadelphia*.

7. For the chronology of Anderson's American tour, see Pecor, *The Magician on the American Stage*, pp. 185–95. For information on the exhibition of Maximo and Bartola in the City of Brotherly Love, see *The Aztecs' Last Week in Philadelphia*.

8. Richard Altick, *The Shows of London* (London, 1968), p. 222.

9. Playbill, author's collection.

10. Playbill, author's collection. An effigy of the Aztecs was also displayed in the New York Museum of Anatomy in the 1870s.

11. A poster commemorating the event, printed in color, is in the collection of the Wellcome Institute of Medicine in London.

12. Edward J. Wood, *Giants and Dwarfs* (London, 1868), p. 438. Items on the wedding from the *Times, Telegraph, Morning Post,* and *Standard,* from which Wood has drawn, are all quoted on the verso of a playbill for the act at the Crystal Palace, April 1870, Harvard Theatre Collection.

13. Robert Bogdan, in *Freak Show* (Chicago and London, 1988), has a good account of the Aztecs and their imitators (pp. 127–34).

14. *New York Dramatic Mirror,* April 8, 1905, p. 15.

15. See playbill in Jacques Garnier, *Forains d'Hier & d'Aujourd'hui* (Orleans, 1968), p. 35. The only death date I have seen for either child (1913, for Maximo) appears in Hans Scheugl, *Show Freaks & Monsters* (Cologne, 1974), p. 105—a book with a peculiar English title, written in German.

16. Carl Scherzer, *Travels in the Free States of Central America, Nicaragua, Honduras, and San Salvador* (London, 1857), 2:234–35.

17. Castaneda received a doctorate in anthropology from UCLA in 1973 by submitting three volumes of field reports revealing his relationship with Don Juan, a mystical Mexican Indian master. Many scholars believe the work to be a complete fiction. For more on the Castaneda story, see Richard De Mille's *The Don Juan Papers* (Santa Barbara, Calif., 1980). A concise summary of the controversy appears in Gordon Stein, *Encyclopedia of Hoaxes* (Detroit, Washington, D.C., and London, 1993), pp. 1–3.

ILLUSTRATIONS

JAY'S JOURNAL OF ANOMALIES

Written by Ricky Jay and published four times a year by the author and W & V Dailey, Antiquarian Booksellers, 8216 Melrose Avenue, Los Angeles, California, 90046, (213) 658-8515. Subscription $90 per annum. ¶ Printed letterpress by Patrick Reagh and typeset in Monotype Ehrhardt with Thorowgood heads on Rives Heavyweight paper. ¶ Designed by Mr. Reagh & Mr. Jay. ¶ The author wishes to thank Susan Green and Larry Vigon for generous assistance in the preparation of this issue. ¶ Comments and corrections to the text are welcomed. ¶ Written and illustrative material, © Ricky Jay, 1997. ¶ All images are from the private collection of the author. Any subsequent use of text or image is permissible only with the express written consent of Mr. Jay.

JAY'S JOURNAL *of* ANOMALIES

VOLUME THREE   NUMBER THREE   1997

The Gnome Fly

SIGNOR HERVIO NANO, the fantastic homunculus, defied conventional taxonomy. Neither dwarf nor midget, he was sometimes billed as the shortest man in the world but was without doubt one of the greatest athletic showmen of his day. "Any description," said a contemporary profile, "must fall very far short of conveying an adequate idea of his reality....His legs do not appear to be more than six or eight inches in length; indeed, one of them is something shorter, yet he moves about with extraordinary agility." His limbs, when full grown, were eighteen and twenty-four inches respectively, from tip of toe to hip, and his arms easily touched the ground when he walked. He appeared "like a head and trunk, moving about on castors."[1] He was said to be small enough to walk under the arm of the famous dwarf Lady Morgan. His head was finely formed and his expression intelligent; down to the waist he appeared to be a normal, indeed muscular, man; but his pelvis was weak and his thighs almost nonexistent, and his right shin and right foot were deformed and his left foot splayed out from his body.[2]

T. COOKE'S
Circus
TENTER GROUND,
Great Prescot Street, Goodmans Fields
SATURDAY, May 2nd. 1829.

BEING FOR THE

BENEFIT
OF
Mr. LEACH,

Late of the Theatre Royal Drury Lane. And positively his last time
OF PERFORMING IN ENGLAND!!!

Who will for this Night only exhibit the MIRACULOUS

FEAT OF RUNNING
UP THE
ROOF
OF THE CIRCUS,
Like a Fly,
Back Downwards!!!

For the First Time in this Country he will Perform his Grand

Antipodæon Decension,

From the Top of the Circus, Down a Ladder Fifty Feet High. on his Hands
Only, in the same manner as Performed by them from the Steeple of
Notterdam in Paris.—With a Variety of New and Interesting Performances
got up expressly for this Evening.

J. W. PEELE, Printer, 9, & 31, New Cut, Lambeth.

According to George Odell, Nano was born Harvey Leach in Westchester County, New York, in March 1804.[3] By 1812 Leach was performing as a dwarf at Bartholomew Fair in London, billed as "The American Youth"; and in 1813 at the Portsmouth Free Market as "the shortest man in the world," with his age given as eighteen (no doubt to distort favorably the impression of his diminutive size). Leach had already begun to exhibit some of the equilibristic stunts that would leave other Lilliputians far behind, and he advanced circuitously but steadily from the ignominy of a "freak" attraction to the celebrity of an accomplished performer. It was observed that he walked down a flight of stairs on his hands faster than any other person could on their feet.[4] He took a pin out of the wall with his mouth, standing upside down on one hand. Balancing on his hands on the top of a chair back, he hurled himself upward and then alighted on the ground, still standing on his hands. After these and similar stunts he challenged anyone to do the like for the sum of one thousand guineas, and was never the poorer for it.

Leach performed at various English venues – St. James Fair, Bristol; Race Week at Newcastle upon Tyne; Nottingham Goose Fair – into the 1820s.[5] At Cooke's Circus he was celebrated with a benefit night on May 2, 1829, which was billed as his last performance in England. Perhaps for the first time, the playbill called the public's attention to the endeavor that was to become Leach's trademark:

Miraculous Feat of Running up the Roof of the Circus, Like a Fly, Back Downwards!!! For the First Time in this Country he will Perform his Grand Antipodæon Decension, From the Top of the Circus, Down a Ladder Fifty Feet High, on his Hands Only, in the same manner as Performed by them from the Steeple of Notterdam in Paris.–With a Variety of New and Interesting Performances got up expressly for this Evening.

Most importantly, Leach's heroic perambulation was wrought without the aid of the suction devices favored by contemporary ceiling walkers.[6] Leach was well on his way to notoriety if not stardom.

For all his talent, he was a cantankerous soul. On March 30, 1830, Leach was the plaintiff in an action against a Mr. Simpson, the manager of the Birmingham Theatre. In November of the previous year, Leach had refused to perform until he was paid the twelve pounds and change he claimed he was owed. He pleaded his case to the audience from a private box, and so aroused their sympathy that spectators pelted the stage with projectiles. When the management tried to have Leach removed by a constable, a riot ensued: benches were torn up and thrown into the pit and much property, including the chandeliers, was destroyed. Leach was handcuffed, carted off to jail, and charged with inciting a riot. He was acquitted, but then turned the tables on his accusers, pressing for a settlement against Simpson for assault and false imprisonment. During these proceedings, Leach was said to have uttered language "rude and unbecoming," displaying such violence that in spite of his diminutive size, it took two men to subdue him. One constable, quoted in the source of this story, a contemporary newspaper account, pronounced him "a sort of pocket Hercules," and another a "very malignant scurvy little dog," epithets that not only amused the courtroom spectators but also led the jury to conclude that Leach was all too likely to have rioted, and they denied his claim.

Without the benefit of a barrister on retainer – much less a jury consultant – Leach was dogged by legal troubles. In 1838 he was accused of "wantonly horsewhipping" a gentleman named John Williams. When Williams, traveling on a pony and rushing to catch a train, overtook Leach's cabriolet on Ludgate-Hill, the little man shouted at the plaintiff. Leach whipped his horse, causing him to fall, it was claimed. When Williams remonstrated, "the defendant, without a word being exchanged, commenced flogging him with his whip in a most violent manner, by which his cheek was cut open, and one of his eyes nearly cut out." At a time when British citizens consider the American justice system to be a branch of the entertainment industry, it should be noted that Leach seemed to treat the courtroom as yet another theatrical venue. He joked his way through the proceedings, occasionally responding in German, Italian, Greek, or French. One witness, a tailor from Fleet Street, reported that the defendant had "lashed the complainant most shamefully," and Leach replied, "I did no such thing; I only cut at a fly which rested on the horse's ear." "Was it of the Gnome species?" asked one of the attorneys. "Oh no," said Leach, "that was behind." Leach was not represented by counsel and brought no witnesses. He hoped to convince the jury that his accuser was merely trying to extort money with trumped-up charges, but "without the least hesitation," they returned a verdict of guilty, and Leach was sentenced to pay a fine of twenty pounds "for wanton cruelty." He vociferously refused an offer of a reduced penalty of ten pounds if he would make restitution, with an apology, directly to Mr. Williams. Leach was apparently judged harshly even by the jury of his peers; according to one newspaper report of January 6, 1839, there were a number of the "theatrical fraternity" in the crowded courtroom that broke into loud applause when the verdict was announced.

Leach could inspire dread as well as astonishment. *The Literary Gazette* noted that he was capable of pursuing a horse at full gallop and then "springing on its back like a monkey.... His mode of fighting, too, was most original; he used to spring in the air, and at the same instant deal a terrific blow upon the antagonist's head, so that he was a very formidable combatant." Leach startled the novelist Edmund Yates, who, according to Raymond Toole-Stott, "walked into a theatre one morning and was petrified with terror to see a singular creature creeping over the chairs and tables with wondrous agility."[7]

Perhaps the British Isles were simply too austere in temperament for Leach, who soon departed for milder southern climes. He performed on the Continent in the 1830s, where his first name was romanticized to "Hervio," and "Nano," the Italian word for dwarf, was adopted as his surname. He was said to have mastered several languages, visited most of the major cities of Europe, and performed for many of the crowned heads (*Memoir*, p. iii). Now the star of his own theatrical extravaganzas, he played Paris, London, Brussels, and the Italian peninsula in the characters of Alnain the Gnome Fly and Wamba the Fire Spirit.[8]

Leach soon aspired to zoological as well as national metamorphosis. An unidentified English newspaper cutting, hand-dated September 17, 1837, announced his success "performing at the Varieties as a baboon, in a piece called *Les Bêtes Feroces de Bois de Boulogne*, to the infinite delight of the amateurs of the Boulevards, and is shortly to come out as a 'Fly,' and crawl about the ceiling of the theatre, &c. What will our ingenious neighbors think of next?" Another account described his encyclopedic and polyglot repertoire of roles and routines:

Sir, On Friday, May 17th, 1839, we shall have the honour to exhibit the Fourth appearance of M. Hervio-Nano-Leach. The King of the Bees, or the Dwarf Alnain The Sorceror-Genius: a grand highly entertaining dramatic tale of enchantment, with songs in three acts, from the French of M. Rochefort, freely translated into Dutch & adapted by the Heer C. Alexander Van Ray; who has also himself provided all the requisite theatrical properties, dresses, new decorations, machinery, scenery, dances, processions, etc. This magical drama was produced expressly for M. Hervio-Nano-Leach at the Theatre Royal Drury-lane in London, & has been performed by him upwards of one hundred & eighteen times there & in the principal cities of Europe, as Rome, Naples, Venice, Milan, Turin, Paris, etc. with universal applauses. In the tale of enchantment abovementioned he will have the honour to perform the part of Alnain, in which are contained seven distinct disguises & characters.[9]

THÉÂTRE FRANÇAIS.

**Monsieur HARVEY-LEACH
(dit L'HOMME MOUCHE)**

Premier Mime des Théâtres Royaux de Druly Lane et de Covent Garden de Londres.

Les Artistes réunis en Société s'empressent d'annoncer aux Amateurs du Théâtre, qu'après une correspondance suivie, ils ont eu le bonheur de réussir à engager pour trois représentations seulement Mr. HARVEY-LEACH, connu par ses Exercices Métempsychosiens et jouissant d'une grande célébrité.

La première représentation qui aura lieu incessamment sera composée de

**LA REINE
DES ABEILLES,**

Pièce Féerie en trois Actes, à Grand Spectacle, ornée de Décors, Costumes et Transformations nouvelles. Mr. HARVEY-LEACH remplira le rôle d'*Alnain* et paraitra sous diverses formes; entr'autres en

MOUCHE, GNÔME, SINGE, PAPILLON &c. &c.
**Il terminera ses exercices par le VOL AÉRIEN,
sous la forme d'une ABEILLE, en s'élançant
du Fond du Théâtre jusqu'au Plafond
de la Salle.**

Jaloux de mériter les suffrages du Public, les Artistes Sociétaires n'ont pas reculé devant les grands frais occasionnés par la mise en scène de ce Spectacle, vraiment extraordinaire et unique par la nature phénoménale, de Mr. HARVEY-LEACH. LA REINE DES ABEILLES sera jouée SEULE; les Machines et Décorations ne pouvant être démontées pour toute autre pièce.

*Afin de ne pas priver les amateurs de la Promenade,
on commencera à 8 heures précises au moment ou la
fraîcheur du soir arrive.*

L'Affiche et les Billets du jour donneront les détails et la distribution de cet ouvrage.

On July 21, 1839, Leach wrote to the prominent dramatist William Thomas Montcrieff (1794–1857), boasting of his European triumphs. He had appeared, he said, as the lead in *La Reine des Abeilles* (The Queen

Bee), and *Le Papillon* (The Butterfly), speaking his part in the Dutch or French as required; and was currently engaged in a "grand equestrian spectacle" before leaving for dates in Rotterdam, Amsterdam, and Hamburg. This immodest itinerary was followed by a specific request for Montcrieff's help with a hippo-drama Leach planned to stage in London, but the missive was chiefly intended to encourage the playwright to produce a magazine piece extolling Leach's exploits.[10]

According to Brown's *History of the American Stage,* Leach made his American debut at the Chestnut Street Theatre in Philadelphia in 1840 as Alnain in *King of the Gnomes,* and he appeared as the Gnome Fly in New York the same year. Although the fly was his main vehicle, for the next few years he appeared on the American stage in a variety of roles: Génie de Feu, Bibbo the Patagonian Ape, and Le Papillon, which Odell pronounced his most astonishing exhibition. Wearing a splendid butterfly costume, Leach traveled "from the ceiling, back of the gallery, to the back of the stage, a distance of 250 feet" (vol. 4, p. 368).

For appearances at the Tremont Theatre in Boston in May he was dubbed the Extraordinary Metempsychosian Actor. As the Gnome Fly and as Sapajou, Baboon to the Prince of Tartary, the playbills noted, Nano had performed by command of the Emperor of Austria at the Coronation at Milan; before the King of Naples at the Festival of St. Rosalie in Palermo; and at Parma for the Empress Maria Louise.[11] In his benefit performance on May 15 Leach re-created the spectacular ascent from gallery to stage, this time in the character of the Queen Bee. Six years later, with Leach still playing the Gnome Fly, Odell referred to him as "the distressing Hervio Nano" (vol. 5, p. 202).

On March 17, 1843, Nano was back in London, now at the Olympia Theatre and teamed with the American giant, Freeman, in a customized production entitled "The Son of the Desert and the Human Changeling." At the conclusion of the performance the pair walked to the footlights in pleasing incongruity, hand in hand, to receive the plaudits of the crowd.[12]

The fall of Mr. Leach from this pinnacle during the 1840s is a story rich in apocrypha and speculation. It is evident that his dizzying rise from exhibited anomaly to theatrical star reversed itself precipitously, and perhaps Leach's predilection for metamorphosis accelerated his

devolution. In the summer of 1846, our protagonist accepted an engagement in which he was exhibited as the Wild Man of the Prairie, the legendary "missing link." His skin was stained and his body covered with a suit of animal hair; he was made to growl ferociously, devour raw meat, and career about the walls and ceiling of his cage like an ape.[13] This unflattering spectacle took place at London's famous home for the spectacular, Egyptian Hall. As recounted by Richard Altick,[14] the playbill and newspaper notice of Saturday, August 29, stated:

Is it an Animal? Is it Human? or is it a legitimate member of Nature's Works? Or is it the long sought for Link between man and the Ourang Outang, which Naturalists have for years decided does exist, but which has hitherto been undiscovered? The exhibitors of this indescribable Person or Animal do not pretend to assert what it is. They have named it the WILD MAN OF THE PRAIRIES; OR "WHAT IS IT?" because this is the universal exclamation of all who have seen it. Its features, hands, and the upper portion of its body are to all appearances human, the lower part of its body, the hind legs, and haunches are decidedly animal. It is entirely covered, except the face and hands, with long flowing hair of various shades. It is larger than an ordinary sized man, but not quite so tall. "WHAT IS IT?" is decidedly the most extraordinary being that ever astonished the world. It has the intelligence appertaining to humanity, and can do anything it sees done, or anything which man or animal can do, speak, read, or write…. Its food is chiefly nuts and fruit, though it occasionally indulges in a meal of raw meat; it drinks milk, water, and tea, and is partial to wine, ale, and porter.

P. T. Barnum, the grand panjandrum of human gullibility, had some interest in the matter, as he explained in his autobiography (New York, 1855): "I was called upon by 'Hervio Nano,' who was known to the public as the 'gnome fly' and was also celebrated for his representations of the monkey. His malformation caused him to appear much like that animal when properly dressed. He wished me to exhibit him in London, but having my hands already full, I declined." Thus it was that two Americans took Leach to London and, Barnum continues, "advertised him as a curious 'nondescript' called 'WHAT IS IT?' and claimed that 'the strange animal' was captured in the mountains of Mexico; that it appeared like a 'wild man,' but could not speak, although it manifested much intelligence. I was let into the secret, on condition of 'keeping dark'"(p. 346). But Hervio Nano was recognized through his disguise, and the imposture was exposed. The money was refunded to visitors.

Barnum concludes the sad story: "That was the first and last appearance of 'What is it?' in that character. He soon afterwards died in London."

Barnum, the master equivocator, is here the egregious liar; he was the instigator and backer of the exhibition. In a letter written from Brighton to his friend and fellow impresario Moses Kimball on August 18, 1846, Barnum confesses: "The *animal* that I spoke to you & Hale about comes out at Egyptian Hall, London, next Monday, and I half fear that it will not only be exposed, but that *I* shall be *found out* in the matter. However, I go it, live or die. The thing is not to be called anything by the exhibitor. We know not & therefore do not assert whether it is human or animal. We leave all that for the sagacious public to decide." Three months later, Barnum confessed his failure to Kimball: "It was *rayther* too big a pill for John Bull to swallow! Still, he has a most capacious throat and stomach!" Arthur Saxon, who also quotes from this letter in his biography of Barnum, speculates that his "unlikely reluctance to acknowledge his own role in this fraud is most likely explained by Leach's untimely death a few months later – brought on, many

thought, by the 'maltreatment' and humiliation he had suffered as the result of his exposure."[15] What prompted Leach to accept this position initially is also worthy of contemplation – one might think of money, or rather the lack of it, as the motivator.

Two days after the debacle at the Egyptian Hall, a reporter from the *Illustrated London News* was chagrined to find the cage empty: "The question of 'What Is It?' immediately induced another of 'Where Is It?' and this led to our asking 'Why is it?' and 'Who is it?'" The next morning's *Times* gave a full report of the fraud.

The gig may have been up, but the stories of this mortal moment of imposture and exposure continued to appear for years. In 1861, Henry Mayhew's strongman ceiling walker recalled his fellow antipodean with feeling: "Harvey Leach . . . he was a tremendous clever fellow. That 'What is It,' at the Egyptian Hall killed him. They'd have made a heap of money at it if it hadn't been discovered. . . . A friend of his comes in, and goes up to the cage, and says, 'How are you, old fellow?' The thing was blown up in a minute. The place was in an uproar. It killed Harvey Leach, for he took it to heart and died."[16]

Wood quotes an account that appeared some twenty years after the fact in the December 29, 1866, issue of the *Illustrated London News*: "Those people who saw through the dodge, but had a kindly humour in them, were not altogether glad when a blundering friend recognized the accomplished actor in his den, and covered him with confusion by insisting on shaking hands and giving him the Freemason's grip, the consequence of which was poor Harvey Leach died of something like starvation."

Fond as I am of the wild man unable to resist the mason's secret handshake, I must relate an even more remarkable tale, recounted by Altick, of the moment of exposure. The famous American lion tamer James Carter is here the debunker.

Deaf to the pleas of onlookers Carter fearlessly entered the What Is It's cage. The monster cowered in the corner under Carter's fearless gaze. Then grabbing its forepaw he "drew the unresisting creature to the center of the cage – with one strong tug tore the shaggy skin all down its back and sides" – and out, sheepishly no doubt came the Gnome Fly. Carter's punchline was said to have been: "And now, as you've been living on raw meat so long, come down to Craven Street and have a broiled steak with me."

The ostensible reason for this ecdysis and exposure was a vendetta against P. T. Barnum, who had denied the loan of his stellar attraction, Tom Thumb, to ride Carter's giant horse George Washington, a twenty-five-hundred-pound specimen, who was exhibited in another room at Egyptian Hall during Tom Thumb's residence. "Carter vowed revenge," Altick concludes, "and it was he who engineered the fatal confrontation" (p. 266).

These apocryphal varia often share the same ending, Leach beaten to death by the defrauded mob. Some trace this violent conclusion to Francis Courtney Wemyss.[17]

Some months later, in March 1847, this obituary appeared:

Death of Hervey Leach, the mortal career of this remarkable individual who earned for himself considerable reputation both in this country and abroad for his clever personifications of the habits and eccentricities of the monkey race under the assumed name of Signor Hervio Nano, terminated after a short illness on Tuesday evening at his residence George Street, Shoreditch. A short time ago deceased exhibited himself at Egyptian Hall disguised as an extraordinary animal captured at the Cape of Good Hope, "Supposed to be the link between the human race and ourang-outang," and called "What is it." The last place deceased performed was at the Standard Theatre in December, last where, notwithstanding the deception having been discussed and made public, he continued to represent "What is it." He was about to start for Lisbon when he was taken ill. He was a native of America and in his 46th year [obviously not as he was born in 1804]. The last request of the deceased was that his body should be presented to Dr. Liston, the

eminent surgeon, not to be buried but embalmed in a glass case, as the doctor had been a very good friend to him.[18]

His remains were sent to University College Hospital in London.[19] According to the obituary in the *Times,* "a very good cast of the entire figure has been made, which will doubtless be shown to those who may be curious in such matters."

As unsympathetic as the little fellow could be, his last days were to be wished for only by his enemies. His fate is all too similar to Tyrone Power's devastating dissolution as a flesh-devouring geek in the film version of William Lindsay Gresham's powerful novel *Nightmare Alley.* But that, of course, was fiction. Even if we are to think of Hervio Nano as a nasty, mean-spirited half man with a seriously inflated opinion of himself, his demise was too, too cruel. I would rather conclude his tale with the hyperbole of the publicist. Leach's profile declared him "a man, who would almost persuade us, by perfection of his goblin feats, that the witching tales of transformation we devoured in our childhood, do not appertain to the fabulous, but belong to the veritable in this wonderful world....His admirable mimicry and daring doings, not merely upon the stage, in the various metempsychosian characters he assumes, as the Gnome, the Baboon, and the Fly, but around and across the house, from side to ceiling, mocking the laws of gravitation, and setting all fear at defiance: these wonderful achievements must be witnessed to be believed" (*Memoir,* pp. i–ii).

Leach's legacy may be chiefly lexographic. He spawned a horde of "human flies" who reached their apotheosis in the daring '20s and depressing '30s. Scores of intrepid, if often unnamed, daredevils propelled themselves up the sides of buildings, hoping to capture the loose change of the throngs gathered below. Harry Houdini, in an attempt to capitalize on the craze, wrote a treatment for a film entitled "The Marvelous Adventures of Houdini the Justly Celebrated Elusive American," which required, among other feats of agility, climbing a wall "human fly fashion."[20] In a letter dated March 8, 1923, Sir Arthur Conan Doyle warned Houdini about that particular folly:

My dear Houdini:

For goodness' sake take care of those dangerous stunts of yours. You have done enough of them. I speak because I have just read of the death of the Human Fly.

Houdini quotes this letter in his *A Magician Among the Spirits* (New York and London, 1924) and remarks:

On March 5, 1923, Harry F. Young, known as "The Human Fly," fell ten stories from a window ledge of the Hotel Martinique, New York City. He succumbed before he reached the hospital. For the benefit of those who do not know, "A Human Fly" is an acrobat who makes a specialty of scaling tall buildings, simply clinging to the apertures or crevices of the outward architecture of such buildings for the edification of an assembled throng, for which he receives a plate collection, a salary, or is engaged especially for publicity purposes. It is not a lucrative profession and its dangers are many. (p. 140)

Fictional accounts of the human fly mirrored the public's fascination with the phenomenon. Houdini's pal and ghostwriter Walter B. Gibson created "The Shadow" using the pen name of Maxwell Grant. In the 1934 novel *Charg, Monster*, the legendary Shadow shimmied up the wall of a building using suction devices on his hands and feet.[21]

The pioneer Philadelphia filmmaker Siegmund "Pop" Lubin, who produced many films between 1897 and 1916, once hired a human fly from a local carnival to simulate Christ's walking on water. A disgruntled Lubin related the less than satisfactory results: "That damn Christ of mine got drunk and fell off a cliff and broke his legs!"[22]

NOTES

1. *Memoir of Hervio Nano, with Portrait*, in *Pattie's Modern Stage, or Weekly Acting Drama Series*, no. 77 (London, c. 1839), pp. i–ii; see also Martin Howard, *Victorian Grotesque* (London, 1977), pp. 78–79.

2. The peculiar combination of being heavily muscled and bantam-sized led the novelist Charles Reade to immortalize him in *It Is Never Too Late to Mend* (London, 1856); quoted in Richard Altick, *The Presence of the Present* (Columbus, Ohio, 1991), pp. 507–8.

3. Odell, *Annals of the New York Stage* (New York, 1928), p. 368, is quoting Joseph N. Ireland, *Records of the New York Stage from 1750 to 1860* (1866; reprint, New York, 1966). T. Allston Brown lists Leach's birthplace as Connecticut in *History of the American Stage* (New York, 1870), p. 215. Brown also mentions a wife who, he says, debuted on September 24, 1841, at the Walnut Street Theater, Philadelphia.

4. This brings to mind Hillary Long, who in the Ringling Brothers Circus in 1917 wore roller skates on his head and a hat on his feet while bouncing down a long staircase; Jean Henri, Napoleon's Tambour Major, who played two drums suspended in the air, with his head hanging downwards; Mr. Carnagy, "The Celebrated Antipathian," who in 1824 exhibited his "incredible Evolutions on the Polandric Pedestal" while he accompanied "the Band in a Trumpet Obligato, standing on his head surrounded with Fireworks"; and countless other intrepid performers who narrowly escape the purview of this article.

5. John Turner, *The Victorian Arena* (Formby, England, 1995), p. 93; and emended in a letter from Turner to the author, August 1996.

6. See *Jay's Journal of Anomalies*, vol. 2, no. 3 (winter 1996).

7. *Circus and Allied Arts: A World Bibliography*, vol. 5 (Liverpool, 1992), entry 13595, recounting a story from *Edmund Yates: His Recollections and Experiences* (London, 1885).

8. Marian Hannah Winter, *The Theatre of Marvels* (New York, 1964), p. 22.

9. These encomia are quoted from items in the author's collection. The second is a handwritten account, probably copy for a subsequent playbill.

10. Autograph letter, signed, on verso of Leach's playbill for his appearance at the Théâtre Français, author's collection. Montcrieff adapted Pierce Egan's *Life in London* for the stage, immortalizing its protagonists Tom and Jerry in a much imitated venture. He also wrote *Rogueries of Nicolas*, a monopolylogue for the great French ventriloquist, Monsieur Alexandre.

11. Playbills of May 8, 14, and 15, 1840, in the Harvard Theatre Collection.

12. Edward Wood, *Giants and Dwarfs* (London, 1868), p. 223.

13. The tradition of the theatrical "man-monkey" was created by the great French acrobatic dancer Mazurier (1793–1828) in *Jocko ou Le Singe de Brésil* in 1825. Its progeny included the Ravel Troupe and the celebrated circus clowns Auriol and Klischnigg; see Winter, *The Theatre of Marvels*, pp. 152–55, 198. Odell seems to have as little praise and sympathy for Klischnigg (Klishnig was his spelling) as he did for Nano (vol. 4, p. 371).

14. Richard Altick, *The Shows of London* (Cambridge, Mass., and London, 1978), p. 265.

15. See *Selected Letters of P. T. Barnum*, ed. Arthur Saxon (New York, 1983), pp. 35–36; and Neil Harris, *Humbug: The Art of P. T. Barnum* (Boston and Toronto, 1973), p. 98. The second letter is also quoted by Saxon in his biography *P. T. Barnum: The Legend and the Man* (New York, 1989), pp. 98, 360.

16. Henry Mayhew, *London Labour and the London Poor* (London, 1861), 3:103. Altick attributes the death-by-disappointment hypothesis to Ireland, *Records of the New York Stage*.

17. See *Twenty-six Years of the Life of an Actor and Manager* (New York, 1847).

18. Hand-dated cutting, March 1847, Harvard Theatre Collection.

19. C. J. S. Thompson, *The Mystery and Lore of Monsters* (London, 1930), p. 87.

20. Kenneth Silverman, *Houdini!!!* (New York, 1996), p. 206.

21. *Charg Monster: From the Shadow's Private Annals as told to Maxwell Grant* was originally published in the *Shadow Magazine*, vol. 10, no. 3, July 1, 1934 (reprinted New York, 1977), p. 11. Gibson also discusses the methods of human flies in *The Book of Secrets* (New York and Chicago, 1927), pp. 92–93. Merko the Human Fly, a major character in Alan Harrington's ingenious novel *The Revelations of Dr. Modesto* (New York, 1955), would have eschewed such mechanical aids.

22. *The Philadelphia Almanac and Citizens' Manual,* ed. Kenneth Finkel (Philadelphia, 1993), p. 72.

ILLUSTRATIONS

JAY'S JOURNAL OF ANOMALIES

Written by Ricky Jay and published four times a year by the author and W & V Dailey, Antiquarian Booksellers, 8216 Melrose Avenue, Los Angeles, California, 90046, (213) 658-8515. Subscription $90 per annum. ¶ *Printed letterpress by Patrick Reagh and typeset in Monotype Ehrhardt with Thorowgood heads on Rives Heavyweight paper.* ¶ *Designed by Mr. Reagh & Mr. Jay.* ¶ *The author wishes to thank Susan Green, Larry Vigon, and the staff of the Harvard Theatre Collection for generous assistance in the preparation of this issue.* ¶ *Comments and corrections to the text are welcomed.* ¶ *Written and illustrative material, © Ricky Jay, 1997.* ¶ *All images are from the private collection of the author with the exception of the watercolor portrait of Harvey Leach, which is reproduced with the kind permission of the Harvard Theatre Collection.* ¶ *Any subsequent use of text or image is permissible only with the express written consent of Mr. Jay.*

JAY'S JOURNAL *of*
ANOMALIES

VOLUME THREE   NUMBER FOUR   1997

Subterfuge at Skittles: or, Bowling for Blacklegs

MATTHEW BUCHINGER, "The Little Man of Nuremberg," born in 1674, was an armless and legless musician, conjurer, and calligrapher. He also demonstrated his skills on the bowling lawn, winning wagers like a modern-day hustler. He could knock down specific pins without so much as touching others. Once he had launched the ball between his fin-like excrescences, it pursued an intricate path of the little man's choosing. In one stunt, the ball traveled a circuitous route between lit candles. In another, it struck two pins on which a glass of liquor was precariously balanced; the glass landed precisely between two other pins without losing a drop of its precious liquid. Buchinger's magical control was described in a contemporary broadside:

> *The Nine-Pins quite surpass my Muse,*   *When one Direction makes it go,*
> *In vain his Art she there pursues,*   *To this, to that, and too and fro,*
> *The wond'rous Wisdom of his Bow[l],*   *Trips up these Pins, and lets those stand,*
> *For surely it must have a Soul,*   *Observing BUCKINGER'S Command.*[1]

The little man's modest assessment of his bowling skills was that he "plays at Skittles or Nine-Pins to a great Nicety."[2]

Today's game of ten-pin bowling is said to have evolved from ninepins sometime in the nineteenth century, but the concept of knocking down objects with the roll of a ball is a pastime of antiquity. During the sixteenth to the nineteenth centuries–the range of my inquiry–the game had many variations and its rules betray a fearless lack of standardization. Unless otherwise stated, however, I refer here to a game in which a bowler hurled or rolled his ball in the general direction of nine pins standing on a grass lawn.[3]

It may surprise us to learn that a sport as thoroughly harmless, domestic, and, some would say, dull as bowling was often thought the equivalent of darker pastimes like dicing, card play, and billiards.[4] But more often than not, bowling was considered a corrupter of youth. Every Tudor monarch enacted legislation against it, fearing that young men would abandon the discipline of archery for this useless indulgence. In 1579 Stephen Gosson warned, "Common bowling alleys are privy moths that eat up the credit of many idle citizens, whose gains at home are not able to weigh down their losses abroad [outdoors], whose shops are so far from maintaining their play, that their wives and children cry out for bread, and go supperless oft in the year."[5] Echoing Gosson a year later, Sir Nicholas Woodrofe, the Lord Mayor of London, addressed his complaint to the Privy Council. He spoke of husbands losing their money while their families went without, and described alleys as "places of the most vicious and disorderly character.... They are the scene of daily drunkenness, blaspheming, picking, cozening, and all kinds of disorder."[6]

In 1591, subterfuge at the game was colorfully described by Robert Greene, the cantankerous Elizabethan playwright who labeled Shakespeare an upstart crow. As a sequel to his *A Notable Discovery of Coosenage*, he issued *The Second Part of Cony-Catching*, and eventually a series conveying a comprehensive picture of contemporary swindles. A "cony" was literally a rabbit, figuratively a sucker. A "cony-catcher," or con man in today's terminology, was the person who took advantage of the "mark." "Coosenage," with its many variant spellings, was a generic term for swindling or deception. Greene

presented a specific if somewhat fanciful account of cheating at bowls, and a definition of Vincent's Law: "common deceit or cozenage used in bowling-alleys, amongst the baser sort of people that commonly haunt such lewd and unlawful places." "Vincent" was another word for the mark. An early chronicler of cant, the language of the criminal underworld, Greene gave a brief glossary of terms used by the perpetrators, some likely of his own invention:

> They which play booty, the *bankers*.
> He that betteth, the *gripe*.
> He that is cozened, the *vincent*.
> Gains gotten, *termage*.

Although Greene acknowledged that some persons of substance and morality populated the alleys (perhaps the ancestors of today's earnest league players), bowling hustlers and their confederate "gripes" and "bankers" (sometimes "bawkers") were always ready to take advantage of a vincent who might happen by. The basic hustle consisted of what modern-day pool sharks would recognize as "playing under speed." A group of "bawkers" would come to the alley in the guise of upstanding citizens, playing "as though they rather did it for sport than gains." A good bowler would play badly until odds were given him. This was called playing "booty," a term that also designated ill-gotten gains, then as now. The vincent was led on, winning small wagers until he "grows proud, and thinks, both by the odds and goodness of the play, that it is impossible for his side to lose, and therefore takes and lays bets freely." The inevitable result was the trimming of the sucker. If the con men came up against a better bowler, they had recourse to a more direct technique, "watering the alley, to give such a moisture to the bank, that he that offers to strike a bowl with a shore [thought to be a kind of curve or hook shot], shall never hit it whilst he lives, because the moisture of the bank hinders the proportion of his aiming."

This repertoire of tricks and wagering scams was near infallible, Greene reported: "So manifest and palpable is their cozenage that I have seen men stone-blind offer to lay bets frankly, although they can see a bowl no more than a post, but only hearing who plays, and how the old gripes make their lays." (In the eighteenth century one John Metcalf, called Blind Jack of Knaresborough, took

sightless participation at bowling a step further. Jack, a spirited character who was blind from smallpox, contracted at the age of four, was an expert rider, sportsman, gambler, musician, practical joker, contractor, and, perhaps most impressively, "a guide over the then undisclosed forest." Around 1737, when Jack was twenty years of age, he took a liking to bowls. He frequented the greens and requested odds of an extra throw for the deficiency of each eye. By these terms he had three shots for his opponent's one. Jack was able to determine the rake of the green by feel, but to aid in his deception, he positioned confederates at strategic spots and had them keep up a conversation, so he could hear them and therefore determine the correct distance to the pins.)[7]

Greene concludes with a warning: "Seeing then as the game is abused to a deceit, that is made for an honest recreation, let this…be a caveat for men to have an insight into their knavery." Greene himself came up short one caveat, when he met his end in a peculiar death fandango attributable to a surfeit of pickled herrings.

If cosenage at bowling was not invariably an elaborate, almost theatrical, ruse, playwrights were nonetheless some of the key authorities about the practice. In *The Black Book* (1604), the dramatist Thomas Middleton offered "The Last Will and Testament of Laurence Lucifer," a wry bequeathing to a fictional band of brigands including Gregory Gauntlet, a highwayman; Benedict Bottomless, a cutpurse; and Francis Finger-false, a dice hustler. Prominent among the group is Humphrey Hollow-bank, a "true cheating bowler and lurcher." Lucifer grants him:

> One-half of all bets, cunning hooks, subtleties and cross-lays, that are ventured upon the landing of your bowl, and the safe arriving at the haven of the mistress, if it chance to pass all the dangerous rocks and rubs of the alley, and be not choked in the sand, like a merchant's ship, before it comes half-way home, which is none of your fault, you'll say and swear, although in your own turned conscience you know that you threw it about three yards short out of hand, upon very set purpose.
>
> Moreover, Humphrey, I give you the lurching of all young novices, citizens' sons, and country gentlemen, that are hooked in by the winning of one twelvepenny game at first, lost upon policy, to be cheated of twelve pounds' worth a' bets afterward. And, old Bias, because thou art now and then smelt out for a cozener, I would have thee sometimes go disguised in honest apparel, and so, drawing in amongst bunglers and ketlers [tinkers] under the plain frieze of simplicity, thou mayest finely couch the wrought velvet of knavery.[8]

Little enough had changed in the alleys that in 1608, Thomas Dekker, another colorful playwright, was able to repeat in *The Belman of London* the description of Vincent's Law from Greene's pamphlet of 1592. Later in the century, however, it was no longer necessary to impress a gang of thugs and to stage an elaborate deception in order to win wagers at bowling. Now there were technical methods, some more deceitful than others. In the first English translation of Jean Leurechon's *Mathematical Recreations* (1633) was a scientific analysis of how a standard configuration of nine pins (here called "keyles," after the French *quilles*) can be struck down with a single throw. More important for our purposes was a method to alter the ball to the cheater's advantage:

> *Of a deceitful Bowle to play withall.* Make a hole in one side of the *Bowle*, and cast molten Lead therein, and then make up the hole close, that the *knavery* or deceit be not perceived. The ball cast at the pins will turn away from them to the weighted side. Those who know of the weighting can adjust accordingly.[9]

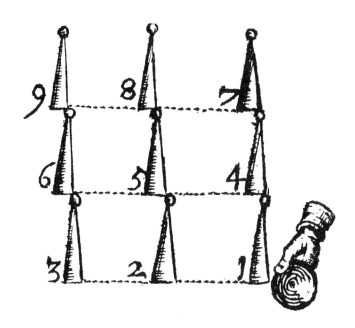

John Cotgrave's *Wits Interpreter, The English Parnassus* (1655) repeats the theory and diagram from Leurechon, but adds a wrinkle to the bowling shot that stretches the imagination:

To make a paire of Bowles to lye near a Jack [this is the lead pin] *as you please.* Divers men peg and put in peggs of Lead into their Bowles in their wheeling or running aside, now instead of those leaden peggs knock in prints of Nailes, or else horsenaile heads very neat and handsome; so that it doth not make the Bowle to rubb.

Then in the toe of your shooe before hand, put a piece of a Loadstone, and then throw your Bowle as neare the Jack as you can when the Bowle is out of your hand, run before it and with that foot draw before your Boule, and it will follow it then where you would have it lye, quickly take away your foot, and there the Bowle rests.

One would be pleased to have a bulldog, let alone a ball, respond so obediently.

In *The Compleat Gamester: or, Instructions How to play at billiards, Trucks, Bowls and Chess* (1674), Charles Cotton, best known for co-authoring *The Compleat Angler* with Izaak Walton, offered a moral inventory of the game, giving, however, no instructions for play. He reveals how little had changed in the hundred years since the cautions of Gosson and Lord Mayor Woodrofe, and forecasts the admonitory tone that commentary was to take in the eighteenth century. "Bowling," he explained, "is a Game or Recreation, which if moderately used is very healthy for the body and would be much more commendable than it is, were it not for those swarms of Rooks which so pester Bowling-Greens, Parks, and Bowling-

Alleys where any such places are to be found, some making so small a spot of ground yield them more annually than fifty Acres of Land shall do elsewhere about the City, and this done, cunning, betting, crafty matching, and basely playing booty."[10]

The proclivity for wagering and deception on the alley caught the attention of Richard Head, the author of the first part of the classic *The English Rogue.* In *The Art of Wheedling or Insinuation* (1675), he outlines various hustles used by the "wheedle," a dissembler or con man. With the hyperbole of the hack and the hustler he explains: "The Wheedle is so dexterous, and so skillful at it, that he will not fail once in five times to knock down a single pin, throwing the Bowl over an house, and though on horse-back, tip down all Nine so certain, and so often, as to make the Loser swear, the Wheedle hath put false Nine-pins on him." The edition of 1684 gives no additional text but does supply for the first time the amusing illustration that can be viewed on the facing page.[11]

In the eighteenth century, the pastime of gaming was frequently addressed in a new genre that sought to provide guidance to the scions of wealthy country gentlemen who, in a rite of passage, would take to the city with their appanage and be lured into various dens of iniquity. In one of the earliest examples, *The Country Gentleman's Vade Mecum or His Companion for the Town,* the author (perhaps one Edward Stacey) tried to dissuade these impressionable young men from ever setting foot in London. Letter 10 in this epistolary work, "In which the Humours, Tricks and Cheat of the Bowling-Greens are exposed," acknowledges that the game was formerly a source of recreation and exercise for gentlemen but had "strangely degenerated from an innocent and inoffensive Diversion to be a perfect Trade, a kind of set Calling and Occupation for Cheats and Sharpers." Even in the preeminent spots such as Mary-bone (Marylebone), the odds of meeting a rook or sharper rather than a recreational bowler were five to one. Unless you were a "master of yourself," he conjectured, you would be seduced into some sort of gaming, and might well repent of it for the rest of your life.

If a stranger came to seek a game, and rolled the dice to choose sides, it hardly mattered who was the partner and who the opponents, as all three players shared in

common the goal of separating him from his money. A subtle distinction was evident between techniques of distraction and out-and-out cheating. In the first category were such diversions as crossing the green as the bowler was about to shoot, "bawling" to him at the moment of delivery, having a kibitzer take his mind off a specific shot, or making him miscalculate by "teizing and confounding him with impertinent Advice to make him forget his Lengths." If this did not leave the victim sufficiently perplexed, the drama became more elaborate. A man would approach and demand the balls in play, saying that they were his personal property—just as the pigeon was growing comfortable with their feel and idiosyncrasies. The con man would offer to supply others of identical weight and size and then introduce into the game gaffed balls that were "back-byast, pegg'd or loaded, or have some other trick used to them, that 'tis impossible to come near the Mark with them." Even if the verdant countryman was not undone by all of the above, he still had to fight off the distracting antics at the greens of "Whores, and Setters, their Thieves, and their Pick-pockets; their false Dice and Cards, and almost all other Engines for Mischief, ready upon occasion."

When *Vade Mecum* appeared almost unaltered in 1746 as *Tricks of the Town*, one could speculate that little had changed on the alleys—or that publishers cared nought for the additional expense of updates and refinements.[12] With minor changes, the work was frequently reprinted into the early nineteenth century.

The scourge of bowling hustlers and other sharpers preying on the English populace was serious enough to warrant governmental action in the early years of the eighteenth century. A Gamester's Law was enacted in 1708, containing "The Form of an Indictment for Keeping a Common Bowling Alley." But the most damaging piece of anti-gambling legislation was doubtless the Act for the better Preventing of Excessive and Deceitful Gaming (1711). It stated that all bets, debts, side wagers, or money lent for "playing Cards, Dice, Tables [backgammon], Tennis, Bowles, or other Games" above the sum of £10 "shall be utterly void." If money in excess of this amount was not returned, the loser could, within three months, sue and be awarded three times the sum lost.

Even more discouraging for the brotherhood of rogues and swindlers was the proviso that if the loss was due to "any Fraud or Shift, Cousenage, Circumvention, Deceit, or unlawful Device," the victim was entitled to recover five times the amount of the sum originally wagered. In addition, such a person would be "deemed

Infamous," and subject to corporal punishment. The act also specified that any person with no visible means of support other than gaming could be approached by a justice of the peace and asked for a security deposit to be kept for up to one year. If the gamester was caught wagering more than twenty shillings, the deposit would be forfeit. Anyone caught fighting over a gaming dispute would forfeit all their "Goods, Chatells and Personal Estate," and was subject to imprisonment without bail in the county jail for two years.

Fairness be damned, Queen Anne excluded herself and friends from the act by adding a clause that these prohibitions did not extend to her majesty's palaces when she or her heirs were present, or to the privilege of leasing such exceptions to others of her choosing, providing their play "be for Ready Money only."[13]

Shortly after Queen Anne's demur, an illustrated broadside was published in London, *The Cheating Biting Sharping Gamester's Sorrowful Lamentation Occasioned by a late Act of Parliament For the Suppressing of all Sorts of Gaming, to the great Grief and Utter Destruction of Rakes, Bullies, Sweetners, Young Fops, and Vagabonds* (London, n.d.). The anonymous author sympathized with the ninety-two thousand families affected, not counting "vast Numbers who has been Murder'd by Quarelling at Gaming," ranging from dukes and counts to tradesmen and commoners, who had suffered loss and anguish at the hands of the sharpers he here attacks. He singles out for attention and illustration deception at cards, billiards, and bowls. In a woodcut of the bowling green we can see not only the participants but also those in the background making wagers on the action. Before his poem on "The Character of a Cheating Gaimster, and his Farewel to the World and Journey to the Devil," he gives us the following verse:

On BOWLS.
A School of Wrangling we may well it call,
For it destroys both Body, Soul, and all;
A Harbourer and Nursery of Vice,
In Short, it is the Devil's Paradise.

Later in the century, attempts to legitimize and standardize bowling were reflected in a fifty-six-page monograph by A. Jones, *The Art of Playing at Skittles: or, the Laws of Nine-Pins Displayed* (London, 1773), and by the broadside *Rules and Instructions for Playing at Skittles,* by a Society of Gentlemen (London, 1786). By now the sport had a history venerable enough to deserve its own record. Mr. Jones extols the virtues of the game as both physical and mental exercise, but prefers earlier versions of the sport that required more skill than those presently in vogue. He cites a description of a skittle frame in use in Lancashire in 1486, and also lists versions of the game favored by the Chinese and Persians.

The instructional broadside reproduced here enabled readers to become grounded in the methods of play. At the center of the illustration may be noted a hatted figure with arms folded across his chest, likely the renowned Samuel Johnson as he frequently appeared in caricatures of the day (see plate on page 111).

While I am loath to follow the shenanigans of skittle sharpers into modern times, I would be remiss not to note some Victorian examples of false play. The 1860 *Autobiography of Lord Chief Baron Nicholson* tells of "magsmen," a popular mid-nineteenth-century term for con men, who baited potential suckers with conversation and then proposed wagers that were readily agreed to but ended in the "cleaning out" of the victims. Often this was effected, Nicholson reports, by skittle sharps.[14]

In *The Gaming Table*, Andrew Steinmetz tells the story of a Frenchman who loses at bowling and literally puts himself "on the send." He goes home for more money only to lose once again to the group of magsmen. (To put someone "on the send" is one of the distinguishing characteristics between the short con, in which the mark is fleeced for all the cash in his pocket, and the big con, in which he is sent back to his home town for more money.) Such swindling had become so commonplace, Steinmetz reported, that the police were instructed to ban gambling on skittles.[15]

The most elaborate treatment of the Victorian skittle sharp is found in Chesney Kellow's *The Anti-Society*.[16] Kellow dubbed his scenario "The Provincial Stranger." The first magsman encounters the stranger, or sucker, and establishes his own supposed provinciality by pointing to Westminster Hall and asking what it is. The sucker is only too happy to explain and is soon drawn into conversation. The con man is "friendly but not effusive, his clothes, his gold hunter, his confident manner proclaim a man of sense and substance. Everything about him encourages trust, and as he by no

A View of a SKITTLE GROUND.

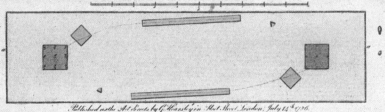

Plan of a double Skittle Ground half an Inch to a Yard.

Published as the Act directs by G. Kearsley in Fleet Street London, July 14th. 1786.

RULES and INSTRUCTIONS for PLAYING at SKITTLES.

By a SOCIETY OF GENTLEMEN.

As the GAME of SKITTLES *is now a favourite Amusement, a general Guide to remove Doubts, and prevent Disputes, is become necessary. Stimulated by these considerations, a respectable Society of Gentlemen (who are esteemed good Players) have been induced to print the following Rules and Instructions, which they have themselves often lamented the want of; hoping they will be found generally useful, but particularly to Learners.*

RULES.

I. THE Bowler must stand at the mark with one foot, and from thence deliver his Bowl fairly out of his hand; which Bowl must run upon the Board, fixed for that purpose, before it arrives at the Frame.

II. If the Bowler should throw the Bowl in such manner as to cause it to run double (as it is commonly called), and any one of the opposite party call out, A foul Bowl; if it has not reached the Pins, the Party must bowl again: but if it arrives at the Frame before the opposite Party called out Foul, whatever number are bowled down are fair.

III. If the Bowler does not cause his Bowl to run along the Board, (or touch it in some part), he loses the benefit of Bowling.

IV. If a Bowl runs clearly through the Frame and knocks down any number of Pins, the Bowl

being impeded in its return back again by one of the opposite Party, one additional Pin must be allowed the person who bowled.

V. If the Bowl passes through the Frame, and in its return back again strikes a standing Pin, immediately after a rolling or live Pin (as it is called) runs against the falling Pin, it shall be deemed fair, because it hit the Pin last.

VI. If a live Pin roll against a standing Pin, and the Bowl comes on its return against the falling Pin, before it is down, it is deemed an unfair Pin, because the Bowl struck it last.

It has been thought necessary to allow the two preceding articles in the manner here given, as more disputes have arisen from these circumstances than from any others; but, by observing whether the live Pin or the Bowl hits the falling Pin last, they may be hereafter avoided.

VII. If the Bowl runs through the Frame, and knocks at the Head-board, although it may have bowled down many Pins, none are allowed fair.

VIII. If the Bowl runs through, or on the outside of the Frame, and knocks, and then runs round the other side of the Frame, without crossing any part thereof, or touching any of the live Pins, the Bowler must stand to take his Tip with one foot upon the spot where the Bowl stopped. And in Tipping from such place, he must take care not to strike the ground with the Bowl before it hit the Pins; if it does, he loses all the Pins he may have struck down.

IX. If in Tipping the Bowl is caught or stopped by one of the opposite Party, and in so doing he stops or impedes a live Pin, he loses a Pin; because he prevented the Tipper from receiving the benefit which might arise from a live or rolling Pin.

X. If an opposite Partner takes up the Bowl in order to prevent its running amongst the Pins, and lets it slip out of his hand, if it hits any of the Pins, he loses one for so doing.

XI. If a person in Tipping gives a sweep round with his hand, and brings down the ninth or any other Pin, by means of his hand or coat sleeve, it is deemed unfair; and he must lose one Pin.— The Bowl is to be clearly and fairly delivered from the hand, both in Bowling and Tipping.

XII. Care should be taken in Tipping not to jump into the Frame immediately after, as in this case he is not allowed any of the Pins he Tips.

XIII. If you Bowl and Tip, for a limited number, at the close of the Game, and throw down more than you want, you must go for Nine.

N. B. In the Ground where these Rules are observed, a disinterested person is generally appointed to Score the Game, and in disputes, (if the case differs from any of those herein stated, which is hardly possible) his decision is, or should be, final.

INSTRUCTIONS.

BOWLING.

THE Art of Bowling well must be acquired in a great measure through practice, yet a little instruction will soon be found very useful, and a proper attention will enable a Learner to become a good Player.

Let the Player hold the Bowl in his Right Hand, with the bias-side from him, with his Left Foot advanced before his Right, which must be at the mark, his body bending towards the Frame, but in an easy position: then, with an equal motion he must throw the Bowl along the Board, at the same time with sufficient strength to reach the Frame; the Left Hand side of the first Pin he should endeavour to hit with the Bowl, which if he can accomplish, he will be pretty certain of bringing Four or Five every time the First Pin is hit in that manner.

He must take care not to aim at the First Pin in a streight direction, but cause the Bowl to form a curved line; by which it will lose something of its force, and strike the Pins with much more certainty of success.

TIPPING.

When the Learner is going to Tip, he should hold the smaller circumference or opposite side of the bias in the palm of his hand, grasping it very strong with his fingers; as few can be Tipped when the Bowl is loosely held; he must place his Left foot, quite clear of the Frame, between the First and Ninth Pin; and his Right Foot behind him, in an easy position, and in such direction that he may with ease hit his Pin in the manner following.

He must strike his First or Second Pins in the middle or largest part, and with the same motion and instant of time deliver his Bowl at the Fourth or Bowl-Pin. Striking them in this manner generally has the following effect.— If you hit the first Pin not quite full, it forces it against the middle or Fifth Pin, from thence to the Seventh, and will frequently rebound to the Eight without any roll.

The Second Pin, if struck well, will knock down the Third, and the Fourth, or Bowl-Pin, will strike the Sixth; and, if the Pins are good, the Ninth is often brought down by some of the rolling ones.

☞ For the benefit of the Learner the Skittles are all numbered in the above Plan.

When the Learner is to Tip for Four upon Game, he should chuse the Pins No. 8, 7, 6, and 4; placing his Left Foot by the side of the Frame, with his toe nearly in a line with the bottom of the Seventh Pin, and Right Foot behind him; he must strike the three Side Pins at one motion, at the same time throwing the bowl at the Pin No. 4.

To Tip for Five, let him place his Left Foot a little to the left of the Pin No. 9, and his other foot behind. He must strike the Ninth Pin to hit the Seventh, the Fifth to hit the Fourth, and the Bowl must knock down the Sixth.

When Six only are wanted, which are generally thought the most difficult, place the Left Foot in a line with the opposite angle of the Frame, and the other Foot behind at a good distance; he must strike the Eighth Pin full in the middle, which will hit the Seventh and Sixth, and with the same motion he should hit the Middle Pin against the Third, and the Bowl should hit the Fourth; by which means he will lay the Six fairly down, and, if not struck hard, without the danger of their rolling, especially if they are tipped down hill; to do which, he must make the Sixth his first Pin.

DIMENSIONS of a DOUBLE COVERED GROUND, by which, and the above PLAN, either a SINGLE or DOUBLE GROUND may be FORMED.

a a The whole length of the inclosed Ground 17 yards and an half. *b b* Breadth of the Ground, from side to side, 4 yards. The Dots shew the curved Line which the Bowl should form. The just proportion of a Skittle is 15 inches round in the largest part, and 12 inches high.——The Bowl should be 18 inches in circumference; each angle of the Frame for the Pins 3 feet 4 inches.——The proportions and distances of every part, as well as those already described, may be ascertained by the Scale.

PRINTED for G. KEARSLEY, at No. 46, in FLEET-STREET, 1786.——PRICE 6d. PLAIN, or 1s. COLOURED.——Entered at Stationers-Hall.

means monopolizes the conversation there is soon quite an exchange of information." The con man uses his skill in interpreting and elaborating on this information to insinuate himself in friendship with the mark: he knows the mark's home town, he is familiar with his line of work, and so on.[17]

Claiming he would like to write to his new friend, "from a well-stuffed wallet he produces a card, which leads to the new friend opening *his* pocket book to put the card safely away." If the sucker flashes sufficient funds, the two are joined by a second player in the mob, who has followed the men from the moment of their meeting. He enters the conversation but unlike the first con man is apparently lacking in charm and is therefore not as well received by the provincial stranger. The conversation turns to sporting and the first con man boasts of his prowess at casting a ten-pound shot. The other men are skeptical and the three repair to a bowling lawn to test the claim. Of course there is inadequate space for the test, and the men decide to play skittles instead. The sucker is drawn into a match in which his new friend bowls against the second con man and wins, causing his "friend" to share in the wealth. Eventually another bowler joins in, the third sharper, and soon the inevitable conclusion is reached. The provincial stranger and his new companion lose heavily.

The first con man, apologetic about the loss, nevertheless extols the virtues of a quick reckoning and pays up immediately. When it is shown that the mark has insufficient funds to pay the debt in full, "the social atmosphere freezes. Now, abruptly, it's three to one; outraged sportsmen against a shamefaced welsher." The men relieve the stranger of all his ready cash and jewelry, down to his silver shirt-stud. Kellow concludes this sketch with an apt passage: "Nothing about the whole business of sharping is more striking than the simplicity of many successful tricks. The skittle-playing charade would have seemed crude to a first-class card sharp, but compared to many of the methods in use at the time it was highly sophisticated." Kellow also introduces the idea that the success of such scenarios was not necessarily owing to the cupidity of the sucker: "One may believe, in fact, that dupes of this sort were caught less by hopes of gain than by that potent lure, a sense of being liked and valued 'for oneself.' What the sharp most

hoped to see in his prey's face was not stupidity but loneliness" (pp. 237–39).

While the modern indoor game of bowling contrasts markedly with these early examples, the most prevalent form of cheating still current on the lanes is the laying back of skill, which lures weaker bowlers into matches with far superior rivals. Kibitzers bet on the proceedings much as they did in the sixteenth-century examples. Proposition bets are also common. I have seen natural left-handed bowlers defeat their opponents right-handed and then be spotted pins to play again, lefty. Before the advent of pin-setting machines, pin boys were often the key to cheating schemes. Working in cahoots with local hustlers shooting against visiting players, they enjoyed a latitude that allowed them to alter the course of the game. They could, for instance, substitute heavy pins or pins that had been refrigerated—both were sluggish and led to lower scores. One simple but ingenious device, insinuated and then quickly removed in the darkness of the pit, was a string lowered between two broom handles that was used to move the seven- and ten-pins slightly off the mark. They were then less likely to fall when an unfavored player hit the pocket with his ball.

Even in the machine-setting era, various methods of advantage play could be instituted. A plug of extra weight in the ball between the holes for thumb and finger would cause more rotation on delivery and greatly aid the shooter. The house proprietors could also be guilty of deception, using an electric sander to produce a subtle groove in the alley that led a ball directly into the pocket. When customers rolled higher scores (they had no idea why their skills were so improved), they were more likely to return to the establishment.

I once heard about a bowling wager that I would love to have witnessed. A man bet that he could knock over the one-pin in its appropriate spot on the alley with an ordinary playing card thrown from the foul line.[18] Apart from the venerable relationship between playing cards and bowling, my own interest in the latter was rekindled by personal experience—not as a teenager forced to rent multicolored footwear but rather as an adult who, claiming to be analytical if not absolutely dismissive toward so-called psychic phenomena, still knows how to hedge a bet.

which no doubt clinched the network sale, was to show a bad film of the slasher variety, along with a superimposed graphic of a bowling scorecard on which X's were to tally the murders. "We've got Brian Doyle Murray as the host," she said, "Run DMC as the guests" (by now I was undaunted by the seeming incongruity), "and the announcer is Richard Burton."

"Do you mean Nelson Burton Jr.?" I asked, conjuring the name of a bowling commentator from the dim recesses of a trivia-laden past. Yes, she agreed, that was, indeed, his name. I wished her well and rang off.

"Did you say Nelson Burton Jr.?" asked my housekeeper, who was then working at my apartment for the first time. "I don't want to appear to be listening in on your calls," she said, "it's just that he's a good friend of mine."

"How do you know him?" I asked.

"I was on the women's professional bowling tour for eleven years," she explained.

When I arrived at my office soon afterward, I found that a package had just been delivered. It contained a shirt, with my name embroidered over the right front pocket and the name of the film on which I had just finished work printed across the back. It was a gift from the writer/director, a customized shirt bedizened with ball and pins, specifically fabricated for the sport of bowling. Jung be blessed, I thought, and headed for the alley… ◉

Some time ago I received a phone call from an ex-girlfriend whom I had not spoken to by design for years. Her voice could still elicit serious pangs of discomfort in me. She was calling, she said, to invite me to a bowling party. I had, I candidly confessed, not the slightest interest in either seeing her or engaging in the sport. "Oh come on," she said, "it's been too long, we'll have some fun." I'd have more fun being the pins than the bowler, I thought, and was enormously relieved to hear the click that indicated another call was waiting. I hastily begged off to speak to an old friend who was a theatrical costume designer. She proceeded to tell me that in her first effort as a television producer, she was doing a show called "Bowling for Horror." The program, she explained, was set in a bowling alley, and the premise,

NOTES

1. *A Poem on Matthew Buckinger the Greatest German Living* (n.p., 1726). The description of the bowling shots is taken from a manuscript in the British Library; see my *Learned Pigs & Fireproof Women* (New York, 1986) for the complete text and a detailed account of Buchinger's life (his name is spelled variously).
2. *This is the Effigies of Mr. Matthew Buchinger*, engraving (London, 1724). Buchinger, it should be mentioned, never grew taller than twenty-nine inches.
3. For sources on the history of bowling, see Robert Craven, *Billiards, Bowling, Table Tennis, Pinball, and Video Games* (Westport, Conn., 1983). On the Internet, Hitchcock's Sports History provided some interesting if uncorroborated material. Less successful was the Web site of the International Bowling Hall of Fame and Museum in St. Louis, which, confoundingly, indicated that the first American description of the game was to be found in *Rip Van Winkle* by Jonathan Swift.
4. Perhaps it was partly that the boundary between gaming and

gambling was murky. For example, the reformed gambler Jonathan H. Green even warned against the evils of playing marbles: "It leads to Sabbath-breaking, to lying, and cheating, and disobedience to parents: also to dishonest practices, theft and crime"; see *Gambling in Its Infancy and Progress* (New York, 1849), p. 17.

5. Quoted in Gamini Salgado, *The Elizabethan Underworld* (Gloucester, England, 1984), pp. 38–39.

6. Quoted in Frank Adylotte, *Elizabethan Rogues and Vagabonds* (Oxford, 1913), p. 94.

7. *The Life of John Metcalf, commonly called Blind Jack of Knaresborough* (York, 1795), p. 34. See also *The Life and Wonderful Adventures of John Metcalfe* (Knaresborough, England, 1877).

8. Reprinted in A. V. Judges, *The Elizabethan Underworld* (London, 1930), pp. 301–2; partially quoted in Salgado, *The Elizabethan Underworld*, p. 39.

9. See page 32 of the 1633 English edition. Both of the methods mentioned here as well as the diagram appear in the Rouen edition of 1628, and likely the first French edition of 1624, but this has not been verified. Leurechon's authorship is persuasively argued by Jacques Voignier in James Hagy's *Perennial Mystics*, no. 9 (Northbrook, Ill., 1991).

10. Quoted from the 1680 edition of *The Compleat Gamester*, p. 34. Cotton also supplies a wonderful commentary on what we would call the "body English" of bowlers.

11. Quotation from the first edition of *The Art of Wheedling or Insinuation* (London, 1675), p. 123.

12. Ralph Strauss, in his introduction to a series of eighteenth-century reprints, conjectures that the success of Ned Ward's *London Spy* set a precedent for pamphlets explaining and satirizing the "modes and follies" of the day; see *Tricks of the Town*, reprint ed. (London, 1927), pp. xiv–xv.

13. *The Act for the better Preventing of Excessive and Deceitful Gaming* (London, 1711).

14. Reprinted in *Rogue's Progress* (Boston, 1965), pp. 25–26. "Lord Chief Baron" Renton Nicholson was not of the legal profession, but rather a colorful scoundrel well versed in London lowlife.

15. *The Gaming Table* (London, 1870), 2:22.

16. Published in Boston in 1970, and in England with the title *The Victorian Underworld*.

17. Commenting on the versatility of the con man in 1552, Gilbert Walker, the probable author, says in *A Manifest Detection of the Most Vile and Detestable Use of Dice Play…*, "Talk about matters of law, he hath plenty of cases at his finger's end;…speak of grazing and husbandry, no man knoweth more shires than he."

18. For other techniques of card throwing, see my *Cards as Weapons* (New York, 1977).

ILLUSTRATIONS

Page 105. Detail vignette from engraving of Buchinger by Elias Beck, probably printed in Germany, c. 1711.

Page 107. Engraved frontispiece from *The Life of John Metcalf*, York, 1795.

Page 108. Woodcut illustration from *Mathematicall Recreations*, London, 1653.

Page 109. Detail from frontispiece, *The Art of Wheedling*, London, 1684.

Page 111. Hand-colored broadside, London, 1786.

Page 113. Engraved title page from *Mathematicall Recreations*, London, 1633.

JAY'S JOURNAL OF ANOMALIES

Written by Ricky Jay and published four times a year by the author and W & V Dailey, Antiquarian Booksellers, 8216 Melrose Avenue, Los Angeles, California, 90046, (213) 658-8515, Subscription $90 per annum. ¶ Printed letterpress by Patrick Reagh and typeset in Monotype Ehrhardt with Thorowgood heads on Rives Heavyweight paper. ¶ Designed by Mr. Reagh & Mr. Jay. ¶ The author wishes to thank Susan Green, Larry Vigon, and Persi Diaconis for generous assistance in the preparation of this issue. ¶ Comments and corrections to the text are welcomed. ¶ Written and illustrative material, © Ricky Jay, 1998. ¶ All images are from the private collection of the author. ¶ Any subsequent use of text or image is permissible only with the express written consent of Mr. Jay.

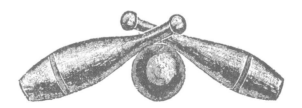

JAY'S JOURNAL *of*
ANOMALIES

VOLUME FOUR   NUMBER ONE   1998

THE ULTIMATE DIET: The Art and Artifice of Fasting

INGESTERS OF STONES, STOATS, AND SWORDS have long compelled my attention and motivated me to wield my pen.[1] In the interests of balanced reporting – a standard infrequently invoked in these pages – I will now suffer the claims of those said to exist sans nourishment of any kind. It is difficult to think of such a culinary regime attracting much attention today, except perhaps from those searching for the ultimate diet. We have, after all, been saturated with the strictures of gurus preaching the cleansing effects of fasting; and we have observed the demise of the hunger strike from the noblest political causes to the plight of Los Angeles gardeners deprived of their leaf-blowers.[2]

In the middle of the nineteenth century, a time when much of the British populace was preoccupied with obtaining minimal nourishment, one Bernard Cavanagh of County Mayo, Ireland, took London by storm when he announced that he would voluntarily consume neither food nor drink for seven days and seven nights. Even today, Cavanagh's abstention from water might turn a few heads. But what should give pause to every medical researcher and investigator of the paranormal is his contention that the supervised fast would be merely an extension of one that had been in progress for more than five and one-half years!

In September 1841, Cavanagh was engaged at the Large Assembly Room in Theobold's-road, overlooking Lamb's Conduit Street.[3] He was confined in a garret some sixty to seventy feet off the ground, the room measuring fifteen by nine feet by seven feet high.[4] After eleven days, on September 15, the exploit was hailed as a success by Drs. Kenny, Brooks, Richmond, and others. But their approbation was not universal. The chamber had not been sealed at either the fireplace or the window, thus allowing not only ventilation but also the possibility that comestibles had been hoisted up from the street below.

Cavanagh next moved to the Hanover Square Rooms where, in view of his sudden celebrity, he charged a half crown for admission. Barely a score of visitors attended him, but each was given a copy of a pamphlet entitled *Memoirs of Bernard Cavanagh*. It stated that when absorbed by devotions he was impervious to cold and pain, that during his long fast he had abstained from speech as well as nourishment, and that in his native Ireland his religious ecstasies had qualified him as a saint. Asked why he was exhibiting for money, Cavanagh animatedly explained that he was raising funds for a chapel from which he could preach. His proclivity for fasting was induced by his religious fervor and, not surprisingly, as he ate less and less he was subject to visitations from the Holy Spirit, the Blessed Savior, and the Holy Virgin. Although as a young man he had eaten butter, bread, milk, and potatoes, he was now unable to eat or drink at all: "It was in vain that he attempted to force food or liquid down his throat as he could not swallow them." Nonetheless, he "partook of, and could swallow 'the blessed sacrament.' It was, he believed, on the Eucharist that he lived."

According to a newspaper account of September 24, when questioned on religious matters Cavanagh "betrayed an imbecility truly lamentable." When interviewed by a fellow Irishman, however, he took the morally proper view that equivocation was preferable to lying:

Q: Is it true you have not eaten for five years?
Cavanagh: Wouldn't I eat if I was hungry?
Q: But do you eat or drink anything?
C: Wouldn't I drink if I was thirsty?
Q: Don't you ever take anything in the shape of food?
C: Wasn't I locked up?
Q: Did they seal the door?
C: Indeed they did.
Q: Did you go out at all during the ten days?
C: Yes, I went to mass once.
Q: And you did not eat or drink anything?
C: I don't want to make anyone believe that I fast.
Q: Answer my question in a straightforward manner. In this little book which I had given to me at the door, I find it stated that … you 'refused' both meat and drink.' Is this true?
C: (quickly) Yes, it is; I did *refuse*.
Q: But did you eat anything notwithstanding your *refusal*?
C: Why, I don't wish to make you believe if you won't.
Q: I am sorry you are a countryman of mine, for I am afraid you are a sad impostor.

Cavanagh also *refused* examination by a doctor who accompanied a reporter from *The Times* of London, declined to answer medical questions on "delicate matters," and passionately disallowed the insertion of a catheter for further monitoring of his functions. In contrast to other newspaper accounts, the *Times* article was pointedly scientific. Curiously, it concluded with a statement by an attending phrenologist, who declared that "the animal propensities of Mr. Cavanagh were very strangely defined."

Enough doubt existed to support a more stringently controlled experiment. On October 12 Cavanagh was placed in a second-floor room furnished with only a chair, table, and iron bedstead. He was denuded and thoroughly examined by a group of doctors who then provided him, without his foreknowledge, a new set of clothes. This time the chimney and window were carefully closed and checked, and sealing wax was affixed to the outside door. In spite of this more thorough approach to Cavanagh's incarceration, his release on October 21 was delayed for three hours when Dr. Edward Blundell, the keeper of the only set of keys, did not appear as planned, and a locksmith had to be summoned to release the faster from his confinement.

Cavanagh was found in good health and spirits, one reporter proclaiming that "he wore the bloom of a fox hunter." A medical examiner found a commendable pulse rate of 72, and pronounced "his tongue foul, his mouth moist, and his breath exceedingly offensive…. He showed no symptoms of a wasted frame, his muscles are exceedingly well defined, and altogether he might be described as being of an iron build of a body." The room, furniture, door, and window were all scrutinized and, most importantly, "no traces of *ingesta* or *egesta* were to be discovered."

Some skepticism remained, however. Cavanagh, it was protested, should have been weighed both before and after the test. One journalist from the *Morning Advertiser* pointed out that sealing wax on the door could be substituted in facsimile, as was frequently done, he noted, with letters in the French post office. The keyhole "was rather large of its kind," he complained, and had not been properly covered.[5]

It was generally acknowledged, however, that Cavanagh had passed the test and that, as one newspaper put it, "his powers of abstinence are extraordinary." But

these short fasts, impressive at the time, did not con-clusively substantiate his claim of having not eaten at all for nearly six years. The notoriety of his London es-capades preceding him, Cavanagh took to the provinces. When he arrived in Reading in November 1841, the fol-lowing playbill was distributed:

EXTRAORDINARY PHENOMENON. The Celebrated Bernard Cav-anagh, from the County of Mayo, who has excited so much atten-tion in the medical and scientific world, on account of his excessive powers of abstinence, which are attested beyond all doubt, is now in this town, and invites all inquirers into the cause of so singular a phenomenon to pay him a visit at the Black Boy [public house], Reading during his stay. A few of his philosophical friends in London, wishing to gain some additional light upon this case, have advised him to give this general invitation, and make no distinct charge for admissions; but as the expense of traveling about the country with his brother, who eats like other men, will be beyond their means, any friendly donation will be thankfully received.

Cavanagh, his brother, and another Irishman named John Tiernan, who is described variously as a showman or servant, held court at the Black Boy public house, an-swering questions. Cavanagh, although he was not under supervision, was said to be continuing his long fast.

Among the attendees was Mrs. Harriet Hatt, the wife of a local laborer. The next day Mrs. Hatt was mar-keting at a considerable distance from the tavern when she noticed a curiously clad figure enter the shop. Although the mysterious customer had tied a handker-chief almost down to his eyes and sported a black nose patch, the eagle-eyed Mrs. Hatt recognized him as the fasting man she had seen the day before. She watched in horror as Cavanagh ordered a saveloy (a cooked dried sausage), threepenny worth of bread, and a quarter pound of ham "cut particularly fat."

Like some fictional sleuth, Mrs. Hatt set out to expose her prey. Racing to the Black Boy, she waited for Cavanagh's return. Eventually he appeared, sans disguise and comestibles. The police were summoned and the unfortunate Irishman was hauled off to stand before the mayor. "Harriet Hatt," reported one journal, "was not the woman to let a saveloy-icide escape unpunished." Neither, apparently, was his Lordship Mr. Chase, who saw to Cavanagh's conviction as a "rogue and vagabond" and had him sentenced to three months at Reading Prison for violation of the vagrancy law. Mr. Tiernan was also convicted as a petty chapman without a license and sentenced to one month's hard labor. Cavanagh's brother left town and avoided prosecution.

Cavanagh, now a cause célèbre in Reading, protested that although he bought the food, feeling hungry for the first time in over five years, he did not eat it, but rather discarded it in a field shortly thereafter, as he no longer felt the urge to sate himself. He was unable to describe the precise whereabouts of the field but was sure he could find it again. This plan was rejected, as considerable time had elapsed, making it unlikely the discards could be located. The *Berkshire Chronicle,* however, reported that a distraught Cavanagh had confessed, "The Lord caused me to be hungry and I did eat." One paper reported these events with glee:

"Fat ham," said the Mayor, as the warrant was read to him. The adipose adjective was appended, and the *posse comitatus* set out to secure the delinquent. His guilt was made manifest beyond the shadow of a doubt.

"What," said the Mayor, "would become of our country – prosperous in commerce, magnificent in war, happy in land, triumphant on the ocean–what would become of us if we suffered Cavanaghs to purchase saveloys?"

There were no dry eyes in the court, save those of the prisoner, who, with brutal insensibility and a strong brogue, exclaimed, "Och! Where's the harm?" The mayor concluded his address by saying that he should put a stop to such porcine outrages, at least for a while, and sentenced him to three months imprisonment–i.e., one month for the saveloy, fourteen days for the bread, and six weeks for the ham "cut particularly fat."

While one might at first think that prison would terminate the career of Mr. Cavanagh, his incarceration provided the perfect opportunity for his vindication. A supervised fast behind bars would finally determine the Irishman's proclivity for traditional nourishment.

It can be assumed that the citizens of Reading awaited the report of Cavanagh's imprisonment with great anticipation. They were quickly rewarded by a document from F. A. Bulley, assistant surgeon to the County Gaol and surgeon to the Royal Berkshire Hospital:

After the closest watching and the strictest care on the part of myself and the turnkeys of the prison to prevent the possibility of clandestinely taking food, I feel satisfied and convinced, in my own mind, that Bernard Cavanagh has not tasted food or drink during the nine days he has been an inmate of the gaol. He remains, notwithstanding the privations he has voluntarily endured, in a state of perfect bodily health, and I cannot detect the slightest alteration in his appearance or spirits.

The good doctor released Cavanagh from his responsibility of hard labor at the treadmill, as likely to be injurious to the prisoner's health.

All Reading was surprised by a reassessment that quickly followed. Dr. Bulley had the foresight (if we may label it as such) to preserve the full bowls of gruel returned by the prisoner, and he determined that the consistency of the broth was thinner than when originally served. In a letter sent on November 28, 1841, he explained

that he [Cavanagh] had taken a portion of it daily and had substituted for it some water which had been given him to drink, or some fluid which I shall not specify, so giving the vessel which contained it the appearance of not having been disturbed. The peculiar smell which it had acquired confirmed me in the latter suspicion.

I believe, notwithstanding the utmost vigilance on my part, and the most scrutinizing care on the part of the turnkeys of the prison, we have been deceived in this trial, and that Cavanagh has, by such stratagem as I have mentioned, contrived to consume a small quantity of the gruel every day without exciting suspicion.

It may be interesting for medical gentlemen to know that the result of this trial has assured me beyond a doubt that Bernard Cavanagh does not possess, as he stated he did, or as in some measure thought, the slightest constitutional or acquired power of controlling the excretory functions.

Cavanagh had performed what, in conjuring terms, would be designated a simple substitution illusion. On the ninth day of his "fast" he became very weak; on the tenth day he obviously ate his food. Later that evening, he collapsed and was given gruel, port wine, and bread, "of which he heartily partook." He quietly served out the full time of his sentence and then faded from public scrutiny. He stayed on in Reading, took an assumed name, and operated a huckster's, or petty goods, shop that eventually failed. He died on August 3, 1845,[6] shortly before the Irish potato famine would have presented him with yet another opportunity to test his skill. Cavanagh's legacy, like that of other eccentrics, is chiefly transmitted in the form of topical and often ironic pamphlets that, through the passage of time and lack of interest, have become very scarce.[7] One of these, *The Very Extraordinary Life and Singular Characteristics of Mr. Cavanagh, The Celebrated Fasting Man* (London, 1841), reports "the sensations experienced by Cavanagh on each of the ten days' confinement," from which I excerpt:

1st day. Very comfortable till evening; went to bed and dreamt of the profit of speculation.

2nd day. Rose early and washed; looked at the water and smelt at the soap–a poor breakfast that! but it must do. . . .

6th day. Looked at my shoes–thought them worth eating. Licking the inner sole, but found it hard to bite.

8th day . . . looked lovingly at my leather breeches, thought they would be very nice stewed.

9th day . . . got up and sat in the arm chair, found it vastly too large; just filled it the first day. Leather breeches missed in the night, shoes missed in the morning. . . .

10th day. At the close of this eventful day, the *Humane Committee* who superintended the affair opened the door and advanced toward the chair in which apparently the unfortunate object of their solicitude was sitting. They touched his hat and coat, which fell on vacancy; his stockings remained upright; as if his legs remained within them; but when his other garments fell, they also fell into the shadow; and at length sad reflections passed in the minds of the Committee, that they had suffered the poor fellow, the identical Bernard Cavanagh, in an excessive paroxysm of hunger, TO EAT HIMSELF! That such was the fact cannot be doubted, as no relic of the body could be discovered to be sent to the Poor Law Commissioners, who felt a very laudable interest in the development of a new principle in curtailing the wants of hungry paupers.

A wonderfully preposterous pamphlet claiming to be an account of the Society of Cavernites was issued in 1858, thirteen years after Bernard's death. The director of the society was said to be Hugh Cavaner (so spelled), "son of the Great Fasting Man, Barney Cavaner." This pseudo-synopsis of a meeting of the society emphasized the well-dressed throng in attendance and attributed their finery to savings accumulated through abstinence. In a speech for neophytes struggling through the first month of fasting, Cavaner recommended the following procedure: a broth was made of common bran and water; it was not consumed but placed in a wading pool, where squishing about in it was said to revive the spirits. Another speaker, Mr. Smith of Uxbridge, mounted the stage wielding a leg of mutton. Wringing from it some liquid, he invited his canine accomplice to sniff it, and the dog promptly dropped his tail and fell down on his side as if dead. This part of the performance being received with great cheering, Mr. Smith said, "You will now see, my friends, what goodness there is in meat."[8]

The meeting ended the way it had started, with the singing of the Cavernite's song:

We want no food anymore,
We scorn the butcher's door;
We'll kill no beast, but christians live,
We'll eat no food, and no food we'll give,
No, no, no, no, not we.

I have chosen to feature Bernard Cavanagh in this disquisition because, to my knowledge, his story has not been chronicled since the time of his death. It should not be assumed that his fasting, or subterfuge in claiming not to eat, was unique. The annals of peculiarity are filled with similar tales of abstinence going back to antiquity, and the amount of material on both religious and performance fasting is extensive, if difficult to corroborate. Here follows an epitome of subterfuge in the service of the ultimate diet.

In the thirteenth century, a Japanese holy man was said to subsist on nothing but tree leaves, and the emperor honored the man's piety by providing him with living quarters close to the imperial palace. When skeptical courtiers investigated, they noticed that his egesta contained grains, and this led to an inspection of the holy man's dwelling and the discovery of a buried cloth bag containing rice. The pious man, taunted with a song, "Grain-dung-holy-man," soon disappeared.[9]

Some early fasters were treated more kindly, and were more inventive in the face of exposure. In the six-

she explained, had at last cured the disorder that prevented her from eating, and owing to his care and wisdom she now enjoyed a healthy appetite.

More wonderful in every respect, however, was the case of Margarete Weiss from Speyer, the subject of an illustrated broadside of 1542. Although she drank water, her only nourishment was said to be from transubstantiation—a wafer would magically float down so that it could be swallowed by the young girl. Tales of Margarete's piety and performance attracted throngs of pilgrims, and tourism flourished. King Ferdinand, showing a healthy disrespect for such nonmonarchial adoration, ordered a thorough examination. Under strict supervision, Margarete soon felt compelled to end her decade-long fast. She grew hungry and confessed her deception. She accused the monks of Speyer of instigating the affair, and of contriving to deliver the wafers fastened to long strands of women's hair, invisible to the naked eye. The revelation of this early conjuring effect did not mollify the king, who ordered that Miss Weiss and her holy brothers pay for their folly with their lives.

Eva Fliegen, a Dutch girl born in the county of Meurs in 1575, was widely known in her day for having survived, for some seventeen years, only on the scent of flowers. As the poet William Davenant (1605–1668) had it, she "lived by her smell / That din'd on a rose, / And supt on a tulip." His contemporaries John Fletcher and Jasper Mayne also contributed to her fame, and she was the subject of broadside ballads and portraits. A pamphlet translated from Dutch into English, published in 1611, gave the most complete account of her history. She had consumed only scent since 1596 and was still inhaling as the pamphlet went to press. Among her severe ordeals was a sadistic experiment perpetrated by the Countess of Meurs, who in 1599 forced the abstemious Eva to taste a cherry. Eva preserved her reputation by feigning a sudden, violent sickness.[10]

One famous fasting girl was Martha Taylor, a young Englishwoman who announced that she had not eaten for a year. Among her many visitors was Thomas Hobbes, who in a letter of October 20, 1668, expressed particular concern that visitors were paying money to witness her ordeal. He does not seem to have worried over the girl's exploitation but rather over the spectators': "Others that see her for curiosity give her money,

teenth century, the Westphalian wonder girl Barbara of Unna claimed to have resisted food for one year. A local magistrate supported her story after observing her for only nine days. Johan Wier, a physician to the Duke of Cleves and an early challenger of witchcraft, greeted Barbara's claims with healthy skepticism, and demanded that she be extradited to his home and supervised constantly for three weeks. After only seven days, she decided that her only recourse was to confess and sit down to eat with Wier, who later argued for leniency in punishing her. The local magistrate was chastised for his stupidity and was asked to instill in the girl an abiding fear of God. Once home in Unna, however, Barbara announced that her long fast had been legitimate. Wier,

ANN MOORE,
The Fasting Woman of Tutbury, Staffordshire.

THERE is living in the village of TUTBURY, in Staffordshire, a woman named ANN MOORE, whose extraordinary and perpetual abstinence from food, has, for a considerable time, been the subject of much wonder and attention. The following is a concise statement of her case:—

ANN MOORE had been in a declining state of health for many years previous to her first attack of anorexy, which she believes to have been occasioned by her attendance on a diseased boy, whose loathsome complaint produced that effect on her imagination, which caused an habitual disinclination for all kind of food.

For some time this remarkable case was treated as an imposition, until Humanity prompted some of her neighbours to represent her distressing state of existence to the neighbouring gentlemen of the medical profession, and to others; who, to satisfy themselves and the public, instituted an examination of the truth of her case, which terminated in proving the facts here stated.

"On the 14th of April, 1807, she took to her bed for a continuance. In the latter end of June following, she eat a few black currants, being the last substance she swallowed. From that time until the examination was instituted, she occasionally took a tea spoonful of water or tea, without sugar or milk; but it occasioned such extreme pain in swallowing, that she was advised by the medical attendant, to refrain from taking any more. For the space of *sixteen* days she was strictly watched, under the direction of MR. ROBERT TAYLOR, Member of the Royal College of Surgeons, London, and every method adopted for detecting the supposed imposition. But the watch ended in proving, that she existed for *thirteen* days, without aliment of any kind, either liquid or solid; at the end of which time, she was better in health than when the examination was established." For the period of *several years* from the time above stated, she has been in the same recumbent state of existence, without the support of nutriment of any kind.

The state of her physical powers, is extremely weak and emaciated; the body resembling a human skeleton more than a living subject; her legs are drawn up in a contracted form, and are quite useless. Her countenance is handsome, and her face has not that emaciated appearance to which her body is reduced, but retains the character of apparent health.

She seldom sleeps, and the position in which she usually sits in her bed, is that in which she is represented in a drawing, taken from life, by MR. LINSELL, and engraved by ANTHONY CARDON, Esq. which portrays her exactly as she appeared soon after the watch had ended. She is able to read with the aid of glasses, and has the Bible generally on the bed before her, which she calls her "best companion." She seems free from superstition, and endures her sufferings with a serenity of mind, that characterizes the Christian in a state of patient and pious resignation.

Her readiness to satisfy any inquiries that visitors think proper to make, gives to every one an opportunity of investigating particulars, and ascertaining facts already given to the public. The curious in physiology or anatomical detail, may be gratified with the particulars of her case by referring to the Medical and Physical Journals, which contain several accounts by medical gentlemen who have examined her.

Croft, typ. Burton.

sixpence or a shilling which she refuseth, but her mother taketh. But it does not appear they gain by it so much as to breed suspicion of a cheat."[11] At least four mid-seventeenth-century pamphlets chronicled Martha's tale. One, John Reynolds's *Discourse upon Prodigious Abstinence* (London, 1669), given before the Royal Society, states that she sustained on "a few drops of the syrup of stewed prunes…or the juice of a roasted raisin…in very small quantities as are prodigiously insufficient for sustenation; she evacuates nothing. …she spits not that I can hear of."

Ann Moore, called the Fasting Woman of Tutbury, is perhaps the most famous of all fasting impostors—not because her accomplishments were in any way more impressive than Cavanagh's but because she happened to be included in numerous nineteenth-century anthologies devoted to eccentric characters. Claiming not to have eaten for years, Ann underwent a supervised fast of sixteen days in September 1808. The results were said to show "conclusive evidence of her veracity." For the next four years she was celebrated and attended by visitors and contributors impressed by her great piety and devoutness. A skeptical physician, Alexander Henderson, published a damning account of her, paralleling her case with that of Anna Kinker, a German woman from Osnaburg who was exposed as a cheater in 1800. (She was said to be particularly adept at methods of concealing egesta, which, exercising restraint uncharacteristic of this reporter, I shall not reveal.) Henderson's publication led to a second supervised fast of one month, commencing in April 1813. After nine days the fast was ended and Ann confessed her guilt. She had been sustained by a number of clever cons. She sucked milk and other nourishing liquids from wet towels used for her toilette, and she also received food from the mouth of her daughter when kissed by her each morning and evening. Her celebrity even reached these shores, where she was the subject of biographies and, like Eva Fliegen before her, of an effigy cast in wax that was exhibited at the Boston Museum about 1813. Ann accumulated more than four hundred pounds from donations before her imposture was revealed.[12]

Perhaps the rage for proposition wagers in the eighteenth century paved the way for the peculiar profession of performance fasting. In 1771 a man from Helpston, near Stamford, was said to have lived on drink alone for seven weeks and two days in order to win ten pounds (and to lose a great many more).[13]

A hundred years later, fasting for money was in full flower. In 1880 the leading exponent of such performance was the English-born, American-schooled, and self-described "eclectic physician," Dr. Henry Tanner. Dr. William Hammond, the debunker of the famous

fasting girl, Mollie Fancher of Brooklyn, offered a stipend of one thousand dollars to anyone able to abstain from food and water for thirty days, but negotiations with Tanner grew contentious. Instead, Tanner undertook a fast of forty days, with small amounts of water, supervised by the United States Medical College. Held before a paying audience at New York's Clarendon Hall, it commenced on June 28. Tanner commanded the attention of the press, which chronicled his trial, and the public, which attended to its details. By the fortieth day his weight had dropped from 157½ to 122 pounds, but he survived admirably (note the "before and after" masthead illustrations). He claimed to have netted only five hundred dollars from the ordeal. He did, however, achieve major celebrity, receiving an avalanche of cards and letters, embroidered keepsakes, and even a pro-

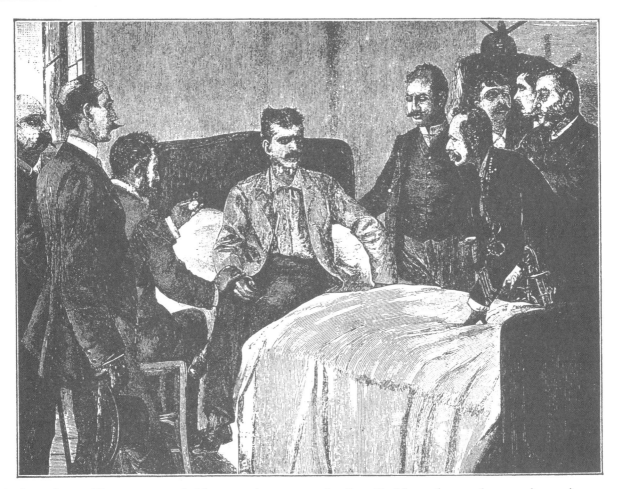

posal of marriage.[14] Tanner repeated this entertainment when lucrative wagers or engagements could be secured. He inspired a number of dueling imitators: Succi, Sacco, Sacco-Homan, Jacques, Merlatti, Cetti, and a host of others, both men and women.

In 1891 the Royal Aquarium of London featured "Jacques the Fasting Man," who was awarded a medal for going fifty days without comestibles (he did smoke seven hundred cigarettes during this interval). In 1894 the same institution featured "a German musician named Berg, who played the piano continuously for thirty hours sustained by Bovril [a popular beef beverage] and biscuits only, which were fed to him by his wife."[15] Although not technically a fast, the performance is more in keeping with my own stringent standards of what constitutes entertainment. In 1901 there was still enough interest in such spectacles to warrant, at the same institution, the exhibition of Augusta Christensen who, as reported in the October 25 issue of *The Showman* magazine, was then entering the last week of her fifty-two-

day fast. On November 29 the same journal announced that the manager of the aquarium would introduce a startling novelty into the world of fasting. Mons. Papuss, the artist in question, would be placed in a glass coffin that would be suspended in a tank of water, at all times to be supervised by "any two or more watchers who...will be paid to see that nothing unfair takes place. During his stay under water the performer will take no food or liquid of any description....Monsieur, however, will be able to console himself with the thought 'Water, water everywhere, and not a drop to drink.'"[16]

Succi, meanwhile, one of the first to beat Tanner's record, was publicly discredited: "It has come to light in his latest attempt to go for fifty days without food that he privately regaled himself on soup, beefsteak, chocolate and eggs." One of those supervising his ordeal was proven to be the provider of the comestibles. The Doctors Gould and Pyle, who provided the account of the exposure, were quick to defend the integrity of exhibition fasting as a whole:

Although all these modern fasters have been accused of being jugglers and deceivers, throughout their fasts they showed constant decrease in weight, and inspection by visitors was welcomed at all times. They invariably invited medical attention, and some were under the closest surveillance; although we may not implicitly believe that the fasts were in every respect bona fide, yet we must acknowledge that these men displayed great endurance in their apparent indifference for food, the deprivation of which in a normal individual for one day only causes intense suffering.[17]

Ricardo Sacco, who became well known in England, was presented by the famous impresario Charles B. Cochran (who confessed to making considerable profit

from this sideshow attraction).[18] On one occasion, Sacco was exhibited in a sealed glass house, and there bettered his record with a fifty-two-day fast. Cochran later confessed, "I will admit that no special watch was kept on Sacco. Therefore I am not in a position to say how far his feat was genuine....he entered his voluntary prison a healthy-looking man, and emerged a skeleton."[19]

W. Buchanan-Taylor, another chronicler of spectacles and amusements, was not so coy. During a fast at the Lesser Free Trade Hall in Manchester, Buchanan-Taylor, then a newspaper reporter, situated himself in the adjacent Theatre Royal armed with powerful binoculars. Sometime after midnight he witnessed Sacco and his managers and their wives sit down to a candlelit dinner for four in the exhibition hall: "They were having a rare tuck-in."[20] Those who were deceived by the imposture did not necessarily enjoy the spectacle. Theodore Feldstead reminisces, in his *Stars Who Made the Halls:* "One of my most gruesome memories was Sacco the Fasting Champion. Here was a man who literally starved to live. Day by day, lying utterly motionless in a glass case, he approached the time-limit...of human endurance, with gaping crowds being admitted to satisfy their love of the morbid. No doubt it was genuine enough, if unutterably repulsive." Feldstead would have been no more pleased by the demise of the worthy Dr. Tanner, who at the end confessed that he fasted because he did not have the money for food; he took his own life, by morphine overdose, in 1893.

Although a work of fiction, Franz Kafka's *A Hunger Artist* magnificently evokes the milieu of the professional faster, exhibiting for a populace that neither cares about nor comprehends what it sees. Both the Polish playwright Tadeusz Rózewicz and the American choreographer Martha Clarke have created pieces inspired by the Kafka story. Joseph Liebling describes with panache the exploits of a champion eater and a champion faster in his 1938 publication, *Back Where I Came From;* and professional fasters worked in European fairs as late as 1950.[21]

The discipline of sustaining oneself from the air alone is sometimes called Breatharianism. Supposedly an ancient yogic principle, it is defined by the *Donning International Psychic Encyclopedia* as living "without food or water by special breathing techniques that enable an individual to be sustained by the spirit." An exponent of Breatharianism named Wiley Brooks, a handsome, very thin black man in his forties, headed the Breatharian Institute of America, and in 1983 claimed not to have consumed anything except an occasional glass of fruit juice for eighteen years. The author of *Breathe and Live Forever*, Brooks insists that one can take gases from the air and turn them into liquids and solids. He is said to excrete waste only through his pores, like trees and plants.

Brooks makes money by lecturing. His fees can be as high as five hundred dollars for helping students make the transition from carnivorism to lesser evils like vegetarianism, liquidarianism, and ultimately nothing at all. Apparently, however, none of his disciples has been able to master Breatharianism. According to a number of sources, Brooks himself has a sweet tooth and religiously observed a junk-food jag between stops on his lecture tour. On one of these outings, a Breatharian coordinator, Kendra Wagner, saw Brooks drinking a Coke. "We felt tricked and deceived," Wagner said, according to a Pacific News Service account. Thirteen of the organization's fifteen officers resigned. An additional article accused Brooks of eating chicken potpies and biscuits in a Vancouver hotel. Lavelle Lefler, whom Brooks called an ex-girlfriend out for revenge, revealed, "The truth is, he sneaks into…fast-food places and eats just like the rest of us."[22]

The thought of Brooks covertly downing a Big Mac is wonderfully reminiscent of Mr. Cavanagh and his ham "cut particularly fat." Indeed, had they existed in 1841, one can anticipate with what rapture Bernard Cavanagh might have contemplated cheese, lettuce, pickles, onions, special sauce, and two all-beef patties on a sesame-seed bun. ◎

NOTES

1. See my *Learned Pigs & Fireproof Women* (New York, 1986), pp. 277–99.
2. Los Angeles gardeners engaged in a seven-day fast to reinstate their gas-powered leaf-blowers–my choice for the world's most senseless and annoying invention (*Los Angeles Times*, January 10, 1998, Metro section, p. 1).
3. The earliest mention of Cavanagh in London is an unidentified cutting, hand-dated August 24, 1841.
4. Unidentified cutting, September 24, 1841. Another account says that the room measured nineteen feet by nine feet and was six feet, eleven inches high. Included with a rare Cavanagh pamphlet I obtained some years ago were a number of newspaper stories of the faster's exploits. These cuttings were pasted on larger sheets of paper, often without the dates or sources of the articles. Whenever possible I will cite specific publications.
5. He was no doubt suspicious that a long straw could have been

inserted through the keyhole, a technique later favored by the estimable conjurer George Marquis for obtaining alcoholic potables from sympathetic bellboys when he was locked in a hotel room to prevent just such imbibing.
6. *Weekly Dispatch*, August 10, 1845.
7. One of the few surviving parodic references to Cavanagh is on the playbill of an acclaimed magician, juggler, equilibrist, and swallower of swords named Ramo Samee, who came from India to seek his fortune in England. In Shoreham on July 11, 1842, it was announced that "[Ramo Samee] will conclude his performance by Swallowing a Sword 2-ft. long!!! This wonderful feat continues to astound the most eminent medical men in London, and is not like CAVANAGH, THE FASTING MAN, AN IMPOSITION." This playbill is reproduced in *Learned Pigs & Fireproof Women*, p. 287.
8. A loyal fasting dog is mentioned by Southey in *Omniana*, quoted in the *Recreative Review, or Eccentricities of Literature and Life* (London, 1824): "A dog which had belonged to an Irishman, and was sold by him in England, would never touch a morsel of food on a Friday. The Irishman had made him as good a Catholic as himself. This dog never forsook the sick-bed of his last master, and when he was dead, refused to eat, and died also" (2:514).
9. D. E. Mills, *A Collection of Tales From Uji* (Cambridge, 1970), pp. 364–65. The reference was provided by John Solt.
10. See Hyder E. Rollins, "Notes on Some English Accounts of Miraculous Fasts," *Journal of American Folklore*, vol. 34, no. 134 (October-December 1921), pp. 357–76. He reproduces part of the 1611 pamphlet and reports that Fliegen was ultimately immortalized in wax. Rollins also gives an excellent survey of miraculous fasts. There is also an account of Fliegen by Henry Wilson and James Caulfield in *The Book of Wonderful Characters* (London, 1869) that pleasantly contrasts her with Pliny's account of an ancient East Indian people called the Astomi, "who have no mouths, and are supported by the smell of roots, flowers and wild apples; and with that of Chinese virgins who are said to conceive by smelling at a rose" (p. 249). Eugen Hollander also mentions Fliegen in his witty and impressive study, *Wunder Wundergeburt und Wundergestalt* (Stuttgart, 1921), and describes a contemporary print that punningly pictures her sitting on a giant fly (*fliege* is "fly" in German). The three sixteenth-century cases noted above are documented by Hollander (pp. 209-16). Lynn Thorndike briefly mentions the fasters from Unna and Speyer, citing early sources, in his *History of Magic and Experimental Science* (New York, 1941), 6:430–31, 516.
11. Walter Vandereycken and Ron Van Deth, "Miraculous Maids? Self-Starvation and Fasting Girls," *History Today* (August 1993), pp. 37–38.
12. A broadside describing the Boston Museum exhibition is reproduced in Richardson Wright, *Hawkers and Walkers in Early America* (New York, 1927), opposite p. 180. Henderson's *An Examination of the Imposture of Ann Moore* was published in London in 1813. A longer account of the case, *Statement of Facts Relative to the Supposed Abstinence of Ann Moore*, by the Reverend Leigh Richmond, appeared the same year. The *Dictionary of National*

Biography contains a succinct and amusing account of Mrs. Moore. Little is known of her life after the exposure, it reports, except her incarceration for "robbing her lodgings."

13. Both the faster and the newspaper are unidentified; *Remarkable Characters* scrapbooks, 2:32, author's collection.

14. *The Human Wonder of the World! The Celebrated Dr. Tanner. A Full Account of his Forty Days' Fast* (Philadelphia, 1880). This is the source of the masthead illustration.

15. John H. Munro, *The Royal Aquarium* (Beirut, 1971), p. 21.

16. This was only one of many acts—playing cards, frolicking, surviving without air—conducted entirely under water, a magic-inspired craze that lasted into the 1920s.

17. George Gould and Walter Pyle, *Anomalies and Curiosities of Medicine* (New York, 1896), p. 421.

18. Typical of the literature sold at these exhibitions was the pamphlet *The Strange Case of Josephine Marie Bedard. A Young Lady, Stout and Active, who has eaten nothing for seven years* (Boston, 1889). It was written by C. H. Webber, Ms. Bedard's sideshow manager, who apparently thought his act's robust physiognomy did nothing to discredit her. She was exhibited at the Nickelodeon in Boston, an establishment with the motto: "More real pleasure can be had for five cents at the Nickelodeon than can be obtained for fifty cents at any other place of amusement in the country."

19. Cochran, *Secrets of a Showman* (New York, 1926), pp. 139–41.

20. *Shake the Bottle* (London, 1942), pp. 77–78.

21. See Laurence Senelick, "Hunger Artist," *The Cambridge Guide to World Theatre* (Cambridge, 1988), p. 465.

22. UPI, AM cycle, April 6, 1983. Mr. Brooks is currently offering a program entitled "A School for the Gods. In this seminar, learn the mechanics of being a three-dimensional God here on the Earth Plane."

JAY'S JOURNAL OF ANOMALIES
Written by Ricky Jay and published three times a year by the author and W & V Dailey, Antiquarian Booksellers, 8216 Melrose Avenue, Los Angeles, California, 90046, (213) 658-8515. Subscription $90 per annum. ¶ Printed letterpress by Patrick Reagh and typeset in Monotype Ehrhardt with Thorowgood heads on Rives Heavyweight paper. ¶ Designed by Mr. Reagh & Mr. Jay. ¶ The author wishes to thank Susan Green, Larry Vigon, Jayme Odgers and Angela Freytag for generous assistance in the preparation of this issue. ¶ Comments and corrections to the text are welcomed. ¶ Written and illustrative material, © Ricky Jay, 1998. ¶ All images are from the private collection of the author. Any subsequent use of text or image is permissible only with the express written consent of Mr. Jay.

JAY'S JOURNAL *of*
ANOMALIES

VOLUME FOUR   NUMBER TWO   1998

Dental Deception

Dentist: A prestidigitator, who, putting metal into your mouth pulls coins out of your pocket.
–The Devil's Dictionary, 1906

AMBROSE BIERCE so defines, and inexorably links, the magician and the molar. But the relationship between conjurers and teeth is of great antiquity.[1] This nexus is reinforced in *Vocabolario della Crusca*, the important and scholarly Italian dictionary, which defines *ciarlatano* ("charlatan") as "one who sells salves or other drugs in public places, pulls teeth and exhibits tricks of legerdemain." Perhaps, as Gerte de Francesco has observed, "the most striking feature of this definition is its association of legerdemain with the ordinary business of peddling."[2] Here we investigate the compelling connection between dentistry, deception, and entertainment. In the early modern period, dentists were public performers, displaying a surprising variety of skills at open-air fairs in front of live audiences. Dexterity, audacity, and a highly developed gift of gab – no conjurer or quack could do without them.

The first known print to feature dentistry, engraved and executed by Lucas van Leyden in 1523, shows an exercise in deception. The patient, mouth agape, is attended by the dentist while his purse is deftly picked by a female accomplice. The sixteenth-century mountebank, or quacksalver (from the Dutch "kwaksalver," or talkative salesman, hence "quack"), often combined the sale of potions with the performance of prestidigitation. James Harvey Young

has written: "At all stages of humanity's concern with the teeth, quackery has brazenly asserted itself." The traveling mountebanks of Renaissance Europe, Young notes, "took it upon themselves to see to the natives' health: to remove from their heads the stones that caused madness, from their eyes the cataracts that caused blindness, to remove from their mouths the teeth that caused pain; and to treat all manner of ailments with the laying on of hands and the prescribing of powerful panaceas. Gaudy costumes, acts of showmanship, and always boastful harangues attracted attention, provoked fear, and promised healing. Sometimes, loud music drowned out the anguished cries of patients."[3] The use of music to mask the moans of dental patients has been discussed in various medicine show memoirs.

The close relationship of dentistry to performance can be seen in the nature of the early retirement elected by Horace Wells, a dentist who used nitrous oxide as a painkiller. In 1844, he arranged a demonstration of tooth-pulling for skeptical doctors at Massachusetts General Hospital. Apparently he ended the application of the gas prematurely and the patient screamed. Wells was hooted off the stage, none of the spectators realizing that they had just witnessed the first successful use of medical anesthesia. Humiliated, Wells left the profession and became an exhibitor of trained canaries.[4] Even before Wells applied nitrous oxide as an anesthetic, the successful magician Mr. Henry presented it as "laughing gas" in a performance that was to be much imitated. Volunteers were selected from the audience of the Adelphi Theatre in London in 1824. Nitrous oxide was administered, and the participants cavorted deliriously about the stage to the delight of the paying crowd.[5]

L ong before scientists and mountebanks chronicled their exploits, early texts offered incantatory cures for toothache or extolled the use of teeth as talismans for various medicinal purposes. Lynn Thorndike, in his eight-volume work *A History of Magic and Experimental Science* (New York, 1923–58), gives several examples. The naturalist Pliny proposed an injection, into the ear nearest an aching tooth, of "the ashes of the head of a mad dog and oil of Cyprus" (vol. 1, p. 68). Others advocated healing a troubled tooth by spitting into a frog's mouth (p. 588), or, as one twelfth-century manuscript suggests, by repeating "seven times in a waning moon on Tuesday or Thursday an incantation beginning 'Aridam, margidam, sturgidam'" (pp. 724–25). To cure "women's diseases," Pliny suggested, one should wear a bracelet containing the first tooth lost by a young boy – providing the tooth had never touched the ground (p. 82), and as he also noted, "serpents flee from a man who wears the tooth of a deer" (p. 84).

Albertus Magnus, a source of many early conjuring tricks, observes that a dog will not bark at a man who holds in his hand the tooth of a black dog – as might be expected, thieves were especially fond of the amulet (vol. 2, p. 574). Newly married couples were urged to seek protection from malign influence by carrying "the pulverized tooth of a dead man" (p. 851), and a late-seventeenth-century reference in the *Journal de Sçavans* immortalized a woman who not only lost a tooth at the birth of each child but also could predict "with certainty," from the state of her teeth, the medical disposition of all her children (vol. 8, p. 443). It is encouraging to note that such pseudo-science was satirized as early as the second century in Lucian's *Philopseudes or Apiston*: "Cleodemus the Peripatetic advises as a remedy for gout to take in the left hand the tooth of a field mouse which has been killed in a prescribed manner, to wrap it in the skin of a lion freshly-flayed, and thus to bind it about the ailing foot" (vol. 1, p. 279).[6]

Perhaps the most famous early story of magical teeth was related in the first important book on ventriloquism, the Abbé de la Chapelle's *Ventriloque ou L'Engastrimythe* (London, Paris, 1772). In 1593, a seven-year-old boy from Silesia, having lost a tooth, supposedly grew another of gold. Many accounts of this miraculous addition were published in works of the day, although La Chapelle surmised that his popular audience would be unfamiliar with these references and find the story fresh. The deception was revealed when a goldsmith, called upon to examine the boy's mouth, announced that a sheet of gold leaf had been applied, with considerable skill, to cover the conventional tooth.[7]

Teeth have ever been the talismans of itinerant performers. Samuel Butler, in his descriptions of various professions and classes of society, defined a juggler – in a way that may remind us of Bierce's dental displacement of assets – as "an artificial magician, that with his fingers casts a mist before the eyes of the rabble, and makes his Balls walk invisible which way he pleases....[He] conveys money out of one man's pocket into another's with much more sincerity and ingenuity than those that do it in a legal way....[and] calls upon *Presto begone*, and the *Babylonian Tooth*, to amuse and divert the rabble from looking too narrowly into his tricks."[8]

In the seventeenth century, volumes devoted entirely to conjuring appeared for the first time in English. A number of these contained tricks or wagers involving teeth. *Hocus Pocus Junior: The Anatomie of Legerdemain* (1634), the first illustrated instruction book of conjuring effects, contained two such items:

L'ARRACHEUR DE DENTS.

C'est toujours sans douleurs que nous continuons d'arracher les dents! Si cet homme a fait entendre quelques cris, c'est la joie d'être débarrassé d'un aussi grand mal qui les lui a fait pousser!...En avant la grosse caisse!

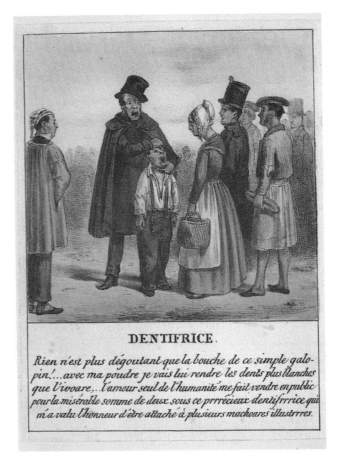

DENTIFRICE.

Rien n'est plus dégoutant que la bouche de ce simple galopin!...avec ma poudre je vais lui rendre les dents plus blanches que l'ivoare...l'amour seul de l'humanité me fait vendre en public pour la misérable somme de deux sous ce prrrécieux dentifrrrice qui m'a valu l'honneur d'être attaché à plusieurs machoares illustrrres.

How to seeme to make a tooth drop out with a touch.

You must have some great tooth in a readinesse; as the tooth of a Hog, a Calfe, or of a Horse; this you must retaine privately in your right hand, and with the same hand take out of your pocket a small cork ball, and having used some Rhetorick to perswade them it is of some excellent property, incline your head, and therewith touch some one of your farther teeth, and immediately let the tooth that you held in your hand drop down, saying, and this is the fashion of Mountebanks, Touch and take.

The second item, *Another conceipt to procure laughter,* involves a wager still performed occasionally under the modern rubric of "bar bets."

Take your ball in one hand, and the tooth in the other, and stretch your hands as farre as you can one from the other, and if any will, lay a quart of wine with him that you will not withdraw your hands [change the position of your arms], and yet will make both of them [the ball and the tooth] come into either hand which they please: It is no more to doe, than to lay one down upon the table, and turne your selfe round, and take it up with the other hand, and your wager is won, and it will move no small laughter to see a foole so lose his mony.[9]

It is reasonable to assume that teeth are not an essential ingredient for the wager.

In 1676 a more dramatic conceit, "To Cure the Tooth-ach," appeared in *Sports and Pastimes, Or, Sport for the City, and Pastime for the Country; with a touch of Hocus Pocus, or Leger-demain,* a volume of conjuring effects authored by the elusive J. M. A man complains of a toothache and the conjurer announces that he will effect a cure. He gives his subject a thimbleful of salt, which he carefully wraps in a small piece of white paper. He instructs the patient to hold the package to his cheek, near the troubled tooth. After a few minutes the subject says he feels much better. The conjurer then asks him to wash his mouth with two spoonfuls of cold water. While the patient departs to perform his task, the conjurer ridicules the conceit and substitutes the salt in the package for a similar quantity of ashes and twists the ends of the paper exactly as he did before. When the subject returns he is asked to hold the packet to his teeth again and to describe how he feels. Pleased with the results, and to the delight of the audience, the man proclaims his surprise that simple salt could be so efficacious. One of the company will say, "Why do you think you have salt in the paper?" The man replies that he saw the magician take salt out of the box and wrap it up. The spectators suggest a wager, to which the patient agrees. When the packet is opened there are no ashes, only salt.

When the company disperses, the conjurer splits the winnings with the patient, who, it must be confessed, is his accomplice. In addition to this collusion, a bit of sleight of hand was necessary, as the conjurer had to switch the packet of ashes for a concealed identical package of salt when his colleague returned from gargling. The author cheerfully concludes, "I have won many a Pinte of Wine by it."[10]

This gambit persisted for many years in the literature of magic. In the series of books called *The Whole Art of Legerdemain, or Hocus Pocus in Perfection*, first penned by Henry Dean in 1722, "To Cure the Toothach" is introduced as an example of one of magic's most fundamental principles, confederacy:

…by confederacy mighty wonders are wrought, which seem incredible and impossible. Some will ask for what reason I do write these things and set them forth in such a manner, for they say, we know them already; my answer is if you do, every one does not; therefore slight not simple things, for you, that seem to be so cunning and so wary, may be imposed on and deceived: what would an ingenious person give, or how far would he go to learn secrets? I myself would have gone twenty miles to have learnt the worst fancy in this book.

In the panoply of magic effects, none has generated more furor than a magician's claim to invulnerability, as expressed by his or, occasionally, her, willingness to be a human target. Versions of the effect have been recorded since the sixteenth century and, in spite of the death of at least a dozen performers, it continues to be exhibited. Most early presentations featured a conjurer's attempt to catch a bullet fired directly at him — on the point of a sword, in a silk handkerchief – or in his grasp, barehanded. In the most popular performance of the stunt, the conjurer offers a bullet that is examined and then marked for identification and loaded into a pistol or rifle that is to be fired by a volunteer from the audience. Bracing himself for a shot aimed squarely at his mouth, the magician orders the volunteer to fire. After staggering like a slightly tipsy party guest, the performer grins triumphantly and the marked bullet is seen to emerge from between his teeth.

The first account I have located of firing directly at the teeth is in a newspaper cutting from 1817 describing a performance at Bartholomew Fair. The Frenchman Monsieur Gobert, husband of the justly famous strongwoman of the same name, thus ended their joint presentation: "by way of climax, [he] loaded a pistol, and having put in a marked ball, he desired one of the company to fire at him. The person obeyed, and Monsieur Gobert caught the ball in his teeth. Bravo! cried an English plumber – who will now say the French cannot stand fire and lead?"[11]

It is not surprising that one of the earliest proponents of the stunt was a dentist. Called Le Fevre, "Operateur pour la Dents," he authored an undated booklet (most likely published in the mid-seventeenth century), *Nouveau livre des plus admirables secrets de ce temps. Expérimentez & approuvez pour la curiosité & récréation des beaux esprits* (The New Book of the most admirable Secrets of the Times. Tested and approved for the curiosity and recreation of the intelligent). In keeping with the tradition of conjurer-dentists, he apparently performed and even taught some of the effects he described. His explanation of the gun trick, however, might have given one pause before seeking his ministrations. His technique for invulnerability to rifle bullets was to rub the "throat" of the gun inside and out with bacon or an onion, which, he assures us, will alter the path of the bullet so the marksman will miss his target. He proffers a similar effect, with an only slightly more practical explanation, for firing a pistol at "a dog or a hat, without hurting the dog, nor piercing the hat."[12]

In the colonies in 1787, the Brenons from Dublin treated residents of New York, and later Massachusetts, to a combination of skills: Joseph Brenon performed convoluted evolutions on the slack wire (he was the fellow who caught a bullet while so balanced, in his handkerchief); his wife performed "dexterity of hand," restoring the head of a decapitated fowl. As a conclusion it was noted, "Said Brenon cures the Tooth Ache without drawing.– No Cure, No Pay. For the Poor Gratis."[13]

The magician Jacob Philadelphia holds a special place in the annals of conjuring as the first of his profession to have been born in the United States. Oddly, Jacob Meyer (his given name) never performed in America but gained great fame in Europe, using the name of his native city and a performance that combined illusions, scientific principles, and ghostly projections. The bombast with which he advertised his feats, and the extremity of the occult powers that he claimed, so angered the physicist Georg Christoph Lichtenberg that he authored a satirical broadside featuring a particularly hyperbolic stunt combining guns and teeth. It was posted in Göttingen, the town where Philadelphia was to give his mystical soirees, in January 1777. I offer some of the text for flavor:

NOTICE

The admirers of supernatural Physics are hereby informed that the far-famed magician, Philadelphius Philadelphia (the same that is mentioned by Cardanus in his book *De Natura Supernaturali*, where he is styled "The envied of Heaven and Hell"), arrived here a few days ago by the mail, although it would have been just as easy for him to come through the air, seeing that he is the person who, in the year 1482, in the public market at Venice, threw a ball of cord into the clouds, and climbed upon it into the air till he got out of sight....

He has had the honour of performing with the greatest possible approbation before all the potentates, high and low, of the four quarters of the globe; and even in the fifth, a few weeks ago, before Her Majesty Queen Obera at Otaheite....

The following are some of his one-thaler tricks; and they are selected, not as being the best of them, but as they can be described in the fewest words:...

He takes two ladies and sets them on their heads on a table, with their legs up; he then gives them a blow and they immediately begin to spin like tops with incredible velocity, without breach either of their head-dress by the pressure, or of decorum by the falling of their petticoats, to the very great satisfaction of all present....

He draws three or four ladies' teeth, makes the company shake them well together in a bag, and then puts them into a little cannon, which he fires at the aforesaid ladies' heads, and they find their teeth white and sound and in their places again.

Philadelphia plodded through his much more pedestrian performance and sheepishly left the city.[14]

As peculiar as was Lichtenberg's hypothetical repertoire, the effect with teeth did have a precedent in the work of a better-known satirist. In 1721, Jonathan Swift authored an advertisement for a fictional conjurer called Emanuel Schoits, "THE WONDER OF ALL THE WONDERS THAT EVER THE WORLD WONDERED AT." This is the final effect in a series of stunts impossible to perform and even difficult to imagine: "He likewise draws the teeth of half a Dozen Gentlemen mixes and jumbles them in a Hat gives any Person Leave to blindfold him, while he returns each their own, and fixes them as well as ever."[15]

The attorney Henri Decremps (whose fame rests not on legal briefs but rather on a series of books he published largely to expose the famous contemporary Italian conjurer Joseph Pinetti) fancifully describes a satirical broadside on the subject of teeth. Decremps introduces a fictional character expressively named "Sieur Pilferer," a rogue and swindler who is also a doctor of pyrotechnics, professor of chiromancy, attendee of thirty-six universities, and visitor to sixty-five kingdoms. An adept in diverse mystic arts, including "appeasing the tempest," Pilferer, according to the playbill, inconveniently posted in Cape Town, "continued to cure tooth ache, not like the empiricists, who wrenched the jaw, but by a method as certain as unheard of, which consists of cutting off the head." Pilferer, anticipating the reluctance of volunteers, added: "to prove that this operation is not at all dangerous, & that it can be made according to the rules of the art cito, tuto & jucunde [swiftly, safely, and pleasantly] he will resuscitate an instant afterwards, after the principles of P. Kirker by Palingenesia.[16]

A number of nineteenth-century prints feature performing dentists, often as, or in combination with, magicians. In 1837 Victor Adam executed a print for *Le Charavari* featuring a troupe of performers; a clown balances on a free-standing ladder in front of a table with conjurer's equipment, and a banner with a large tooth trumpets a dentifrice. In the *Album Comique de Pathologe Pittoresque* of 1823, an Aubry print juxtaposes an ornately dressed sword-wielding conjurer and a dental examination. At approximately this time an artist called Courtin designed a marvelous album of hand-colored lithographs, *Spectacles en Plein Vent*. This panoply of outdoor entertainment featured a wide array of street performers: peepshowmen, checker-playing dogs, ladder balancers, very strong women, cups-and-ball

conjurers – and, of course, dentists. These plates (both reproduced here on page 129) demonstrate the techniques of mountebanks while the captions evoke the colorful speech used to seduce the audience. In *L'Arracheur de Dents,* a drummer drowns out the patient's painful wail as the dentist announces: "We continue as always to pull teeth with no pain! If this man had been made to listen to some testimonials, he might have known the joy of being rid of the tremendous ache his teeth have caused him! Get your money ready!" In the second plate a cheapjack pries open the mouth of a child and hawks his dentifrice by announcing: "There is nothing more disgusting than the mouth of this simple ragamuffin!…with my powder I will make these teeth whiter than ivory….only the love of my fellow man makes me offer for public sale at the miserably low price of 2 sous this precious toothpowder, which has honored me by being applied to many worthy jaws."

The startling effect of a conjurer firing a pistol to punctuate the disappearance of his own tooth graces at least two extremely rare magic chapbooks originally issued in 1812: *The Whole Art of Hocus Pocus containing the most dexterous feats of Slight of Hand,* and *The Complete Conjuror; or Art of Legerdemain*, both published by Thomas Tegg. Each featured a hand-colored illustration of this effect by George Cruikshank (opposite) as the frontispiece. Oddly, neither book describes the vanishing tooth effect in the text, but the familiar wager accomplished by switching the package of ashes is included.

In 1832 *Hutchins' Improved Almanac* published a "Yankee peddler" story entitled "Slight of Teeth." Peter Snicker, the goods seller, motions to the fireplace and challenges a Dutch tavern owner, "Will you bet a dollar I can't bite an inch off that red hot poker?"

"Wy, you great Yankee fool," said the Dutchman, "I knows you can't do it."

"Well now," returned the peddler, "I'll bet you my load of tin-ware and other notions, against the amount of my [dollar] bill, that I'll do it."

The peddler moved the red-hot iron toward his teeth but stopped an inch short of the end and bit the air. The Dutchman scoffed that he could have done the same, but the peddler reminded him that the wager was to bite an inch *off* the poker, and so collected his dollar.

In 1853, Johann Nepomuk Hofzinser, the great Austrian sleight-of-hand artist, was a guest at an important function. An intriguing young woman was also in attendance, and someone remarked on the beauty of her teeth. "Let me show them to you," she said, and removed the teeth from her mouth and placed them in a cup that was then circulated among the confounded diners. The cup was eventually handed to Hofzinser, who covered it for a moment. He lowered his hand to show that the teeth had vanished. He gestured to the woman whose dazzling smile revealed that the teeth had returned to her mouth. It was in this way that Hofzinser introduced his wife to polite Viennese society.[17]

The tale of a fortuitous encounter between a conjurer and a magic-loving dentist was published in 1944 in *Al Munroe's Magical Miscellany*, an eccentric journal promulgated by mimeograph. Munroe obtained this story, "Every durned word True," only with "considerable persuasion" from Ed "Pop" Reno, then 83, and affectionately billed by Munroe as "the grand old man

of magic." Reno had planned to spend the weekend in Dodge City before a Monday show at Bloom, Kansas. On the train to Dodge City he ate a sandwich, "a big fat one," and broke the bridgework on his teeth. At two o'clock Saturday afternoon, when he made an emergency visit to a local dentist, he was told that a new plate could not be completed in under five days. But Reno had a Monday show. The dentist saw the point, said, "Get in the chair," and went to work. He pulled nine teeth and then, doing his own lab work and vulcanizing with the aid of an assistant, kept Reno "in and out of the dental chair" until two o'clock Sunday night. He did tricks for the dentist, his wife, and two boys. The work was done in time, and the dentist charged only twenty dollars. "He must have liked my tricks," Reno concluded, "and the fast work of the dentist and his assistant certainly saved the day for me."[18]

As a breed, magicians suffer from having to conceal their most important work, although a good conjurer will sometimes take advantage of a situation so perfectly that he can barely resist revealing his ingenuity to those he has just astounded. Occasionally this is because he wants to disclose a magical effect whose inner workings are more interesting than what was seen by the spectators. At other times he may perform so effortlessly that his deception, in the words of the legendary Erdnase, may not be "suspected, let alone detected."[19] So it was with the greatest illusion of the respected conjurer T. Nelson Downs. From an obscure beginning in Marshalltown, Iowa, Downs became a major attraction in vaudeville. One of the first and unquestionably one of the best magicians to specialize in a specific branch of the art, he performed on stage conjuring only with pocket change. Billed as "The King of Koins," Downs headlined in America and Europe in the early years of this century. His greatest effect, he related privately, was performed not on the stage but off. At every meal that he ate in company he would dab at his mouth with a handkerchief before eating, and at the end of the meal he would do the same. This seemingly natural gesture belied some serious sleight of hand. As he commenced eating he substituted a set of false teeth that aided him in chewing and, at the end of the evening, exchanged them for the first set. As he colorfully expressed it, he switched his "lookers for his choppers."[20]

NOTES

1. As early as the tenth century, the famous Arabian physician Rhazes warned of the dangers of letting a quack get too close to one's mouth: "There are so many little arts used by mountebanks and pretenders to physic, that an entire treatise would not contain them....[They say] they can draw snakes out of their patients' noses, or worms from their teeth. No wise man ought to trust his life to their hands." Quoted by C. J. S. Thompson in *The Quacks of Old London* (London, 1929), p. 21.

2. De Francesco offers the remark and the citation in *Power of the Charlatan* (New Haven, Conn., 1939), p. 4.

3. James Harvey Young, *American Health Quackery* (Princeton, N.J., 1992), p. 107.

4. Sadly, Dr. Wells's distress also manifested itself in his tossing sulfuric acid at prostitutes. While incarcerated for his crime in The Tombs, the famous New York prison, he obtained and administered chloroform to himself before cutting his wrists with a razor. "The history of anesthesia is filled with drama, intrigue and skullduggery," wrote Ralph Moss in his review of a chronicle of the subject, *We Have Conquered Pain* by Dennis Fradin.

5. See Edwin Dawes's chapter on the use of nitrous oxide on the stage in *The Great Illusionists* (Secaucus, N.J., 1979), pp. 71–81.

6. Lucian is responsible for divulging a number of magic principles in an exposure of the pseudo-prophet Alexander of Abonutichus. See Lucian's *Reply to Celsus*, quoted in Thorndike, *A History*, vol. 1, pp. 277–79. For more on these magical effects see the recently published essay by W. Kalush, *Some Uses for Paper in Magic, 180 A.D.–1774* (Atlanta, 1998).

7. La Chapelle mentions earlier works on the subject by De Fontenelle, Fullanous, Horstius, and Helmstad. A discussion of the "gold tooth" and the literature it spawned is contained in Thorndike, *A History*, vol. 8, pp. 371–73.

8. Butler is quoted by Sidney Clarke in *The Annals of Conjuring*, reprint ed. (New York, 1983), p. 51.

9. *Hocus Pocus Junior: The Anatomie of Legerdemain* (London, 1634), sig. E4 recto and verso.

10. J. M., *Sports and Pastimes* (London, 1676), p. 8.

11. Unidentified cutting, hand-dated September 1817; "Bartholomew Fair Scrapbook," author's collection.

12. *Nouveau Livre*, pp. 3, 7.

13. Isaac Greenwood, *The Circus: Its Origin and Growth prior to 1835* (New York, 1909), pp. 79–80.

14. An important account of Philadelphia appears in Dawes, *Illusionists*, pp. 93–98. Like the exposure of psychics in more recent times, the episode seems to have had no deleterious effect on Philadelphia's career.

15. Jonathan Swift, *Irish Tracts and Sermons* (Oxford, 1948), pp. 285–87.

16. It is unlikely that the broadside was issued, but an overzealous reader of Decremps produced a version in *The Magician* (March 20, 1909), p. 45.

17. The source of the story is an article in the paper *Das Fremdenblatt;* see Richard Hatch's translation of *The Magic of J. N. Hofzinser* (Omaha, 1985), p. 12.

18. *Al Munroe's Magical Miscellany*, October 1944, p. 3.

19. S. W. Erdnase, *Artifice, Ruse, and Subterfuge at the Card Table* (n.p., 1902), p. 83.

20. Conversation with Dai Vernon, March 1974.

ILLUSTRATIONS

Page 127. *The Dentist*, engraving by Lucas van Leyden, 1523.

Page 129. *L'Arracheur de Dents & Dentifrice*, hand-colored lithographs by Courtin from *Spectacles en Plein Vent*, Paris, n.d.

Page 131. Woodcut of decapitation from a playbill of Professor Krosso, London, hand-dated February 1852.

Page 132. *Clown*, hand-colored engraving by George Cruikshank from *The Complete Conjuror*, London, 1812.

Page 133. Johann Nepomuk Hofzinser, *carte de visite* (Vienna, 185?).

Page 134. Silhouettes of T. Nelson Downs in various poses from his act from *Modern Coin Manipulation*, London, 1900.

JAY'S JOURNAL OF ANOMALIES

Written by Ricky Jay and published three times a year by the author and W & V Dailey, Antiquarian Booksellers, 8216 Melrose Avenue, Los Angeles, California, 90046, (323) 658-8515. Subscription $90 per annum. ¶ Printed letterpress by Patrick Reagh and typeset in Monotype Ehrhardt with Thorowgood heads on Rives Heavyweight paper. ¶ Designed by Mr. Reagh & Mr. Jay. ¶ The author wishes to thank Susan Green, Larry Vigon, Tim Tobin, Bill Kalush and Bob Read for generous assistance in the preparation of this issue. ¶ Comments and corrections to the text are welcomed. ¶ Written and illustrative material, © Ricky Jay, 1998. ¶ All images are from the private collection of the author. Any subsequent use of text or image is permissible only with the express written consent of Mr. Jay.

JAY'S JOURNAL *of* ANOMALIES

VOLUME FOUR   NUMBER THREE   1999

Suspensions of Disbelief

S ADDUS, FAKIRS, AND SNAKE CHARMERS have conjured a vivid and long-lasting image of Indian magic, but truth be told there is little in the repertoires of Western performing magicians that can be traced to the land of the Ganges. Nevertheless, one of the most compelling motifs, the suspension of a human being in midair, was initiated by a Hindu conjurer early in the nineteenth century.

"The Air Man," as he was evocatively called, carried a four-legged stool about eighteen inches high, a brass bar or pole about three feet in length, and a rolled-up deerskin. The bar was affixed to the stool, under cover of a blanket held by assistants, and then the deerskin was placed perpendicular to the bar. The magician "mounted" his apparatus and the blanket was lowered. He was seen sitting cross-legged in air, about four feet above the ground, the only point of contact with the equipment being his right wrist, which rested on the animal skin.

The conjurer and his illusion garnered substantial attention, and there are numerous appreciative descriptions that unfortunately disagree on such key points as his name, his age, his motives, and the type of apparatus he used. The earliest account I have located appears in a work called *Descriptive Letter Press to the Indian Microcosm* (Madras, 1827). The book features twenty hand-colored lithographs depicting Indian life as exemplified by various trades, such as water carrier, boat man, carpenter, corn grinder, and basket maker. A very few copies include the two additional plates that are reproduced here, accompanied in the original by a page of text dated 1828. These plates are not recorded in any collation of the 1827 publication.

According to the *Indian Microcosm*, the performer was a Cuddapah Brahmin called Sheshal (of a caste much higher than that normally associated with the performance of street entertainments), described as a thin middle-aged man wearing a rose-colored chintz gown, light waistband, and dyed yellow turban. He sported a neatly trimmed beard and around his neck was a row of large Pundaram beads. He appeared at the government house in Madras, where his airborne stance continued for a few breathtaking minutes. His eyes were half-closed, his left hand was configured in a recognizable posture of prayer, and the beads rested in his right hand. Then Sheshal was once more surrounded by his blanket-toting minions, and under the cover they provided he made his descent. His paraphernalia – the skin, the pole, and the stool – were then made available for inspection by the baffled spectators.[1]

According to R. A. Davenport's anonymously issued *Sketches of Imposture, Deception, and Credulity* (London, 1837), the conjurer was capable of staying aloft for *forty minutes*. An unidentified eyewitness notes that a hollow pole of bamboo was affixed to the stool by means of a brass joint. The deerskin here becomes "a kind of walking-crutch" covered with "a piece of common hide." When the conjurer descended, hidden by the blanket, the spectators "heard a gurgling noise, like that occasioned by wind escaping from a bladder or tube, and, when the screen was withdrawn, he was seen again on *terra firma*." In a conclusion more inclined toward credulity than imposture, Davenport states that the Brahmin died "without communicating his secret," seven years before the publication of *Sketches*; and "though

Dancing on Nothing.

attempts were made to explain it, none of them were satisfactory. It was asserted by a native that it is treated of in the Shasters [the Hindu sacred canon], and depends upon the art of fully suppressing the breath, and of cleansing the tubular organs of the body, joined to a peculiar mode of drawing, retaining, and ejecting the breath – an explanation which leaves the mystery as dark as ever" (pp. 287–88).

An article published in *Scientific American* in 1846 – within the magazine's first full year of publication – introduced a variation called "Dancing on Nothing," celebrating it as "one of the most astonishing wonders exhibited by the jugglers of Hindustan." The audience was admitted into a curtained chamber where they witnessed the performer standing on a square box about two feet high. He held a cane that rested on top of a nearby tree stump and, after a formal bow, commenced to dance on the box, with the encouragement of the crowd. A rascal would suddenly jump forward and mischievously remove the box. "Then appears the wonder of the performance; for the dancer without being in the least discommoded – not even appearing to notice the abstraction of the box – continues dancing as before. This having continued for a short time, he stops, bows, thanks and dismisses the audience, who leave him standing without any other connection with the earth than by way of the cane and the stump." This bears no resemblance to any other Indian version of the effect I have encountered.[2]

The World of Wonders, a Record of Things Wonderful in Nature, Science, and Art (London, c. 1868) cites another eyewitness account of 1828. In this instance the tools were laid open for scrutiny before the performance: the pole, of hollow bamboo, was two feet long and two and a half inches in diameter and was affixed to one of two brass stars inlaid on the seat of the stool, while the skin, here described as antelope hide, was four inches in circumference. "The man then concealed himself in a large bag. After a delay of five minutes, during which he appeared to be very busy under the shawl, he ordered the covering to be taken away, and was discovered sitting cross-legged in the air." In this posture he remained for more than half an hour, "counting his beads as if this new mode of sitting was no exertion to him. A large bribe was offered to induce him to reveal his mode of performance, but he declined to explain the secret" (p. 324). Such discretion should not surprise us, as the *Indian Microcosm* notes that the illusionist performed at "Gentlemen's gardens at Madras, where exhibiting himself he is very largely rewarded."

Thomas Frost included the effect in *The Lives of the Conjurors* (London, 1875) but subscribed to the error that the original unnamed Indian died in 1830 and that a second performer called Sheshal exhibited the effect in Madras in 1832. A Dutch writer, Francis Valentijn (1656–1727), described an earlier version (from about 1700) where the subject sits on sticks arranged to form a tripod. The conjurer removes one stick, then a second, and finally the third, leaving the fellow suspended in the air. Valentijn reported the experience of a friend, who fortunately had the foresight to run his own stick under the performer (much in the manner of a modern-day magician passing a hoop around a levitating figure).[3]

The earliest description of a levitation illusion in the East precedes the Valentijn account by almost four hundred years. Ibn Batuta ("the traveler" in Arabic), a native of Tangiers, visited the mysterious lands of China and India in 1325 and completed a manuscript account of his journeys thirty years later. An English translation was published in the early nineteenth century. Ibn Batuta chronicles the Eastern effect that was to inspire so many Western conjurers:

I was once in the presence of the Emperor of Hindustan, when two of these Jogees [Yogis] wrapt up in cloaks, with their heads covered (for they take out all their hairs, both of their head and arm-

pits, with powder) came in. The Emperor caressed them and said, pointing to me, This is a stranger, shew him what he has never yet seen. They said, we will. One of them then assumed the form of a cube and arose from the earth, and in this cubic shape he occupied a place in the air over our heads. I was so much astonished and terrified at this that I fainted and fell to the earth. The Emperor then ordered me some medicine which he had with him, and upon taking this I recovered and sat up: this cubic figure still remaining in the air just as it had been. His companion then took a sandal belonging to one of those who had come out with him, and struck it upon the ground, as if he had been angry. The sandal then ascended, until it became opposite in situation with the cube. It then struck it upon the neck, and the cube descended gradually to the earth, and at last rested in the place which it had left. The Emperor then told me that the man who took the form of a cube was a disciple to the owner of the sandal: and, continued he, "had I not entertained fears for the safety of thy intellect, I should have ordered them to show thee greater things than these." From this, however, I took a palpitation of the heart, until the Emperor ordered me a medicine which restored me.[4]

The levitation of performers in theatrical productions had been noted as early as 431 B.C.E. as the conclusion of Euripedes' *Medea*, and numerous ascents were witnessed in medieval religious pageants; but the means by which these flights were executed were often not invisible to the beholders.[5] The suspension illusion performed by Sheshal caught on throughout Western Europe and traveled to the Americas as well. Its appeal owed less to the Indian's performance than to its adaptation by the great French conjurer Jean Eugene Robert-Houdin. He dispensed with the curtain-wielding protectorate and presented the effect in full view, and he displayed his subject, his son Eugene, in a position parallel rather than perpendicular to the stage. These innovations were as naught, however, compared to his claim that he accomplished the effect by administering ether to his son.[6]

Beginning in 1847, ether was used as an anesthetic by inhalation in surgical procedures. It was a stroke of genius for Robert-Houdin to yoke these profoundly dissimilar phenomena, the Indian suspension illusion from the ancient East and the latest therapeutic inducement of unconsciousness. Robert-Houdin not only revamped the technical aspects of the mystery, he also placed them within the context of a hotly debated public issue. And he did so with full awareness of the affinity of magic and medicine: "The insensibility produced by inhaling ether began to be applied in surgical operations; all the world talked about the marvelous effect of this anesthetic, and its extraordinary results. In the eyes of many people it seemed much akin to magic."[7]

Robert-Houdin conjectured that if the scientists were able to enter his "domain," turnabout was fair play. "With the seriousness of a Sorbonne professor"–but one who knew he was fanning the flames of controversy–he announced his production, "The Ethereal Suspension," and proposed to demonstrate a marvelous new property of ether. His six-year-old son stood on a stool and extended both of his arms while a thin pole was placed under each of them. His eyes closed and his body sagged as a bottle was uncorked under his nose. "When this liquid is at its highest degree of concentration," said his father, "if a living being breathes it, the body…becomes in a few moments, as light as a balloon" (*Memoirs*, p. 312). The stool that the boy stood on was pulled away, leaving him supported by the thin rods alone. Next, the father placed the child's right hand on his own head and carefully removed the pole from underneath the child's right arm. He was now suspended by only a single stick that extended from his elbow to the stage floor. Robert-Houdin was now ready for the denouement: with a single finger he effortlessly lifted his son's feet until the child's body was suspended horizontally in midair, apparently in a state of ether-induced sleep.

The pseudo-scientific basis of this illusion created a furor mixed of approbation and concern for the child. Robert-Houdin was excoriated by letters in which outraged parents "severely upbraided the unnatural father who sacrificed the health of his poor child to the pleasures of the public. Some went so far as to threaten me with the terrors of the law if I did not give up my inhuman performance" (*Memoirs*, p. 215). But far from exposing his son to danger, Robert-Houdin had planned his illusionary attack on more than one front. The bottle decanted under the child's face was empty; backstage meanwhile, in the words of Robert-Houdin, "someone poured ether onto a very hot fire shovel, so that the vapour diffused into the room." A marvelous combination of verisimilitude and misdirection.

Robert-Houdin's later version of the same effect, introduced on October 10, 1849, was even more mystifying. The stool and rods had rested directly on the stage, but now, while the child was suspended in the same horizontal position, the pole supporting him was bal-

anced in the center of a footstool that itself was balanced on a wooden plank. In what appeared yet a further defiance of the laws of gravity, one of the supports holding up the plank was then removed. Many explanations were proffered by the confounded spectators. One writer insisted that the child was not human at all but an ingenious automaton. That Robert-Houdin consciously conveyed such an impression is confirmed by William Manning, who describes the boy's entrance and exit thus: "Houdin led his handsome boy by the hand to the footlights to make the most mechanical of bows to his audience." The father then administered the ether and performed the suspension. "This was always the final trick of a performance," Manning continues, "and when the curtain fell, and was raised again in obedience to the recall, father and son came walking most gravely forward, and the effect of this slow movement was to make half the world believe that the boy was not flesh and blood at all, but a marvelous automaton!" (*Recollections of Robert Houdin*, pp. 13–14). Those familiar with the *modus operandi* might proffer another explanation of the studied downstage perambulation.

In 1848, London audiences could witness three major magicians performing the illusion: Robert-Houdin at St. James's Theatre, Compars Herrmann at the Haymarket, and John Henry Anderson at the Strand.[8] The effect was far more often imitated than exposed, and after Robert-Houdin's retirement from the stage it became a staple in the repertoires of countless magicians, notably the Frenchman's rivals, Robin, Jacobs, Herr Alexander, Compars Herrmann, and Anderson.[9] Anderson, the self-styled "Caledonian Necromancer and Great Wizard of the North," was a master of advertising bombast and publicity and a larger-than-life figure on the British stage. He devised a derivative but original presentation called "Suspension Chloriforeene," billed as an "extraordinary new scientific wonder performed by a child of 5 years of age sleeping in the air while under the influence of condensed chloriform [*sic*]."[10] Herrmann, a conjurer of considerable reputation, performed a variant in which he concluded the effect by marching the child and the rod by which he was still suspended down a runway that led from the stage over the orchestra pit into the audience. Here he once again placed the stick into the floor, showing that the child could apparently be suspended at any location.[11] Compars's brother Alexander, another member of this magic dynasty, also featured the illusion, with his wife Adelaide as the subject.

Hamilton [Pierre Chocat], Robert-Houdin's designated disciple, performed a major revision of the effect at the Théâtre Robert-Houdin on January 16, 1860. Hamilton placed a youngster on a stool and then, grasping only one strand of his hair, suspended him from it. The program offered a poetic depiction of the child's own confident voice:

L'ENFANT ENLEVÉ PAR UN CHEVEU

Je suis l'enfant du prestige,
J'escamote tous les soirs.
Le sorcier qui me dirige
M'a donné tous ses pouvoirs.
Approchez,
Ecoutez, regardez;
Et puis, applaudissez![12]

This presentation, too, was widely imitated, notably by Robin (Henry Joseph Donckèle), the Frenchman who performed it in Egyptian Hall in London in 1862 as "A New Sensation Wonder Illustrating Archimedes Problem"; and by Ernst Basch in Germany, as pictured on the cover of this issue.[13] In 1864 J. M. Macallister presented an appealing innovation that he named "The Cataleptic Couch, or, the Triumph of the Magic Art." His sole contribution was to place the perpendicular pole of support on a diagonal (see illustration in opposite column).[14]

ANDREWS HALL!
CENTRAL COURT, WASHINGTON STREET.

MACALLISTER'S SOIREES MAGIQUES!

EVERY EVENING AT 7 3-4,
WEDNESDAY & SATURDAY AFTERN'NS at 2 3-4
COMMENCING

MONDAY, March 21, 1864.

PROF. J. M. MACALLISTER, son, pupil of, and successor to the late PROF. A. MACALLISTER, whose eminently successful career at the Old Boston Theatre, Federal Street, in the year 1851, must still be remembered by many. PROF. J. M. MACALLISTER'S Entertainments are after the style of his father, but immensely improved by many years of study and close application. The most noted feature being the

ENTIRE ABSENCE OF APPARATUS!

Depending upon the nimbleness of his fingers, and doing more with his bare hands than any other Magicians, with their tinsel trappings and half a dozen confederates. During his short season in Boston, in addition to a choice selection of those,

WONDERFUL ILLUSIONS!

Made so celebrated by his father, he will introduce upwards of

ONE HUNDRED NOVELTIES!

Invented, planned, and performed only by himself; including the most Wonderful and Startling Illusion, entitled

☞ THE CATALEPTIC COUCH!!
OR, THE TRIUMPH OF THE MAGIC ART.
(Invented and Performed only by PROF. J. M. MACALLISTER.)

TICKETS 25 CENTS.   RESERVED SEATS 50

To be had at O. Ditson & Co.'s, H. Tolman & Co.'s, and at the Hall. DOORS OPEN AT 2 O'CLOCK, AFTERNOONS. 7, EVENINGS

J. H. & F. F. Farwell Printing Office, 119 Washington St., Boston.

The illusion underwent numerous technical refinements and evolved through new methods of presentation devised by some of the most colorful practitioners of the prestidigitational arts. In his monumental *Modern Magic*, Professor Hoffmann (Angelo John Lewis) describes a temporary eclipse of interest after Robert-Houdin's retirement: "The trick fell comparatively out of notice till it was revived in a new form by the Fakir of Oolu in England, and contemporaneously by De Vere on the Continent."[15] The new *mise-en-scène*, however, did attract considerable notice. While suspended in midair, a beautiful young woman would assume various costumes and characters.[16] In an appendix to a later edition of the Hoffmann book, Arprey Vere mentions an even more dramatic technical advance: the final rod was removed, leaving the woman without any visible means of support. This was billed as "The Last Link Severed" by the Fakir of Oolu (actually an Englishman named Alfred Silvester who had worked with the famous ghost-manufacturing Professor Pepper as a scientific demonstrator at the Royal Polytechnic Institution).

At the conclusion of his Artistic Performance the Entranced Young Lady [his daughter Daisy] is Suspended by Two Solid Silver Pedestals. The Fakir's Mysterious Magnetic Power is Gigantically brought into requisition and actually Removes Each Support and leaves the object floating in Mid Air. "Defying the laws of Gravitation." This Novelty must Astound and Electrify all Beholders![17]

The other figure to whom Hoffmann attributes the renaissance of suspension was Charles De Vere, also an Englishman, whose real name was Herbert Spencer Williams but who spent most of his time on the Continent. According to Hoffmann, he had recently "greatly heightened the effect of the trick—the lady being made to rise spontaneously from the perpendicular to the horizontal position, and to continue to float in the air after her last ostensible support had been removed." But the shift in position was actually patented by another, J. Morris, in 1873.[18]

Baron Hartwig Seeman patented a "device for suspending persons in mid-air without visible support" in 1882 for a version of the illusion that he called "Elektra." Seeman, a prominent Swedish magician, toured around the world and ended his career in the United States. The

The Fakir of Oolu

primary subject of H. J. Burlingame's *Around the World With a Magician and a Juggler* (Chicago, 1891), Seeman claims (in a narrative McKinven politely calls "romanticized") to have been inspired by an Indian fakir called Convinsamy. When the Indian magician found Seeman familiar with the basic suspension illusions, he showed him the miraculous levitation of a young Indian girl in a standing position; she "gradually moved her arms and feet to the right and then to the left, ascending slightly in the air she slowly turned her face and then her body towards us." Seeman debuted the piece – after what he described as six years "intuiting" and mastering it – at the New York Academy of Music in 1880.[19] The subject of Seeman's version of the effect was his daughter, who, executing all of the maneuvers in a standing position, demonstrated more freedom of movement than was previously thought possible. Using modern theater stagecraft, Seeman ushered in an approach to the illusion that is still valued by modern-day magicians.

Three legendary figures performing early in this

century, J. N. Maskelyne, Harry Kellar, and Howard Thurston, all made use of Indian personae in their respective presentations of the levitation illusion. "The Entranced Fakir," which premiered at Egyptian Hall in London on April 16, 1900, featured Maskelyne's partner George Cooke playing a befuddled Indian magician floating in midair on a well-lighted stage. Harry Kellar, the preeminent American magician who was heavily influenced by Maskelyne, presented "The Levitation of the Princess Karnac" in 1904, and when Howard Thurston succeeded Kellar in 1908, he too presented the Karnac levitation. The patter of both Kellar and Thurston included a saga of tutelage by Hindu conjurers in India.

Yet more recent accounts of the suspension follow the original trajectory from East to West. In 1936 a

South India tea planter named P. T. Plunkett gave the *Illustrated London News* a rapturous account, complete with photographs, of a suspension that bore remarkable similarity to the feat attributed to Sheshal in 1828. *Time* magazine, in a story with photographs in the issue of June 29, 1936, quoted Plunkett's conversation with an Indian fakir, Sibbayah Pullavar, who explained that "he had been 'levitating' for twenty years, that his family had been doing it for hundreds."

Steve Martin's provocative one-act play, *Patter for the Floating Lady*, opens with the following story:

Magician: On my recent trip to India, I traveled in a small village far, far away from civilization. I had heard about an Indian fakir with extraordinary powers who lived in this village. One of his powers was the ability to levitate a woman, to cause her to float in the air with no visible means of support. I happened to see a demonstration of this in person, outdoors, on a hot summer day. This fakir, or mystic, took two bamboo poles and stuck them into the sand. Then, he looked toward his assistant, a very modest woman – modest but, I must say, very beautiful in her plainness – and hypnotized her. She then sat in the lotus position between the two poles which she lightly touched with her fingers. There was no noise in the crowd who stood motionless in a semicircle around them. Then, slowly, inch by inch, she rose up; she was suspended in the air. The circumstances were so simple, there was no question of trickery. As I stood there watching her float in the hot, desert air, I said to myself, "That's something I'd like to do to Angie."[20]

The sustained appeal of this illusion over literally thousands of enactments owes less, I believe, to cunning technical advances than to the ontological transformations in the image itself.... At the beginning, one sees the Air Man, inscrutable, sitting cross-legged in prayer – such grace, such mystery, such power, that one is inclined to forget the brigade of sycophants under his blanket.... The scene shifts to an elegant theater in Paris, where the most refined and successful conjurer in the land takes the hand of his young son and exposes him to the dangers of medical anesthesia. The father kicks away rods and stools and with a single finger lifts his son to a position of exquisite repose.

And now one sees the startling image of a child suspended by a single human hair.... Once again the scene shifts, and one sees not a child but a beautiful young woman who moves from vertical to horizontal without the aid of a single finger. She is so comfortably suspended that she is able to assume the costumes and identities of her more famous and groundworthy counterparts. She moves and shifts, and vogues her way to your heart. Again, a change, and now one sees a woman rising to take her place in the heavens.

Finally one is asked to suspend disbelief as a beautiful woman lies on a couch and a handsome young conjurer drapes her body with a thin sheet. It is a disturbing image, on the threshold of this world and the next. She rises slowly. Is she shedding her mortal coil? She ascends higher and higher, and suddenly, amid a clap of thunder and a flash of lightning, the sheet is whisked away. Not a trace remains of the woman who has captured the heart and the imagination. She has vanished into thin air.[21] ◉

NOTES

1. *Descriptive Letter Press to the Indian Microcosm* (Madras, 1827 [1828]), with lithographic title page, where there is a printed pasteover of the words "Indian Microcosm" covering the misprint "Indian Micricosm"; text from first unnumbered leaf. This work clearly identifies the pictured performer as Sheshal. An article from the *Saturday Magazine* (London, 1832) claims that Sheshal was the name of a second purveyor of this illusion after the death of the original performer – an error that has been repeated by a number of historians. Yet other midcentury reports call him Sheshah. Other disputed elements include the skin on which his arm rested (identified as antelope rather than deer) and the pole (sometimes bamboo is mentioned, a more deceptive illusionary material than brass). An issue of *People's Magazine* (June 14, 1833) reports the account of an unidentified correspondent writing from Tanjore who witnessed the illusion in Madras: "I saw him exhibit four times, and each time tried my utmost to discover the secret but without success. A large bribe was offered to induce him to reveal his mode of performance, but he declined."

2. Although uncorroborated, as far as I know this quirky presentation and the method suggested in the article are fully viable; see *Scientific American*, vol. 1, no. 52 (September 17, 1846).

3. Sidney Clarke, *The Annals of Conjuring* (reprint ed., New York, 1983), p. 266. Clarke does not cite the book, but says it was written about 1700. Francis Valentijn's five-volume travelogue, *Oud ennieuw Oost-Indien*, was published in Dordrecht, Holland, between 1724 and 1726.

4. *The Travels of Ibn Batuta; Translated from the Abridged Arabic Manuscript Copies...by The Rev. Samuel Lee* (London, 1829), pp. 161–62. Sidney Clarke quotes the passage in *The Annals of Conjuring*, pp. 264–65, noting that the cubic figure was most likely the Yogi sitting in a cross-legged posture; and since the

spectators were sitting on the ground, the man need not have been more than three or four feet off the ground to justify the perspective "over our heads." Clarke is prudently skeptical of the drug-induced perceptions of the chronicler. Accounts of impossible illusions are common in the literature of conjuring. In the December 1947 issue of *Britannia and Eve*, Douglas K. Gordon reported that he walked completely around a suspended Hindu boy while waving a stick under him, fully convinced that "he was actually floating in air." As Sam Sharpe notes, the photograph accompanying the article was conveniently taken before the stout stick that supported the child was taken away. See *Oriental Conjuring and Magic by Will Ayling*, with an index by S. H. Sharpe (Devon, England, 1981), p. 125.

5. See John A. McKinven, *Stage Flying* (Chicago, 1995), an excellent study of these techniques; the device used in *Medea* and the ascension of both Aphrodite and Artemis in Euripedes' *Hippolytus* are discussed on p. 1.

6. Milbourne Christopher, in his *Illustrated History of Magic* (New York, 1973), identifies six-year-old Auguste Adolphe Robert-Houdin as the participant (p. 145), but this is unlikely. William Manning, in *Recollections of Robert-Houdin, Clockmaker, Electrician, Conjuror* (London, 1891; reprint ed., Chicago, 1898), states that another son, Eugene, served as subject during the English engagement (p. 13).

7. *Memoirs of Robert-Houdin King of the Conjurers*, translated by Lascelles Wraxall, with introduction and notes by Milbourne Christopher (New York, 1964), p. 214.

8. In Germany a version called Suspension Éthéréenne featured "The Greek Woman Floating Freely in Air." See Stephan Oettermann, *Alte Schaustellerzettel* (Frankfurt, 1980), plate 2.

9. Houdini, in *The Unmasking of Robert-Houdin* (New York, 1908), gives a distorted history of the illusion in an attempt to downplay the Frenchman's contributions.

10. Robert-Houdin comments on the puffery of his rival Anderson in his *Memoirs*, pp. 224–27.

11. Sam H. Sharpe, *Salutations to Robert-Houdin* (Calgary, 1983), p. 96, quoting from Burlingame, *Alexander Herrmann: The Great Magician and His Tricks*.

12. [I am the famous child / Who performs tricks every evening / The magician who directs me / Has granted me all of his powers / Approach / Listen, look / And then, applaud.] See Michel Seldow, *Vie et Secrets de Robert-Houdin* (Paris, 1970), p. 147.

13. See Edwin D. Dawes, *Henri Robin, Expositor of Science & Magic* (Balboa Island, Calif., 1990), pp. 38–39. The Basch playbill is from *Schausteller Gaukler und Artisten* (Essen, Germany, 1980), vol. 1, p. 135. It is incorrectly dated c. 1840. These bills and broadsides, mostly from the Prater in Vienna, were from the collection of Albert E. Fischer and subsequently dispersed at auction; this sheet is now in the collection of Volker Huber. Basch, who became a well-known maker of magic apparatus, was one of four brothers who engaged in the profession of conjuring. The image, redrawn, was also used by the conjurer Adrien, who performed the effect in

France in 1861, and in a trade catalogue of the prominent Parisian magic manufacturer, Voisin.

14. Macallister claimed to be "son, pupil, and successor to the late Prof. A. Macallister," the well-known Scottish magician and former assistant to the important French conjurer Philippe. Playbill for Andrews Hall, Boston, March 21, 1864; author's collection.

15. *Modern Magic* (London, 1876), p. 495. Robert-Houdin's levitation was long remembered; Jules Verne, for instance, refers to it in describing the effects of weightlessness in his *From the Earth to the Moon* and *Around the Moon*, originally published in Paris, 1865–1869: "And immediately divers other objects, firearms and bottles, abandoned to themselves, held themselves up as by enchantment. Diana [a dog], placed in space by Michel, reproduced without any trickery the wonderful suspension practiced by such as Caston and Robert-Houdin. Indeed the dog did not seem to know that she was floating in air" (quoted from the Heritage Press edition, New York, 1970, p. 272).

16. This was a variation of "poses plastiques," or living pictures, introduced in the equestrian performances of the great rider Andrew Ducrow at Astley's Circus early in the nineteenth century; see A. H. Saxon, *Enter Foot and Horse* (New Haven and London, 1968), p. 35.

17. See David Price, *Magic: A Pictorial History of Conjurers in the Theater* (New York, London, and Toronto, 1985), for a reproduction of the Fakir's bill. Price notes that the Fakir occasionally preferred to be called Hadji Mahommed Salib. *Punch* magazine once referred to him as "The Great Isuarian Trompydeuxvilist."

18. See John A. McKinven, *Roltair "Genius of Illusions," Plus a Review of Historical Levitation Patents* (Lake Forest, Ill., 1980), p. 27. Morris was manager of the popular and intriguing Dr. Lynn, "The Talkee-Talkee Conjuror," who over a long career was associated with many magic presentations under various names and billings. Lynn demonstrated a double-suspension illusion at this period, most likely employing the mechanism described by Morris. That he performed the effect with two girls at opposite sides of the stage is confirmed by Charles Waller in *Magical Nights in the Theatre* (Melbourne, 1980), p. 75; and by an undated illustration in the *Programme of Dr. Lynn the Wonder Worker*, in the author's collection.

19. Burlingame, *Around the World*, pp. 55–56. Lee Siegel, in *Net of Magic* (Chicago, 1991), speculates that Covindsamy, so spelled, may be the same levitating fakir mentioned by Louis Jacolliot in his *Occult Science in India and Among the Ancients* (New York, 1884). Siegel provides a survey of descriptions of the suspension illusion.

20. Steve Martin, *Picasso at the Lapin Agile and Other Plays* (New York, 1996), p. 103. The levitation, seen on the stage much as described, was designed by Jim Steinmeyer and constructed by John Gaughan.

21. This description is of the "Asrah" levitation and vanishing lady created by the brilliant Belgian conjurer Servais LeRoy in 1905. Part of the illusion's appeal was its play on a cliché, legion levitating ladies in the repertoires of numerous magicians. Now LeRoy's version, too, has been replicated countless times.

ILLUSTRATIONS

JAY'S JOURNAL OF ANOMALIES

Written by Ricky Jay and published three times a year by the author and W & V Dailey, Antiquarian Booksellers, 8216 Melrose Avenue, Los Angeles, California, 90046, (323) 658-8515. Subscription $90 per annum. ¶ Printed letterpress by Patrick Reagh and typeset in Monotype Ehrhardt with Thorowgood heads on Rives Heavyweight paper. ¶ Designed by Mr. Reagh & Mr. Jay. ¶ The author wishes to thank Susan Green, Larry Vigon, Bill Kalush, John McKinven, Jim Steinmeyer, and Christian Fechner for generous assistance in the preparation of this issue. ¶ Comments and corrections to the text are welcomed. ¶ Written and illustrative material, © Ricky Jay, 1999. ¶ All images are from the private collection of the author. Any subsequent use of text or image is permissible only with the express written consent of Mr. Jay.

SUSPENSION ÉTHÉRÉENNE

JAY'S JOURNAL *of*
ANOMALIES

VOLUME FOUR   NUMBER FOUR   2000

The Automaton Chess Player, The Invisible Girl & The Telephone

D AI VERNON, the great sleight-of-hand performer whose life spanned the twentieth century, inspired this encomium: "In the performance of good magic the mind is led on, step by step, to ingeniously defeat its own logic." This is a story of logic and ingenuity, science and deception – and magic. It is the tale of an eighteenth-century thinking machine that couldn't think and yet influenced the industrial revolution and led to the invention of the telephone.

It begins in 1769 at the court of Maria Theresa, where the empress was witnessing the performance of François Pelletier. A man who demonstrated a curious combination of magnetism and illusion, he was one

of a new breed, a performer-cum-scientist. Among the most raptly attentive members of the audience was the learned and inventive Hungarian baron, Wolfgang von Kempelen. Whether it was the baron or the empress who threw down the gauntlet is not known, but by the end of the evening the baron had promised to return in a year with an invention that would bring the court to new heights of wonder. He was more prophetic than he knew, for Kempelen's device was to attract the admiration of a remarkable roster of philosophers, scientists, and hucksters, from Benjamin Franklin to Walter Benjamin.[1]

Returning to Schönbrunn Palace even before the prescribed interval, Kempelen debuted a turbaned wooden and metal figure of human stature, festooned in Turkish habiliment. The effigy, whose face was carved with an intense, brooding expression, sat behind a cabinet 3½ feet long, 2 feet wide, and 2½ feet high. He was richly caparisoned in robes lined with ermine and he sported an imposing turban that added to both his stature and his mystique. To the surface of the cabinet was affixed a chess board 1½ feet square. To begin the demonstration, the doors and drawers of the cabinet were thrown open, preempting the audience's suspicion that a human operator was concealed within the machine. Gears and wheels were displayed as a candle was passed behind the dimmest parts of the interior. The Turk's robes were unceremoniously thrown over his head to allow inspection from the rear, and even the interior of his physique was disclosed through a small door opened beneath his trousers. The entire structure was mounted on casters so that the cabinet could be revolved and viewed from all angles. As one eyewitness, Karl Gottlieb von Windisch, marveled, "Do not imagine, like many others, that the Inventor shuts one door as he opens another; *the entire Automaton is seen at the same time uncovered, his garments turned up, and the drawer opened, as well as the doors of the chest.* It is in this state that he rolls it from one place to another, and that he presents it to the inspection of the curious."[2]

Its skepticism allayed, the audience was eager for play to begin. Red and white ivory chess pieces were removed from the long drawer at the bottom of the cabinet and placed on the board. The Turk was allowed the honor (and advantage) of the first move. So that he could move his arm to manipulate the pieces, a long pipe was

removed from his left hand. A pillow, on which he would rest his arm while his opponent contemplated a response, was inserted under his elbow. The adversary, chosen because of his considerable skill at the game, was instructed to move his pieces to the exact center of the squares to enhance the Turk's ability to grasp them.

A small wooden casket was removed from the cabinet and placed on an end table near but not touching the automaton. During the match Kempelen occasionally opened the casket and gazed inside, preventing any but himself from viewing the contents. The specific purpose of the casket, other than Kempelen's acknowledgment that it was the very motivating power of his invention, was not discussed. (Note the casket on the left of the Chess Player in the illustration on the cover.) The mechanism was wound with a large key. A clockwork drone was heard and the Turk, after surveying the board, moved his left hand from the pillow and grasped a pawn, moved it forward two squares, and deposited the piece on the fourth rank. The opponent responded and the game was under way. Kempelen repeated the winding process after each dozen or so moves. When capturing his rival's piece the Turk would remove it from the board and then place his own piece on the vacated square. When the Turk threatened the player's queen, he courteously nodded his head twice; when the king was in check he nodded three times. It was soon obvious that the machine was able not only to play within the known parameters of the game but to play well. Indeed, very well. Eventually the adversary moved and the Turk refused to respond. This, Kempelen explained, signified the end of the game: checkmate—a victory, the first of many, for the automaton.[3]

It is difficult to fathom the profound effect that the Turk had on the courtiers present. As Windisch later wrote of the performance, "I know not whether all the spectators underwent the same impression; I, at least, thought I perceived on the faces of many of them, marks of extreme surprise. An old lady, above all the rest, who, without doubt, had not forgotten the tales with which her infancy had been amused, crossed herself, heaving a devout sigh, and went and hid herself in a distant window seat, that she might no longer remain so near a neighbour to the evil spirit, which she verily believed, must animate the machine."[4]

THE AUTOMATON CHESS PLAYER

It is also difficult to fathom the effect the Turk had on Kempelen himself, whose dismay was directly proportional to his success. He downplayed his own ingenuity, implying (truthfully, as we shall see) that the Turk relied on a simple secret rather than a complex system that replicated human thought; but admiring observers preferred to endorse the latter. (Kempelen was not the last to reject the flattery of scientific explanation; Houdini, later to be a player in this very drama, rebutted the accounts of scientists who claimed that he dematerialized his corporeal body to effect miraculous escapes.)

The great "automaton," one must now reveal, was not an automaton at all. The machine depended on a hidden director, a fully grown man who maneuvered within the casing so as to appear invisible and yet could determine his opponent's moves and respond accordingly. A director who changed many times over the career of the Turk, and who, depending on his skill, could at times be almost invincible during play. Yet, although the human agency of the Chess Player has been exposed countless times, these explanations are often full of misinformation. Even now there are no more than a handful of people who can explain it precisely.[5] Of the many mistaken explanations, the most often repeated was that the machine was inhabited by a dwarf, a small child, or an amputee.[6]

Kempelen referred to his own invention as a "mere bagatelle," and it is no wonder he returned to Pressburg anxious to resume other experiments. Nonetheless, the fame of his creation was such that he was forced to tolerate numerous interruptions from importunate dignitaries. In frustration he disassembled the machine, explaining that it had been damaged in travel. The furor abated for a time, but in 1781 Emperor Joseph II, like his mother Maria Theresa an early witness to the Turk, asked Kempelen to present the Chess Player to the visiting grand duke and duchess of Russia. Kempelen refurbished the figure for the occasion and it was triumphantly displayed to the dignitaries of the court, who unanimously urged the inventor to take the Turk on tour and granted him an extended leave. Kempelen was in need of funds for his more serious endeavors, and he consented. Hiring a Herr Anthon to front his exhibition and a strong if not brilliant chess player (whose name has not survived) to direct the machine, he embarked on a grueling concert tour through France, England, and Germany.

If the Turk triumphed on this tour – and, in spite of published exposures of his *modus operandi*, he did – his creator's attentions were consumed by more substantive matters. In London, on March 6, 1784, Kempelen submitted to the king, via Lord Sydney as secretary of state, a patent request for "A New Reaction machine, set in motion by Fire, Air, Water, or any Fluid, and applicable to any other Machine or Engine requiring a Moving Power in any Direction whatever."[7] In the document, Kempelen stated that the device "was entirely new, and hath never heretofore been invented." The machine was a variant of a steam engine of the first century, attributed to Hero of Alexandria. Kempelen harnessed the propulsive force of steam jets used by Hero and produced the rotary motion of an industrial engine, incorporating a safety valve to prevent explosions.[8] Even though this device apparently generated less power than the steam engine invented by James Watt in 1769, and significantly improved by him in 1781, the patent was awarded to Kempelen on April 10, 1784.[9]

Wolfgang de Kempelen

Although Kempelen continued to be interested in the steam engine (Ewart notes that at the end of his European tour Kempelen "returned to Vienna where he …tried to improve…upon the steam Engine of Boulton and Watt" [*Chess*, p. 41]), his major passion was to create a machine that could accurately replicate human speech. The pursuit of the guttural grail had enlisted an array of eccentric crusaders for centuries, including such oracular impostors as the head of Orpheus on the island of Lesbos, and the figure constructed by Alexander of Abonutichus, exposed by Lucian of Samosata. Albertus Magnus was said to have constructed a brazen head that was destroyed by an irate Thomas Aquinas; Friar Bacon created a speaking figure whose attempts at articulation were thwarted when the lab assistant failed to summon him at the precise moment called for by the simulacrum, who uttered, "Time is …time was…time is past," and was never heard from

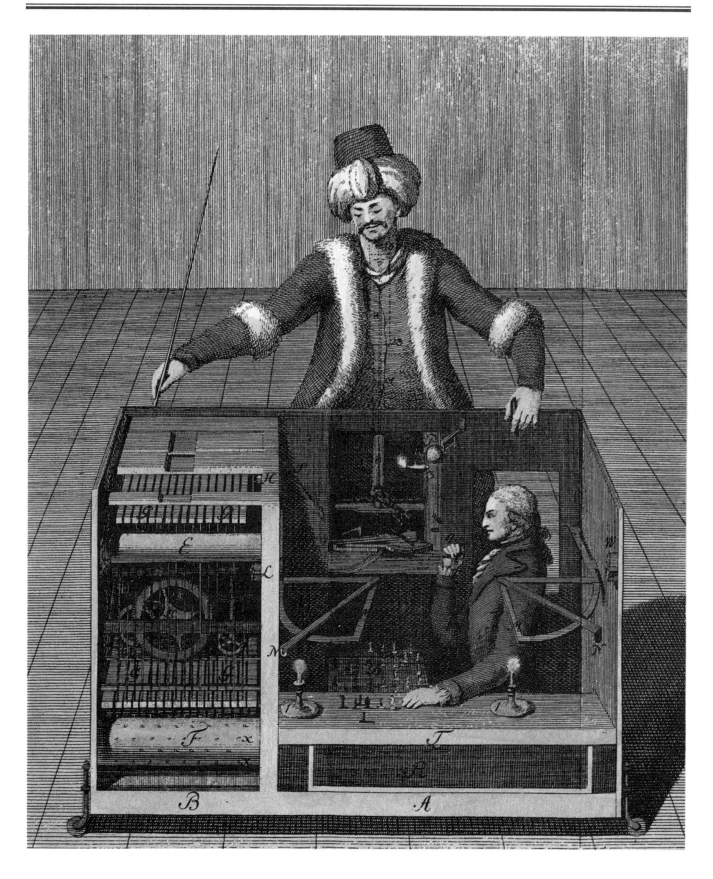

again. Talking heads were attempted in the seventeenth century by Thomas Irson and Athenasius Kircher (both were commissioned to please royalty, Charles II of England and Queen Christina of Sweden, respectively); while von Helmont, the alchemist, analyzed mechanical speech in his *Short Explanation of the True Natural Hebrew Alphabet*. Descartes, who occasionally alluded to automata in his philosophical comparison of man and machine, anticipated the invention of a mechanical speaker.[10]

In the third quarter of the eighteenth century, the Imperial Academy of Science in St. Petersburg sponsored a competition to discover "whether one can construct an instrument like that called the *vox humana* in an organ that will accurately express the sounds of the vowels."[11] Although Kempelen did not enter the competition, he had been experimenting on his own speaking machine from the time he began work on the Chess Player. He started by searching for a musical instrument that would approximate human speech; finally — inspired by a bagpiper — he affixed a pipe to a flute, added the bell from a clarinet, and attached the hybrid device to a bellows. When Kempelen cupped his hand over the bell in different ways, the instrument made some vowel-like sounds, authentic enough that Kempelen's family wondered what new house guest was praying excitedly in a strange language. Eventually he was able to refine his device; his right hand operated keys, his elbow controlled the bellows, and his left hand manipulated the bell-like mouth of the machine. He was able to reproduce consonants and even string together specific sounds into words and sentences.[12] After more than twenty years of conscientious experimentation Kempelen published his work on phonetics, *Mechanismus der Menschlichen Sprache* (Vienna, 1791), simultaneously issued in French as well. Despite these impeccable credentials, the reputation of Kempelen's speaking machine was damaged by association with imposture — not merely by its proximity to a fraudulent automaton on the curriculum vitae of Kempelen — but by its resemblance to an even better-known sham.

In 1784, while Kempelen was exhibiting the Chess Player in London, that same city welcomed an attraction called "A Speaking Figure," which also came to be known as "The Invisible Girl." According to a contemporary playbill the figure, about the size of an infant and

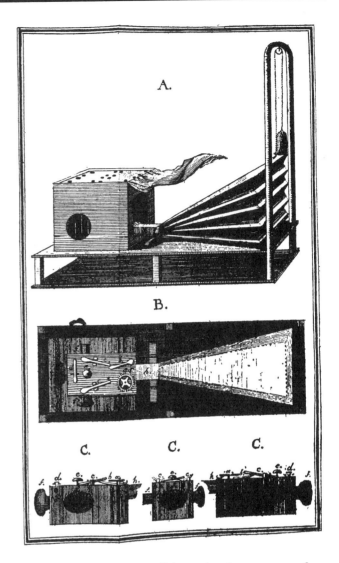

A.

B.

C.   C.   C.

suspended in the air by ribbons (to demonstrate freedom from outside agency), would answer any question posed by members of the audience. These questions could be either spoken aloud or whispered, as could the figure's response. Nor was language a barrier, as the effigy was fluent in French, English, German, and Italian — "any tongue," claimed the advertising sheet, which also announced that she had come directly from Paris and Portugal, where she had enjoyed royal patronage; and from Spain, where she had been interrogated by the Inquisition. My copy of the playbill is glossed in the hand of an eyewitness, who notes: "The question is conveyed to the figure thru a tin tube fixed in the mouth and the answer received by the same tube on the persons putting his Ear to it. The voice is undoubtedly a human one but nothing appears more inconceivable than the

from this tube, with no figure in sight, a little girl's voice could be heard to answer questions posed by the spectators. *The New Wonderful Museum and Extraordinary Magazine*, compiled by William Granger, posited the preposterous – although in view of explanations of the supposed Lilliputian inhabitants of the chess machine, unsurprising – theory that the chest concealed "a really invisible girl, a dwarf much smaller than that of the King of Poland. If this is the fact, it must be only from twelve to fifteen inches in length, and about five or six in thickness; this being all the space of the chest which cannot be seen, it being behind the communicating tube."[13] One of the most famous versions of the Invisible Girl consisted of a small copper globe from which four trumpet mouths extended, and these provided answers to whispered questions. According to Charles Dickens, admiring the Invisible Girl more than half a century later, "the ball was suspended in mid-air between four upright posts and united at the top by four horizontal rails like the framework of a table. Bent wires springing up from the posts, converged to an ornamental centre. …This was all the visitors saw."[14] (See illustration on the left of the masthead.)

During the first English run of the exhibition in 1784, one Philip Thicknesse, an astute but clearly eccentric fellow, authored a pamphlet attacking and exposing not only the Invisible Girl but the Turk as well, *The Speaking Figure and the Automaton Chess-Player Exposed and Detected*. Thicknesse was a friend of Benjamin Franklin, who not only had the Englishman's exposé in his library but also played against (and lost to) the Turk in a celebrated match in Paris.[15] While Thicknesse admired what he saw as the limited creativity of the entertainments (he does refer to Kempelen as "a very ingenious man"), he resented the large admission price (each attraction cost five shillings), noting, "when I see such men, I say, collecting such an immense sum of money in this Kingdom, to carry to some other by mere tricks; tricks inferior to many slights of hand which are shown for two-pence, my indignation rises at the folly of my Countrymen, and the arrogance of the imposing strangers."[16]

Perhaps the eyewitness to the exhibition read the Thicknesse account, as he added to his copy of the playbill: "A similar figure to this was afterwards shown & the

modesty which is conveyed thru the tube as no possible communication is discernible with the figure and no body stands near it or even in the same room but those who are questioning it[;] it answers perfectly well."

Defying geographical borders and numerous exposures, Invisible Girls appeared in Europe, Canada, and America at the end of the eighteenth century, and variations with exotic descriptions lasted well into the nineteenth. One early account related by the abbé Sicard in the *Gazette de France* described an "Invisible Girl" displayed in a transparent glass cabinet suspended from the ceiling of a Parisian residence by four chains. A horn speaking tube was attached to one of its extremities, and mode explained which appeared to be by corresponding tubes with trumpet mouths[,] one in the figure[,] the other placed as near it as it can be so as to be concealed from the spectator. An interval of 2 feet is not too much[;] it is not necessary the tubes should correspond with great nicety, and the mouth of one of them at least may be covered with [any] substance [such] as fine paper & when once the voice is received into the tube it may be conveyed to a considerable distance & the tube bent at any angle" (see illustration on page 152). The method depended on a combination of various speaking tube techniques, which originated in ancient temple trickery directed at auditors no less astute.

In a pattern that students of deception will recognize, exposure often did not harm the popularity or viability of these attractions, and proprietors proved resourceful in using negative publicity. When the exhibitor of one Invisible Girl performing in the provinces in 1796 decided to sell his debunked attraction and call it quits, he engaged in an eighteenth-century version of political spin: "The mystery she [the invisible girl] possesses is altogether unsolvant; she freely forgives them their abortive curiosity, and is resolved notwithstanding the boasted discernment of her would-be detectors, to see company till Saturday night next at her apartments, the late White Lyon Inn, in Lynn, during which time she will convince every impartial spectator and auditor, that her secret is still her own, and shall remain so, in spite of the eyes of *Argus*, the ears of *Midas*, or idle *Rumour* with her hundred tongues. Admittance One Shilling Each."[17]

Because of a gratuitous association with this hoax, Kempelen's legitimate research into the production of human speech was virtually ignored.[18] At the end of his tour he returned home to scientific and courtly duties. In a long and distinguished career, Kempelen was also an accomplished dramatist, an engraver of landscapes, and a designer of theaters. He constructed a water works that supplied Bratislava Castle and another to draw water from flooded salt mines in Transylvania. He designed a bridge to cross the Danube and a fountain for Schönbrunn Castle. He invented a printing machine for the blind, and implemented a plan to thwart terrorist attacks on the city of Banat.[19]

After Kempelen died in 1804, the Chess Player enjoyed an impressive renaissance in the hands of Johann Nepomuk Maelzel, the Viennese (he was actually born in Regensburg, Bavaria) musician, mechanic, inventor, and showman. He built ear trumpets for his friend Beethoven and improved the metronome. Maelzel purchased the Turk from the baron's family and exhibited it once again, often in combination with his own automata and panoramas. Having constructed and patented two acrobatic figures that said "mama" and "papa" as they performed their evolutions on the slack rope, Maelzel now refashioned the Chess Player to speak the word "échec" when placing his opponent in jeopardy. Maelzel showed the machine successfully in Europe and crossed the Atlantic for the first time in 1826. Although Americans embraced the Turk and garnered kudos for its presenter, the repeated exposures had now gathered greater momentum. The most celebrated of his debunkers was Edgar Allan Poe, whose account was published in the *Southern Literary Messenger* in 1836. In Boston a woman attended the show, armed with an exposure claiming that a hidden director inhabited the Turk and viewed the board through its vest. She challenged the exhibitor to cover the figure during play. A contemporary journal not only presents a compelling account of the proceeding but also gives us a sense of the showmanship of Maelzel. He asks the woman to return in a few days, and when she renews the challenge he briefly feigns to have forgotten his offer; eventually he relents:

> Approaching the androides, he took the plume from the turban. Then receiving a cloak from a little girl on the first seat, he wrapped it closely around the *vest* and *head* and *body* of the automaton. Over this cloak he wound the shawl of the lady. Over this covering he tightly fastened other pieces of cloth, and some music paper which he found on the piano forte. All this being done, Mr. M turned to the audience and invited any one to play with the androides. In a few moments the challenge was accepted. A buzz now arose throughout the hall; the curiosity of the spectators was on tiptoe. "Can he play *now*?" whispered numerous voices; all were indeed anxious to see if the automaton could perform in this novel condition. Then there was dead silence. You might have heard a pin drop. Presently the game commenced; and the automaton made his moves, one after another, and vanquished his enemy with as quick and relentless a hand as ever. The lady and her companions were astonished. They told Mr. M they were satisfied. The test was real, and the victory complete; and the audience joined in a general burst of applause and admiration.[20]

After eleven years in the United States, Maelzel left for what was to be an ill-fated engagement in Cuba. William Shumberger, the talented hidden director (once described as a dissipated Prussian hunchback),

succumbed to yellow fever on the island, and Maelzel died during the return voyage on July 21, 1838.

The Turk deteriorated for two years in a warehouse on the Philadelphia wharf, but was then purchased and revitalized by a consortium headed by Dr. John Kearsley Mitchell, who was both a friend of Maelzel and the personal physician of Edgar Allan Poe when the famous writer lived in Philadelphia. Following a briefly renewed interest in his capers on the chessboard, the Turk was relegated to a corner of the Chinese Museum at Ninth and Sansom Streets. His son, Silas Weir Mitchell, also a well-known physician, who later coined the term "phantom limb,"[21] was on hand at the automaton's demise when the Chinese Museum caught fire on July 5, 1854. Mitchell eulogized the Turk: "Already the fire was about him. Death found him tranquil. He who had seen Moscow perish knew no fear of fire. We listened with painful anxiety. It might have been a sound from the crackling woodwork or the breaking window panes, but, certain it is, that we thought we heard, through the struggling flames, and above the din of outside thousands, the last words of our departed friend, the sternly whispered, oft-repeated syllable, "*Échec! Échec!*"[22]

Serious scientists were also inspired by Kempelen's machine. The Reverend Edmund Cartwright had viewed the Chess Player with awe in 1784. Already intrigued by Awkright's cotton mill, Cartwright proposed to his friends that there would soon not be enough hands in the nation to spin that precious commodity and that a mechanical device might do such work. Cartwright invoked the Chess Player: "Now you will not assert, Gentlemen, that it is more difficult to construct a machine that shall weave than one which shall make all the variety of moves required in that complicated game." Using this logic, illogical though it was, Cartwright was led to construct and patent a power loom in 1785, and an improved version in 1787. It was to have an enormous impact on the industrial revolution; by 1833 more than a hundred thousand of his machines were in operation.[23] It is unlikely Kempelen ever knew of his Victorian progeny.

More importantly, Kempelen's machine captured the imagination of Sir Charles Wheatstone (1802–75). A remarkably diverse scientist, he is known today for the Wheatstone Bridge (which measures electrical resistance), the concertina, the stereoscopic viewer, and pioneering efforts in telegraphy. Wheatstone also built a model of Kempelen's speaking machine, and in 1863 he entertained a serious speech researcher and his teenage son with a demonstration. The son was especially taken by the device. Wheatstone loaned them his copy of Kempelen's book on the speaking figure; the lad's name was Alexander Graham Bell.[24]

Bell's imagination was sparked by yet another speaking machine: the "Euphonia" of Joseph Faber, who was billed as the "Premier Calculator and Land Surveyor to the Emperor of Austria." The talented, troubled, and elusive Faber is not easily chronicled and his speaking machine not easily categorized; it was both a remarkable technical innovation and, for intermittent periods, a performance sensation. Faber was most likely born in Freiburg around the turn of the century, and like Kempelen he served the Austrian court. He began

exhibiting a speaking machine early in the 1840s but continued working on improved models that for a time, unlike Kempelen's machine, performed in costume. He experimented with both genders but most often bedizened his figure as a Turkish man.[25] Undated newspaper cuttings from Germany in the early 1840s detail both Faber's successes ("he has satisfactorily solved the difficult problem which baffled even the excellent mechanic Kempelen when he was working on his speech machine") and his fragile health ("[Faber], whom illness temporarily kept from carrying on his performances, is well again and will continue with them"). "Faber," says the *Kunstwelt*, "may properly be called the Prometheus of modern times." After demonstrating his creation for the courts of Austria, Prussia, and Bavaria, Faber appeared in London in 1846 at the Egyptian Hall (a traditional venue for illusion, later to become the most famous magic theater in the world). He played a concealed keyboard to make his figure enunciate not only words but also phrases, sentences, and even simple songs. According to a newspaper advertisement of April 8, "it has held conversations sufficient to fill a volume."

Shy, withdrawn, and encumbered with a thick accent, Faber was an odd candidate to grace the world's stages with his invention, but so he did, and with no less a promoter than P. T. Barnum. The great showman saw Faber in London and engaged him for a tour, once again obfuscating the line between science and entertainment and transmogrifying the inventor into a performer.[26] Barnum wrote to his colleague and confidant Moses Kimball on August 18, 1846: "The speaking automaton has paid all the expenses from Philadelphia to London, and is now clearing $300 per week with prospect of a great increase next year in the *season*."[27]

After an interval of nearly thirty years Barnum again hired the Euphonia under the direction of a "Mr. and Mrs. Faber" for the tenting season of 1873. According to the *New York Tribune* of January 16, Barnum pressed this Faber into forfeiting £200 for canceling an appearance at the Vienna Exposition – and instead receiving $20,000 (a figure almost certainly inflated) from Barnum for a stand with his circus.[28] Barnum's description of Faber's machine makes one anticipate with delight the achievements of modern science abetted by creative copywriting: "It not only speaks loudly and distinctly the rich round words of *die Mutter-Sprache*, but gives also the mellifluent liquids and sibilants of the Italian and French, the euphonism of the Castilian, as well as the *terrors* of our own English vernacular."[29]

The Euphonia was duly vetted by scholars. Joseph Henry, the Princeton professor and "foremost American scientist of his day," viewed the machine in Philadelphia in 1846. Henry realized there "was no ventriloquist or concealed speaking tube," and that Faber's contrivance was a marked improvement over Wheatstone's version of Kempelen's speaking machine. He was tantalizingly close to the discovery of the telephone when he wrote to a friend: "The keys could be worked by means of electromagnetic magnets and with a little contrivance, not difficult to execute, words might be spoken at one end of the telegraph line, which had their origin at the other....Thus the same sermon might be delivered at the same minute to all."[30] During its long performing career, the possibility of fraud or illusion in the Euphonia was sometimes addressed, owing to a lingering association with invisible girls, ladies, and fully grown women; or to an audience unable to fathom its scientific principles. One case not before discussed, to my knowledge, appears in an endorsement by a Professor Pettigrew, a lecturer on anatomy and physiology, who observed the machine privately before the proposed visit of the queen in 1846. It is quoted on a bill from St. James' Assembly Rooms: "I feel that I was bound to use every exertion to detect a fraud, if such there should be; I therefore perhaps have to apologize for having asked you to move the Figure to another part of the room; and also to make the Figure pronounce the word LINGUA, which I wrote in pencil, and which was not uttered by any individual save the Instrument. Upon farther examination and reflection since my visit, I cannot look upon the Figure as a mere piece of mechanism. I consider it as the successful result of a mind gifted with the strongest reasoning and calculative powers and I cannot but think that it is the country rather than yourself that is honored by its exhibition."[31]

Faber was showered with praise, but apparently it did not ease his troubles. After his first tour with the American promoter, it becomes increasingly difficult to track his whereabouts. According to the Wurtzback *Biographical Lexicon*, Faber took his own life somewhere in the United States around 1850.[32] No further details of this often repeated story are given. It contradicts the scenario that I now propose, fragmentary though it may be.

In 1868, Miss Marie Trunka, the twenty-year-old proprietor of a cigar store in Vienna, mentioned to a customer named Samuel Husserl (described in a euphonious pejorative as a Hungarian Hebrew) that her uncle had willed her a speaking machine that he had completed only a few days before his death. Trunka and Husserl joined together to exhibit the figure and billed themselves "Professor and Mrs. Faber," but on their second visit to America they ran into problems brought on by incompatibility and low attendance. A motion for their separation was heard by Judge Van Vorst of the Circuit Court. According to the *New York Herald*, Mrs. Faber charged "abandonment, cruelty, drunkenness and gambling – the last vice, she alleges, absorbed the many thousands of dollars they made in their exhibitions. He [Joseph Faber né Samuel Husserl] denies that he has ever been cruel to her or that he ever married or abandoned her." The speaking machine was at the time pledged for debt to the proprietor of the hotel. The judge directed the jury to the verdict of separation on the grounds that they were married, she was abandoned, and they had resided in the state a sufficient amount of time to validate the proceedings. Mrs. Faber waved alimony and court payments, and Mr. Faber, although he did not attend the hearing, was said to be "pleased with the result" as he was saved "from going back to Ludlow Street Jail, where he has been confined pending the suit."[33]

PROFESSOR FABER'S TALKING-MACHINE.

The owner of the device at the time of the court proceeding was Joseph Wehrle, the proprietor of the Belvedere House hotel at the corner of Eighteenth Street and Fourth Avenue. In April of 1885, Husserl, still signing himself "Faber," wrote to Alexander Graham Bell asking him to intercede on his behalf in an attempt to regain the speaking machine. Thus Bell became a participant in the fascinating but confusing story of the ownership of the Euphonia. We know that Bell wrote to Wehrle, assuming the debt, now four hundred dollars, and asking for the machine to be sent to him C. O. D. Faber was to follow his machine to Bell's home in Washington but was unable to keep the appointment. Although the correspondence is sketchy and incomplete, it becomes clear that Faber now wants his machine,

which had been transferred to Bell's possession, returned to him. On April 25 Bell writes that he is willing to extend another five hundred dollars to Faber, but "I cannot undertake to deliver your machine to you until you have either repaid me the amount advanced or given me other security." Bell wrote again the same day in the attempt to buy the piece outright: "I beg to offer you the sum of one thousand dollars for your automation speaking machine." Perhaps unwilling to appear as if taking advantage of another's misfortune, particularly one who had asked for his help, he offered Faber the alternative of an additional five-hundred-dollar loan, agreeing to return the machine when the money was repaid. Bell even issued a general notice stating this as his position. Faber's response, in full, was, "I will not sell my talking machine for less than eight thousand dollars. Please let me know if you will deliver my machine to me today." (Apparently this figure had been previously discussed, as on April 20 Bell wrote to the president of Columbia College asking if that institution had plans to purchase the Faber machine for the same sum. I have been unable to locate a reply.)

Later on April 25, the lawyers were called in. Bell asked for any further communication to be directed to his attorney, J. H. Saville, and on April 29 Saville wrote to Bell of an attempt by a Mr. Wolf, on behalf of Faber, to secure the machine. Wolf and Saville agreed to what seemed a fair proposal, but Faber, instead of accepting the offer, impulsively asked for an additional hundred dollars. Saville wrote, "I have declined to do this as most unreasonable." To the displeasure of Faber, Bell must have actually displayed the machine, as the next day Faber acknowledged his receipt of three hundred dollars from Bell, "for services in exhibiting my talking machine, and in further satisfaction of any and all claims and demands." The following day Faber signed a note to Bell for a two-hundred-dollar loan at six percent interest. Evidently Bell returned the machine, as Saville sent all the correspondence to him with a note that concluded, "congratulating you on getting rid of what was a great nuisance."

The speaking machine, however, was not silenced. On December 14, J. C. Gordon of the National Deaf Mute College alerted Bell that it might be available for purchase. He suggested that it "ought to be bought if practicable and cared for in some museum. The present parties bear no business with what is really an historical curiosity." Indeed, the same day a note on the stationery of the Belvedere House was received from a Mr. Herrmann [?] acting on behalf of Mrs. Faber, "in hope that you yet remember the introduction I had to you at the convention held at the deaf and dumb asylum." It announced that Mrs. Faber was in possession of the machine, as she "has been deserted by her husband who has left for parts unknown and being now in sorest distress she wishes to dispose of the machine."

The following day Bell received a letter from a Victor Hawley also claiming to be an agent acting on behalf of Mrs. Faber, "now the *sole* owner in reduced circumstances [who] is thereby necessitated to dispose of it." Hawley had a specific motive in brokering the transaction: "I want to be frank with you that I am anxious to exhibit the machine to the public. I tried to arrange with Mrs. Faber but could not – as she prefers to sell the machine. If you should buy it, – I should be glad to arrange with you to exhibit it – I was connected with the Edison Phonograph Co. as exhibitor and expert when the phonograph had its career." Bell appears not to have been moved to any further action.[34]

Thirty-two years later Bell was to have a brief correspondence with a deceiver of another kind. It is not surprising that Harry Houdini, not only a mystifier but also a student of deception, should have approached the famous inventor:

March 13, 1917:

Dear Prof. Bell,

May I intrude on your good nature to settle an argument, regardin[g] the Faber Talking Machine, (about 44 years ago,) and from information I have gleaned hear that at that . . . time your Late father, offered a prize to you three boys as to who could make a machine to imitate the sounds mechanically.

Rumor has it that you won the [prize], and therefore it has caused me to write this letter.

P. T. Barnum brought the Faber Machine to America engaging the nephew of Faber the inventor in 1873, and the contention is that it was an illusion with a man concealed behind two mirrors who did the talking, whereas I claim, that it was an honest mechanical contrivance.

We have agreed to abide by your decision, and trust you will favor us by deciding this question, as much as it is in your power.

If I *mistake not* – Mr. Faber stopped at the old St. Lawrence Hotel in Montreal at the time you witnessed the machine.

Thanking you for a reply I beg to remain sincerely yours,

Harry Houdini

P. S. I am mailing you one of my books, The Unmasking of Robert Houdin, on page 90 you will see the Faber machine illustrated. H. H.[35]

Bell favored Houdini with a reply on April 6. After thanking him for the book he clarified a number of issues:

I had the opportunity in Washington, a good many years ago, of seeing and examining the Faber Talking Machine, and have no hesitation in saying that it was an honest mechanical contrivance and not an illusion with a man concealed behind two mirrors who did the talking. . . . It was Sir Charles Wheatstone's talking machine, which was a reproduction of the celebrated machine of the Baron De Kempelen of the 18th century, that led my father to offer a prize to his boys.

Although I have been unable to locate Houdini's response, it is possible to conclude from the following missive that he did not know about Kempelen's speaking machine (in *The Unmasking*, Houdini refers only to the Chess Player). Bell writes from his summer home in Nova Scotia on June 28, 1917:

I believe that the De Kempelen who "projected" the chess automaton on the public is the same Baron De Kempelen of the talking machine. De Kempelen published a book fully describing this last mechanism, with plates and illustrations, and it was from this description that Sir Charles Wheatstone reproduced his talking machine. Sir Charles was once kind enough to lend the book to my father, when I had the opportunity of studying it.[36]

The fate of the Faber machine lacks the magnificent clarity of the Turk's demise. Why, one must ponder, did Bell choose not to reveal his involvement with the Euphonia? Bell and Houdini play cameo roles in this drama of the convergence of magic and science. Others in

THE AUTOMATON CHESS PLAYER

the dramatis personæ include the father of computing, Charles Babbage; the architect John Carter, who made detailed notes and sketches of the machine in the 1780s; and Napoleon, who displayed bad manners in his match against the Turk in 1809. Cervantes exposed a false speaking head in *Don Quixote*, and the *Tales of Hoffmann* fictionalizes the Turk. Wordsworth mentions the Invisible Girl in his *Prelude*, and Mrs. Trollope, the novelist and mother of Anthony, actually exhibited the elusive lady in America. You can read about these topics in the criticism of John Ruskin and Walter Benjamin; the poetry of Thomas Moore and Hannah Flagg Gould; the novels of John Dickson Carr and Robertson Davies; and the works of Goethe, Balzac, Hawthorne, Emerson, and Thackeray.

What the inventors Kempelen, Farber, and even Bell transgressed was not merely the boundary between science and amusement but the far more profound one distinguishing the human from the mechanical. Their magical ingenuity was in giving a human face, and voice, to technology, forming the modern partnership in which man and machine would together surpass their previous limits – beyond anyone's wildest dreams. ◉

NOTES

1. Most accounts name Maria Theresa as the provocateur, but according to *Observations on the Automaton Chess Player by an Oxford Graduate* (London, 1819), the challenge was instigated by Kempelen, who "dropped a hint that he thought himself competent to construct a piece of mechanism which should produce effects far more surprising and unaccountable than those she [Maria Theresa] then witnessed" (p. 12).

2. *Others* might say that Windisch only thought he saw all the doors open at the same time. The history of the automaton Chess Player has been related numerous times, with varying emphasis and accuracy. Whenever possible I have relied on contemporary accounts. Karl Gottlieb von Windisch's *Briefe über den Schachspieler des Herrn von Kempelen* was published in Pressburg and Basel (in both German and French editions) in 1783. The English version, felicitously entitled *Inanimate Reason, or a Circumstantial Account of that Astonishing Piece of Mechanism,* was published in London in 1784; quotations here derive from the second British edition, *Letters of Mr. Charles Gottlieb De Windisch on the Automaton Chess Player* (London, 1819); see p. 17. Most useful were George Allen's "The History of the Automaton Chess Player" in *The Book of the First American Chess Congress* (Philadelphia, 1859); and *Chess: Man vs. Machine,* by Bradley Ewart (San Diego, New York, and London,

1980). Especially valuable were the Maelzel Papers at the American Antiquarian Society; the John G. White Chess Collection at the Cleveland Public Library; and the George Allen Chess Collection at the Library Company of Philadelphia.

3. The Chess Player had apparently been victorious at some preliminary games in Kempelen's home in Pressburg before arriving in Vienna.

4. Windisch, *Letters*, p. 11. James Cook Jr. speculates that the old woman's great fear of the figure may have been based on its Turkish aspect, as Vienna had often been threatened by Ottoman forces; *Winterthur Portfolio*, Chicago, vol. 30, no. 4 (winter 1995), p. 240.

5. See Ken Whyld, *Fake Automata in Chess* (Lincolnshire, England, n.d.), which lists some four hundred accounts. The casket that stood to the side of the machine was completely nonfunctional; it was designed as a piece of magician's misdirection.

6. The "small" theory appeared most recently in the accounts of the matches between Garry Kasparov and Deep Blue, the IBM computer; see "Computer in the News: Kasparov's Inscrutable Conqueror," by Robert D. McFadden *(New York Times*, May 12, 1997). The annals of history are replete with such instances of self-perpetuating errors. I myself contributed to the mistaken belief that Munito, the most famous learned dog of the nineteenth century, and possibly of all time, was a poodle. When I belatedly obtained the pamphlet *Historical Account of the Life and Talents of the Learned Dog Munito,* published by his trainer in London in 1817, I was shocked, shocked, to learn that the dog was in fact the progeny of a hound father and a water spaniel mother: "He is endowed with the understanding of both the species he descends from, though he resembles his mother most." The source of the error can no doubt be traced to an illustrated broadside that sometimes accompanied the pamphlet, which featured Munito coifed in an elaborate sculpted and shaved "do" that today we associate with the poodle breed. Over the years, artists pictured the dog as increasingly poodle-like, and written accounts accepted the faux pedigree.

7. Original patent request papers signed by Kempelen; author's collection.

8. A slightly later version of Kempelen's patent request was signed by two witnesses, one the presenter of the Chess Player, Herr Anthon (giving his first name as Jos[eph], for the only time of which I am aware). Was the other one, "George Aust.," the director of the machine?

9. Letter to the author from John McKinven (February 7, 1999), who points out that although the Kempelen machine did function, it did not generate much power. He notes that more sophisticated steam engines were already in use.

10. An apocryphal bit of Cartesian scandal concerns the great philosopher's supposedly constant companion, a lifelike automaton of his illegitimate daughter Francine, delegated to a specially prepared case. An eighteenth-century source recounts that after they had embarked together on a sea voyage, a suspicious captain entered Descartes's room, opened the case, and upon discovering its contents tossed the offending automaton overboard. See Stephen

Gaulkroger, *Descartes: An Intellectual Biography* (Oxford, 1997), pp. 1–2.

11. Linda Strauss, *Automata: A Study in the Interface of Science, Technology, and Popular Culture* (Ph.D. dissertation, University of California, San Diego, 1987), p. 119. The same competition is also discussed in Thomas J. Hankins and Robert J. Silverman, *Instruments and the Imagination* (Princeton, N.J., 1995), pp. 188–89. The authors suggest that the competition was instigated by the great mathematician Leonhard Euler, who wrote about the mechanical articulation not only of vowels but also of complete words. Euler, incidentally, created a beautiful solution to "the chess knight's tour," a complicated problem in which a knight was made to occupy every position on the chessboard. This stunt was often demonstrated by the automaton Turk.

12. A version of Kempelen's machine is now at the Deutsches Museum in Munich (see illustration on page 151).

13. Granger, *The New Wonderful Museum and Extraordinary Magazine* (London, 1803), 1:40–41. The dwarf of the King of Poland, whom Granger does not identify – only noting that he used a wooden shoe for a cradle – was Nicholas Feny or Ferry, commonly known as Bébé.

14. *All the Year Round*, September 24, 1870. The Invisible Girl took many forms other than those described here: a mermaid, a friar, or a caricature of a black man.

15. Franklin also befriended Kempelen and shared an interest in musical glasses with the Thicknesse family. Franklin invented a version of the glass harmonica in 1761 – probably the same year that Ann Ford, Thicknesse's third wife, wrote the first known manual for the instrument, *Instructions for Playing on the Musical Glasses* (though it must be noted that their instruments differed consider-

ably). Thicknesse also crossed paths with Louis Dutens, a Huguenot refugee from England, who resided on the Continent and enjoyed a reputation as a man of letters. Dutens, who visited Kempelen in Pressburg, authored the first account of the Chess Player to appear in English (*Gentleman's Magazine*, July 24, 1770). Thicknesse dismissed him as "a French clergyman who was showing her [Ann Ford] some trinckets." See Philip Gosse, *Viper: The Querulous Life of Philip Thicknesse* (London, 1952), p. 237. Some measure of the man may be intuited from a codicil in which Thicknesse willed one of his sons "my right hand, to be cut off after death . . . that such a sight may remind him of his duty to God, after having so long abandoned the duty he owed his Father who once affectionately loved him" (p. 271).

16. See Richard Altick, *The Shows of London* (Cambridge, Mass., and London, 1978) on the gullibility of the English public. Altick also gives an absorbing account of the Chess Player and various speaking machines.

17. Playbill, Lynn, England, February 20, 1796.

18. Kempelen had even intended to fashion his machine into the shape of a little girl, because the sounds it made seemed to him childlike, and he wished to show that the machine reflected a developing work rather than a completed project; see Ewart, *Chess*, pp. 27–28.

19. Slavomir Ondrejovic, *Wolfgang von Kempelen and his Mechanism of Human Speech*, n.p., September 1996.

20. *American Magazine of Useful Knowledge*, Boston, February 1837, p. 198.

21. In an odd postscript to this tale of science and magic, Dr. V. S. Ramachandran recently initiated a treatment to retard or eliminate the acutely painful persistence of sensation in the imaginary limbs of some amputees. He created a crude magician's cabinet by placing a small vertical mirror inside a cardboard box. The patient then viewed the reflection of his or her normal hand in the mirror and was asked to move it around until the reflection appeared to be superimposed on the felt position of the phantom hand. The patient thus had the illusion of observing two hands. Ramachandran referred to one such treatment as "probably the first example in medical history of a successful 'amputation' of a phantom limb," and remarked that the patient "seemed to think I was some kind of magician." See V. S. Ramachandran and Sandra Blakslee, *Phantoms in the Brain* (New York, 1998), pp. 48–50.

22. Maelzel often exhibited the Turk on the same program with his panorama called the "Conflagration of Moscow" – thus his fearlessness in the face of fire. The Mitchell eulogy is quoted by Ewart, *Chess*, p. 122. Additional material on Maelzel may be found at the American Antiquarian Society. Some of the biography above is drawn from Joseph Earl Arrington, "John Maelzel, Master Showman of Automata and Panoramas," *The Pennsylvania Magazine of History and Biography* (January 1960), pp. 56–92. Maelzel's speaking figures are discussed in *Manuel Complet Des Sorciers, ou la Magie Blanche* (Paris, 1831). A wonderful re-creation of the Turk was recently fabricated by John Gaughan of Los Angeles.

23. Ewart, *Chess*, p. 37.

24. Robert Bruce, *Bell: Alexander Graham Bell and the Conquest of Solitude* (1973; reprint, Ithaca, N.Y., and London, 1990), p. 35. Some of this material is discussed in Hankins and Silverman, *Instruments*, p. 219; and Ewart, *Chess*, p. 28.

25. It is not clear if this was an homage to Kempelen or a salute to the Orientalism of the period. Although engravings depict Faber's machine as either male or female, the only known photograph, in the Meserve-Kunhardt Collection, shows it with a woman's head, sans body.

26. According to Barnum, "my agent exhibited it for several months in Egyptian Hall, London, and also in the provinces"; George S. Bryan, ed., *Struggles and Triumphs: or, the Life of P. T. Barnum* (New York, 1927), 1:399–400.

27. *Selected Letters of P. T. Barnum*, ed. Arthur Saxon (New York, 1983), p. 35. There were conflicting reports on the success of the attraction, but it is clear that its drawing power fluctuated precariously.

28. P. T. Barnum, *Struggles and Triumphs* (Buffalo, 1873), p. 772. According to the Kundhardt biography, *P. T. Barnum: America's Greatest Showman* (New York, 1995), p. 63, "Barnum exhibited later versions well into the 1870s, with a sign offering $10,000 to anyone who could match the device. When he first heard rumors of Edison's talking machine, Barnum quickly took down the sign."

29. W.C. Crum, *Illustrated History of Wild Animals and Other Curiosities contained in P.T. Barnum's Great Traveling World's Fair, Museum, Menagerie, Polytechnic Institute, and International Zoological Garden* (New York, 1873), pp. 73–74.

30. All quotations in this paragraph from Bruce, *Bell*, pp. 4–5. Hankins and Silverman argue that Bruce overplays this connection to the invention of the telephone (*Instruments*, p. 218). Years later, in 1875, the second Faber asked Henry to underwrite the speaking machine but he refused; David Lindsay, "Talking Head," *Invention & Technology*, vol. 13, no. 1 (summer 1997), p. 62.

31. Playbill, London, [1846].

32. *Biographical Lexicon*, vol. 4, pp. 124-25, quoted in *Schausteller Gaukler und Artisten* (Essen, 1980), vol. 2, p. 423.

33. *New York Herald*, undated, but before December 15, 1885. The reporter notes that the speaking machine "has taken no part in the controversy but remains perfectly silent." Bruce suggests the date of the original Faber's death as the late 1860s and states that an unnamed niece received the machine (*Bell*, p. 82).

34. Even the stationery used by Faber presented a dissembling history, including a long newspaper quote: "The machine is the product of continuous labour and study of two members of the same family. It was begun in 1815 by one Joseph Faber, and so far elaborated in 1841 that it was exhibited that year to the King of Bavaria. The originator, dying, bequeathed the machine to his nephew, the present owner, also named Joseph Faber, who had been associated with him in its construction, and since it became his property Herr Faber has almost doubled its powers of articulation." Letters from Faber to Bell dated April 9 and April 15, 1885; letter from Bell to Joseph Wehrle dated April 16; and two letters from Bell to Faber dated April 25, 1885. All correspondence from the collections of the Manuscript Division, Library of Congress.

35. Reproduced from the originals in the Manuscript Division, Library of Congress. Houdini was an obsessive collector of materials on magic and theater. *The Unmasking of Robert-Houdin* (New York, 1909) was his history of conjuring, presented in a mean-spirited attempt to discredit the great French magician from whom he adapted his stage name. Houdini gives a confusing history of Barnum's involvement with the speaking machine on pp. 89–91. The argument Houdini describes seems like a ploy to elicit Bell's response. See also *The Memoirs of Robert-Houdin* (London and Philadelphia, 1859) for an entertaining but largely fictional account of the Chess Player, and the play *La Czarine* (Paris, 1868) by Jules Adenis and Octave Gastineau, for which Robert-Houdin constructed a replica of the Turk. According to David Lindsay, in "Talking Head," in 1879 Faber's speaking machine was presented in a room adjoining the Théâtre Robert-Houdin in Paris.

36. The two Bell letters are reproduced from the originals in the Harry Ransom Humanities Research Center, University of Texas at Austin.

ILLUSTRATIONS

JAY'S JOURNAL OF ANOMALIES

This is the final issue of this periodical written by Ricky Jay and published by the author and W & V Dailey, Antiquarian Booksellers, 8216 Melrose Ave., Los Angeles, California, 90046, (323) 658-8515. ¶ Printed letterpress by Patrick Reagh and typeset in Monotype Ehrhardt with Thorowgood heads on Rives Heavyweight paper. ¶ Designed by Mr. Reagh & Mr. Jay. ¶ The author wishes to thank Susan Green, Larry Vigon, Jayme Odgers, Mary Wolfskill, Cathy Henderson, Jim Steinmeyer, Arthur Freeman, Volker Huber, John Gaughan, Jim Green, William Kalush, John McKinven, and Dan Chariton for generous assistance in the preparation of this issue. ¶ Comments and corrections to the text are welcomed. ¶ Written and illustrative material, © Ricky Jay, 2000. ¶ All images are from the private collection of the author. Any subsequent use of text or image is permissible only with the express written consent of Mr. Jay.

AFTERWORD

I HAVE NO MEMORY FOR DATES. I was surprised, therefore, to discover in my disorderly files a draft of the first issue of *Jay's Journal of Anomalies*, dated January 1993, over a year before the first magazine was published. Even more surprising was to find the draft, and drafts of the first four issues, handwritten on yellow legal pads with a calligraphic fountain pen. Eventually I obtained a word processor, learned how to type, and was transformed from a Luddite into a computer-challenged magazine publisher. In some ways I still yearn for those simpler, more tactile times. My calligrapher grandfather, who also taught me sleight of hand, and a childhood fascination with the great American Type Foundry in Elizabeth, New Jersey, where my best friend's father worked, initiated my lifelong appreciation of the book arts.

The major catalyst for the journal was the pursuit of a higher standard of illustration, type, and paper than the mainstream publishers of my earlier work were able to provide. I wished to do justice to materials collected over long years in my areas of interest – conjuring, unusual entertainments, confidence games, the biographies of eccentric characters. My expectations of print media were honed during the five years that I was curator of one of the largest repositories in these fields, the Mulholland Library of Conjuring and the Allied Arts. I have no aversion to fine-press limited editions, but I am unmoved by manufactured rarities – works intended to be scarce rather than achieving that distinction by the natural process of decay and attrition. The idea of a small-run fine-press book intrigued me less than a periodical with high production values – a magazine printed letterpress on mold-made paper, with tipped-in color plates to present the illustrations I cherished with dignity and clarity. An anomaly devoted to anomalies.

Sharing my passion for handsomely printed items were William and Victoria Dailey, owners of a rare-book firm in Los Angeles, who are talented and tasteful designers and publishers of elegant small volumes. I had purchased many items from them over the years, and based on my large eyes and small purse they had publicly designated me their worst customer. It then seemed prudent for us to enter into a business relationship, and with me, they became the publishers of *Jay's Journal*. Andrea Braver, a long-time colleague, initially edited the text, but the production of twin boys curtailed her activities on the production of the magazine. Susan Green, who had provided capable advice on my book *Learned Pigs & Fireproof Women* years before, was enlisted as editor before the first issue went to press. Her patient analysis of my convoluted prose has ensured lively debate that improved the final result, and I am genuinely grateful for her help and friendship.

The introduction of Patrick Reagh to this mix was essential. Patrick and I were first allied through a lecture and demonstration I gave at the William Andrews Clark Memorial Library of UCLA. This function was intended to be a fund-raiser for the institution (which was then providing me with a carrel for my research on *Learned Pigs*), and its administrators were necessarily unwilling to add to my personal coffers. In lieu of a fee, they proposed that Mr. Reagh, regarded as one of the finest letterpressmen in Southern California and certainly the only one who played a mean salsa piano, produce a commemorative broadside. I did not play a good hand of poker, and the deal was immediately sealed. I am thus able to record the date of this event with impunity – October 31, 1984 – because it appears on the very handsome keepsake that he set by hand and produced on his fine old Heidelberg automatic single-revolution cylinder press in Glendale. The impending first issue of the magazine took me straight to his door there. He agreed to print the publication and to collaborate with me on the design. After experimenting with a number of sample formats we decided to print the body text in Erhardt, eleven points on thirteen, with Thorowgood heads. We selected Weiss for the banner line and agreed to vary the masthead vignettes as appropriate for each issue. Pat has long since become a trusted friend, and we have worked together on numerous projects.

Recent issues of the journal have been written and edited via e-mail from various destinations in North America and Europe and have been printed in Sebastopol, California, where Patrick now resides. He has ingeniously adapted computer technology to letterpress printing. My friend Larry Vigon of the renowned design firm Vigon/Ellis has provided generous assistance with color printing, and I am especially grateful for his work on the dust jacket of this volume.

I am not certain that I ever imagined my ideal reader sitting at a desk penning provocative letters in reply to each issue, but I must confess I did envision the *Journal* delivered into the hands of Robert Lund, who was a journalist for various Detroit automotive publications and the proprietor of the American Museum of Magic in Marshall, Michigan. Beyond our kindred interest in the vagaries of human achievement, he exhibited a compassion and generosity of spirit rare among serious collectors. He taught me much and he is sorely missed.

For their help and encouragement, I remain indebted to the contributors who were acknowledged in the colophons of each issue; and, for their continuing support, to Robert Bookman, Dan Chariton, Stan Coleman, Persi Diaconis, Steve Freeman, Jonathan Galassi, John Gaughan, Lawrence Green, Joy Harris, Volker Huber, Bill Kalush, Bill Liles, David Mamet, Ethan Nosowsky, Bob Read, Winston Simone, Mark Singer, Andrew Solt, John Solt, Jim Steinmeyer, Dan Waldron, Lawrence Weschler, Michael Weber, Steven Zax, and Michael Zinman.

The "editorial style" for the journal was constantly evolving and somewhat informal. The procedures changed markedly during the years of publication, and no decisions we made anticipated simultaneous republication of all the issues. In the first few magazines, for instance, we applied the term "sic" to errors within quoted texts. We soon abandoned this intrusion as grating, and the reader is asked to assume that quotations are as they appear in the original sources. Our chagrin at discovering inconsistencies is more than compensated for by our joy at reviewing and republishing these issues for a larger audience. We have taken advantage of this process by correcting some of our more egregious errors while allowing variations in bibliographic and typographic form to stand. We hope our readers will regard these incongruities as quaint or arcane. As always, corrections, emendations, and comments are warmly encouraged. The engagement of our readers is often responsible for the updates which follow.

I.
The Faithful Monetto & The Inimitable Dick

Although I had investigated the exploits of sagacious animals in *Learned Pigs*, I continued to pursue scholarship in brute creation. The keen-eyed Andrew Edmunds provided an unrecorded print that inspired the first issue of *Jay's Journal*. The illustration of the faithful Monetto showed a blatant attempt by the dog's trainer to capitalize on the notoriety of a more famous canine star, Munito. I used this premise to expound on the theme of dogs purloining the acts of other dogs. I am able to record but not, I assure you, to condone the exploits of a dog called Minetto who performed in New York at Peale's Museum in July 1827. I should also add that much of Munito's most accomplished repertoire

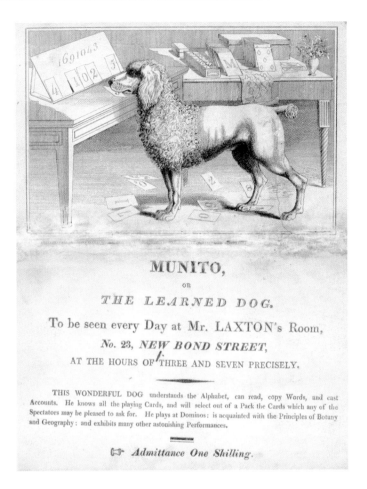

MUNITO,

OR

THE LEARNED DOG.

To be seen every Day at Mr. LAXTON's Room,

No. 23, *NEW BOND STREET*,

AT THE HOURS OF THREE AND SEVEN PRECISELY.

THIS WONDERFUL DOG understands the Alphabet, can read, copy Words, and cast Accounts. He knows all the playing Cards, and will select out of a Pack the Cards which any of the Spectators may be pleased to ask for. He plays at Dominos: is acquainted with the Principles of Botany and Geography: and exhibits many other astonishing Performances.

☞ *Admittance One Shilling.*

CHOCOLAT-LOUIT

4 _ Le Chien Munito.

had been exhibited in that metropolis as early as 1796 by a dog in the employ of Gabriel Salenka at the Assembly Rooms on Cortlandt Street.

Since the publication of the first issue, Munito himself has caused me some embarrassment (see page 159, note 6 for a full explanation). My blunder in mistaking the headliner for a poodle should be forgiven by tolerant readers, who may consult his portrait on the trade card for Chocolat-Louit in Bordeaux and the more reliable likeness on the broadside for his appearance at Laxton's Rooms in 1817. The text establishing the pedigree for his noble mix of hound and water spaniel was published the same year. Both items were kindly provided by the imaginative Jim Burmester. I was able to elaborate on the international scope of Munito's tour when I unearthed playbills for his appearances in Austria and Finland. At the marvelous collection of Christian Fechner in Bordeaux, I found the rare pamphlet *On En Parlera Longtemps De L'Histoire Singulière et Plaisante Arrivée au Palais-Royal, dans une des Séances du célèbre Munito.*

Although I did not formally request comments, corrections, or emendations to the text until the third issue of the magazine, a few thoughtful subscribers responded from the beginning. Laurence Senelick, a writer on popular culture and the Fletcher Professor of Drama at Tufts University, was to become my most consistent commentator, combing his collection for materials to augment my own. He staked his ground by sharing a fine postcard image of a Loïe Fuller dog. Jack Rennert, the authority on posters, drew on his collection of Loïe Fuller imitators to show me a lovely lithograph of Miss Dublin, an extraordinary household cat trained to perform Loïe's act. Patricia Corrigan, a reporter and critic for the *St. Louis Post-Dispatch*, wrote to take umbrage at my less than reverential characterization of the original "La Loïe."

From Jonathan and Lisa Reynolds I have obtained the original text of the doggie drama *The Caravan*, presented in December 1803 at Drury Lane by Richard Brinsley Sheridan. After reading the play, I concluded that those who caricatured Sheridan and his canine star, Carlo, for the "debasement of the stage" had exercised admirable restraint. I obtained one particularly good example drawn by C. Williams that features Sheridan studying a playbill for a *Growlo Drama* with an impressive likeness of Carlo, who is presenting similar fare for the producer to ponder.

I have acquired a playbill for Clark's "Collies of Knowledge," as well as a personal favorite for "Boswell, the Unusual Eater of Bern." Through the good graces of Michael Zinman, a signed copy of the rare *Kepler, A Biography*, once in the collection of the New York Public Library, found its way to me. It is the true story of a mighty mastiff whose keen ability to identify butchers was his greatest claim to fame. The predictor of the Kentucky Derby and the World Series, "Jim the Wonder Dog," who met his maker on March 18, 1937, will be resurrected, I am told by Roy Blount, Jr., in a modern motion picture coming soon to a theater near you.

Harry Houdini has made many appearances in the

A FRIENDLY VISIT to the DRAMATIC MANUFACTORY or Preparations for next Season

BOSWELL

THE UNUSUAL EATER OF BERN

This wonderful phenomenon of nature has exhibited before Royalty and Men of Science.
He grinds and swallows stones with as much ease as a person would Crack a Nut and Masticate the Kernel.

His capacity for ingesting flints, pencils, nylons, sandals, towels (hand and bath) and all manner of Rugs,
Runners and Carpets -- showing a special predilection for the Iranian Tabriz -- is universally acknowledged.
This performer exhibits a Fondness for Unmentionables worn by both sexes but a preference
may be noted in articles more likely to be donned by the *Female Gender*.

SITS
ON COMMAND!

STAYS
ON COMMAND!

He is a character of Singular Capabilities, Handsome Visage, and a Wry Personal Demeanor known to melt the
frostiest embankments of the Swiss country-side. This canine curiosity occasionally answers to the name of
BOSWELL or LITTLE ANDREW PITOOTSNIAK. It is generally acknowledged, however, that the appellation of
"TOUT MANGE" is a more accurate description of his nearly limitless Capacities of Voraciousness. He is said in
the enormity of his appetite even to surpass his cousin, the Noble WALTER,
formerly known far and wide for his accomplishments in this arena.

☞ IN THE ZERMATIAN ALPS HE IS ALSO KNOWN AS SIDEROPHAGUS, OR EATER OF IRON. ☜

Much like the swarthy Francis Battalia immortalized in John Bulwer's *Anthropometamorphosis:
Man Transform'd; or the Artificiall Changling*, BOSWELL is capable of ingesting a half peck of pebbles which,
when he shakes his body, may be heard to resonate as if they were Rattled in a Sack.

Although not a bibliophagist (Thank the L---! Thank the L---!) he is a connoisseur of the arts and his literary
pretentions are too well known to be ignored. It is fair to say that although their initial reception was not
universally heralded, his *Sketches by Boz* and his *Life of Samuel Johnson* are now
highly regarded and eagerly discussed in the salons of the *beau monde*.

This remarkable performer may be seen by appointment in the Commodious Large Rooms of the proprietress,
C----A-- V-----, (the celebration of whose date of birth this broadside commemorates).

N. B. Visitors may feed him a bunch of keys, a handkerchief or a set of sewing needles
which he will devour as readily as though they were gingerbread.

magazine's pages. He found a spot in the initial issue for his exhibition of the canine escapologist "Bobby, the Handcuff Dog." I mentioned a precursor of this act, Emile, a Newfoundland appearing in a French circus. I have learned of another Newfoundland, Nelson, who was also able to break free of restraints and had an altogether sterling career as reported in the biography of his master, the showman Sam Wild, titled *The Original, Complete, and Only Authentic Story of "Old Wilds,"* edited by "Trim" (William Broadley Megson, London, 1888). Nelson was capable of fetching a live canary in his mouth without ruffling a single feather.

I have also learned of Houdini's account of a performance in Treibsee, Germany, written when he was a correspondent for the *New York Dramatic Mirror*. Houdini reported in July 1905 that the canine soldiers re-enacted a battle of the Russo-Japanese War in which the dogs representing the Japanese were of course victorious. A marksman in the audience, not in sympathy with this outcome, "calmly drew a pistol and shot several of the Japanese dogs dead." The sharpshooter was arrested by the German police, who demanded a fine of 8,000 marks for killing "the best dogs of the troupe." Houdini also noted that the gunman was still being held as a "prisoner of war," as he was unable to make restitution.

Shortly after the publication of the issue on Munito, the singer Katy Moffatt alerted me to the disappearance of Oscar, "the world's only canine hypnotist." According to unlikely articles in both *USA Today* and *The Detroit News*, Scottish police confirmed that Oscar was indeed missing and that his sold-out appearances in Edinburgh were to be canceled. Hugh Cross, the owner and presenter of Oscar, offered a reward for the return of his talented Labrador, but warned the unsuspecting public to avoid looking the dog straight in the eye, as "that's how he hypnotizes people." The following day one Ronan Smyt found Oscar, avoided his mesmeric gaze, and collected $7,716 dollars from a pet-food manufacturer and a keg of beer from the pub in which the dog was performing.

Portrait of PHILIP HOWORTH at the age of four years, a child of extraordinary size and strength, in the CHARACTER of the INFANT HERCULES.

2.
Edward Bright: The Gazing Stock and Admiration of all People

Although I have little material to add on Mr. Bright himself, I have augmented my holdings on giant children with a number of prints and playbills. My favorite is a mezzotint executed in 1812 by G. Dawe of four-year-old Philip Howorth, "a child of extraordinary size and strength." He is represented grasping serpents "in the character of the Infant Hercules." A close second is a likeness of the baby Everitt, who was introduced in the issue. He is shown – all three feet three inches of him – in this engraving from 1780 at just eleven months (see page 170). A recent arrival to the archives is a playbill of Master Pierce, the Gigantic Shropshire Youth. According to his billing in this issue, he was a child of fifteen months who weighed a mere 42 pounds. At age sixteen he had filled out to 420, or a neat 30 stone. At seventeen, Master Smith, the Yorkshire Giant Youth, outweighed his rival by 70 pounds. I am fond, too, of Miss Mary Jane Youngman, the Wonderful Dwarf Giantess Just Arrived from Australia. At her London appearance in 1865, Ms. Youngman was fifteen years of age and had attained a modest 188 pounds.

Doris's Museum was a late-nineteenth-century establishment for cheap entertainment located on Eighth Avenue between Twenty-seventh and Twenty-eighth Streets. It was the venue for an event at which Ms. Youngman, had she been in New York, would have been well received. Massive size is trumpeted in this unusual example of the copywriter's rodomontade. Some of the most celebratory language may teeter on the brink of political correctness:

FAT WOMEN'S CONVENTION.

Doris's animated, astonishing, adipose tissue. More Fat Women in Convention Assembled, – Arranged in one massive group, – than were ever assembled before on earth. The Men who assembled at Washington last week were not a marker compared to The Big Women who assemble at Doris's this week. Their United Weight is Over 5 Tons! They are immense, huge, gross, obese, mighty, monstrous, marvelous, magnitudinous, mountainous and mammoth beauties, and looming over all is The Beautiful Alice, Her huge and beauteous form clad in her grand Parisian Bridal

Dress, – a marvel of Nature in a marvel of Worth's. The bridal dress was procured at an immense cost and required 132 yards of satin to make it. Alongside of this Regal Queen of Obesity will be seated Her Lilliputian Husband, whose Weight is 98 pounds. They were married in Boston by the Rev. W. W. Dowd, on the 22 Feb. last, – 3 weeks ago.

Mʳˢ EVERITT and her SON, — The GIGANTIC INFANT;
Born 7ᵗʰ Feb: 1779 at Enfield Paper Mills, Middlesex;
whose true dimensions at the Age of Eleven Months, were as follows:

His height 3.3 — Round his Breast 2.6 — Loins 3.1 — Thigh 1.9 — Leg 1.2 — Arm 0.11 — Wrist 0.9
He is of a prodigious weight, lives entirely on the Breast, is healthy, and very good
natur'd: was not remarkably large when born; but since the Age of
five or six weeks, has increased to the amazing size he is now of.

London, Published as the Act directs, as Jan: 1780, by W.Richardson York House N°31 Strand.

3.
The Bonassus: Verbal Deception Deciphered

Since the chronicling of Bonassus, the generosity of Donald Heald has led to the acquisition of a number of new broadsides. Clarence Wolf was good enough to provide the rare Spooner pamphlet quoted in the text. One of the great pleasures of producing *Jay's Journal* has

been the kindness of scholars, often unknown to me, wh answered queries and supplied information. I wa especially delighted by a conversation with Richar Reynolds, an expert on performing animals, whom I ha heard speak but had never met. I was so taken not onl by Mr. Reynolds's knowledge but also by his charmin Southern accent and turn of phrase that I recorded ou conversation in my personal journal on November 17 1994:

"Mr. Reynolds, my name is Ricky Jay. Fred Dah linger at Circus World Museum suggested that I cal you. I'm writing a piece on the exhibition of th Bonassus and I'm interested in examples of scientifi names being used and misused to attract audiences a the circus."

"Why, Mr. Jay, I do believe I've heard your name Did you give a talk at one of the circus historical meet ings on menageries?"

"No, on the exhibition of trained fleas," I say.

"Ah, yes, that would be it."

"Mr. Reynolds, could the Bonassus possibly hav been considered uncommon in 1821?"

"Why, to the contrary, Mr. Jay; in 1821 the Bonassus or American bison, was the most numerous hoofe quadruped on the face of the earth!"

"Would you happen to know what the cynocephalu was, or the guzzerat?"

"The cynocephalus, I have heard of that."

"I think it might be a primate," I say.

"Well, I'll look here under apes. No, I don't see it."

"How about baboons?" I suggest.

"Yes, yes of course, it's the *papio cynocephalus*, th yellow baboon from East Africa!"

"I am interested in the zimbo," I say, "and som other creatures as well, like the bovalapus."

"Yes, that was a water buffalo; you know, Christie's Show in 1920 advertised a pterodactyl."

"Are you a naturalist by profession?" I ask.

"No, I am an attorney."

"Then I guess you have some experience in seman tic subterfuge?"

"Yes, Mr. Jay, I use sophistry on a daily basis, and I am interested in the concept of using scientific nomen clature to deceive."

One of the minor pleasures of revisiting these issues is the opportunity to restore tidbits that we reluctantly eliminated because of the constraints of space. Two avid subscribers, the scholar of Japanese John Solt and the bookseller Ann FitzSimons, requested the additional verses of the Bonassus poem originally given on page 23. While I had hoped to restore all seventeen hyperbolic stanzas, my prudent publishers have proposed this compromise:

His darken'd brow, sagacious eye,
  And beard that trails along:
Thou easier wilt by sight descry,
  Than if detail'd in song.

Like Etna, by an earthquake shook,
  His swelling chest will rise
Nor can the visitor o'erlook
  The fire in his eyes.

In infancy secur'd by man,
  To Europe dragged away;
Come see the animal who can,
  For short is here his stay.

He who in nature's power could reign
  O'er hills and valleys green,
Is now bent down by slavery's chain,
  And may in peace be seen.

Yet still his restless, daring soul,
  Exists in tenfold rage;
No power can his fire controul,
  Or dare with him engage.

The fairest form that ever breath'd,
  The QUEEN to England true,
With condescending hand hath wreath'd
  Bonassus' lofty brow.

The first of all the British land,
  Hath to bonassus been;
A glorious emblem see him stand,
  Protected by the QUEEN!

The QUEEN the nation and the laws,
  We always will obey;
And e'en Bonassus will have cause
  To hail the QUEEN's right day.

Ye who in nature's forms delight,
  That seldom have been known,
Bonassus waits you, day and night,
  He always can be shewn.

So various are the brutish race
  Within his form combin'd,
None can his generation trace;
  It beat the powers of mind.

His eyeballs restless as the flash
  That darts the living fire;
And when we see his motions rash,
  We fear but must admire.

He never whines, he never roars
  His breath is always still;
Mild as the gale that sweeps the towers
  On Zion's holy hill.

But when enrag'd, nought can constrain
  The furies of his mind;
And could he burst his galling chain
  He'd leave "no wreck behind."

Then haste ye who are nature's friends,
  Bonassus calls you here;
For time he'll make you all amends
  Now count your shilling dear.

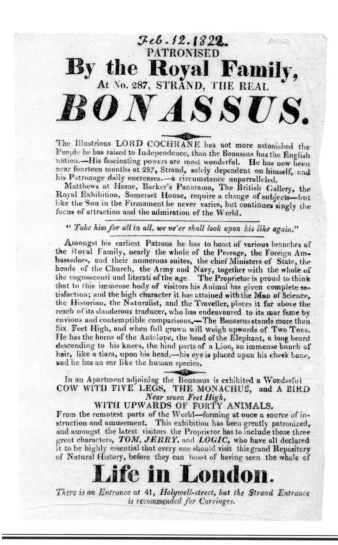

Feb. 12. 1822.
PATRONISED
By the Royal Family,
At No. 287, STRAND, THE REAL
BONASSUS.

The Illustrious LORD COCHRANE has not more astonished the People he has raised to Independence, than the Bonassus has the English nation.—His fascinating powers are most wonderful. He has now been near fourteen months at 287, Strand, solely dependent on himself, and his Patronage daily encreases.—a circumstance unparralleled.
Matthews at Home, Barker's Panorama, The British Gallery, the Royal Exhibition, Somerset House, require a change of subjects—but like the Sun in the Firmament he never varies, but continues singly the focus of attraction and the admiration of the World.

" Take him for all in all, we ne'er shall look upon his like again."

Amongst his earliest Patrons he has to boast of various branches of the Royal Family, nearly the whole of the Peerage, the Foreign Ambassadors, and their numerous suites, the chief Ministers of State, the heads of the Church, the Army and Navy, together with the whole of the cognoscenti and literati of the age. The Proprietor is proud to think that to this immense body of visitors his Animal has given complete satisfaction; and the high character it has attained with the Man of Science, the Historian, the Naturalist, and the Traveller, places it far above the reach of its slanderous traducer, who has endeavoured to its mar fame by envious and contemptible comparisons.—The Bonassus stands more than Six Feet High, and when full grown will weigh upwards of Two Tons. He has the horns of the Antelope, the head of the Elephant, a long beard descending to his knees, the hind parts of a Lion, an immense bunch of hair, like a tiara, upon his head,—his eye is placed upon his cheek bone, and he has an ear like the human species.

In an Apartment adjoining the Bonassus is exhibited a Wonderful
COW WITH FIVE LEGS, THE MONACHUS, and A BIRD
Near seven Feet High,
WITH UPWARDS OF FORTY ANIMALS.
From the remotest parts of the World—forming at once a source of instruction and amusement. This exhibition has been greatly patronized, and amongst the latest visitors the Proprietor has to include those three great characters, *TOM, JERRY,* and *LOGIC,* who have all declared it to be highly essential that every one should visit this grand Repository of Natural History, before they can boast of having seen the whole of

Life in London.

There is an Entrance at 41, Holywell-street, but the Strand Entrance is recommended for Carriages.

4.
Fact & Crucifixion

No matter how wondrous the advantages of spell checkers and global searches for the orthographically challenged, the downside can be substantial, especially with proper nouns. One ill-considered stroke on the keyboard and we had turned the hapless Chami Khan – who had certainly suffered enough, having willingly spent a number of days nailed to a cross in several venues – into "Kahn." The name may invite inconsistency, polyglotally: in front of me is a Spanish-language newspaper that gives "Chammi Kann" in a caption to his photograph and "Chami Kkan" in the accompanying text.

I remain grateful for the use of the wonderful portrait of Chami done in 1994 by the cartoonist Peter Kuper, which appears on page 31. Since *Fact &*

Crucifixion was published I have acquired a number of less spectacular depictions and some newspaper cuttings about Chami. Mike Caveney located in his archives a prepossessing account of Chami's stint on a cross in his native Venezuela. In a letter to Phil Calhoun, a resident of Pasadena and a director of the Los Angeles Adventure Club, Gladys Abbott described Chami's condition after his attempt at a ten-day crucifixion in Maracaibo, Venezuela, in January 1957: "Chami is fine again although he was not able to stay the ten days he did manage 145 hours [the newspaper accounts say 100 hours] and he felt that he could have done it if he had had more time in preparation. Please get in touch with me if there is any possibility of a booking on the coast. We have arranged what I believe is an excellent presentation and one which could do only 'good' if it were presented. If there are any possibilities, I feel sure that we could get together on terms."

Another exponent of stage crucifixion was Paul Diebel, whose torture act was prominent in the 1920s. According to Milbourne Christopher in *Mediums, Mystics, and the Occult* (New York, 1975), Diebel headlined at the famous Scala Theatre in Berlin, where spectators saw his left forearm impaled on a dagger. They were invited to view the blade close up, which extended some four or five inches outward from his skin: "Then he would approach the footlights and under a powerful spotlight make drops of blood ooze from his chest to form a cross." For a finale, a metal bolt shot from a powerful slingshot would penetrate his body; he would then pry the bolt loose and bow to applause. Jim Steinmeyer, whose wide knowledge often benefited *Jay's Journal*, mentioned a Diebel reference in the work of Charles Fort. In *Wild Talents* (New York, 1932), Fort quoted from the New York *Herald Tribune* of February 6, 1928: "In Munich recently, [Diebel] remained nailed to a cross several hours smoking cigarettes and joking with his audience."

One day I was discussing human "horses" with the equestrian and attorney Stan Coleman. He was reminded of the controversial technique used by a Brooklyn football coach of his acquaintance to select players. He would prick with a pin those athletes vying for a berth on his squad. "Some kids just don't feel the pain," he told Stan. "Those are the ones I want on my team."

5.
The Smallest Show on Earth: or, Parasites for Sore Eyes

Great fleas have little fleas upon their back to bite'em,
And little fleas have lesser fleas, and so ad infinitum.
— Augustus de Moran

Bertolotto, the renowned flea impresario, issued a playbill announcing his departure from 209 Regent Street for a new address a few doors down at 238 Regent Street. He warns his public that the proprietors of "a peep-half-penny street show" have "established their Box of Fleas" in his vacated premises and urges one to "Beware of Imposition at 209." He trumpets his royal patronage: Her Royal Highness the Princess Augusta, Their Majesties the King and Queen of the French, the King and Queen of the Belgians. As a bonus Bertolotto displays "Perpetual Motion By Magnetism" and "A Variety of Optical Illusions causing Roars of Laughter." A rival exhibition of "Industrious Fleas formerly at Regent Street," now removed to Somerset Gallery, offered a twelve-flea orchestra, "playing on different Instruments of proportionable size, the Music is audible," while four fleas indulged in a hand of Whist. A particularly sturdy specimen was shown hauling a fully rigged "Man of War, 420 times the weight of the insect."

Richard Wiseman of the Psychology Department at the University of Hertfordshire, who was preparing a piece on the flea circus for *Fortean Times*, alerted me to a strange fashion accessory sported by seventeenth-century Frenchmen who "demonstrated their depth of feelings for a loved one by catching a live flea from their partner's body and wearing it on a gold chain around their neck." From Jonathan Gestetner I was able to obtain, after much unpleasant dickering, a mid-eighteenth-century playbill of a London show of flea-drawn miniatures. The show was "seen and admired" on February 29, 1764, by John Henry Mauclerc, an aficionado of eclectic exhibitions. The device was displayed at the toy shop in the Haymarket – three years earlier than the version mentioned in this issue, as announced in *The Gazetteer and New Daily Advertiser.*

In view of my abiding fondness for fleas, I reluctantly proffer an advertisement that illustrates the depth to which greedy promoters have fallen in insect entertainment, from *Billboard Magazine* of May 20, 1933:

Signor Bertolotto's
EXTRAORDINARY EXHIBITION
OF THE
INDUSTRIOUS
FLEAS,
AND
Perpetual Motion !
PATRONISED BY
Her Royal Highness the Princess Augusta ; Their Majesties
the King and Queen of the French ; the King and Queen
of the Belgians ; the Nobility and Gentry, &c. &c.
REMOVED FROM 209, TO
238, REGENT STREET,
OPPOSITE HANOVER STREET,

Caution to the Public !
SIGNOR BERTOLOTTO
Having REMOVED his celebrated Exhibition from 209, to 238, Regent Street, the Proprietors of a peep-half-penny street show, availing themselves of Signor Bertolotto's popularity, have established their Box of Fleas in his former exhibition room, with the intention of catching any person who, not being informed of the Removal, may become an easy prey to the Imposition. It becomes Signor Bertolotto's duty to the Public, as well as to his character, to expose the trick, that the curious may not be made to pay a shilling for what has been shown to thousands for a half-penny about the Streets.
To prevent this please to remark that Signor Bertolotto's Name is on all his bills, and that the Exhibition
Is Removed to 238,
OPPOSITE HANOVER STREET.

The Industrious Fleas
Will continue to Dance a Waltz, Playing on Musical Instruments, a Game at Whist, Flirting, Fighting, a Duel with Real Swords, Pulling a Bucket from the Well, Drawing a First Rate Man of War, 120 Guns, Coaches, Gig, the Great Mogul and the whole of the First Train of the Liverpool Railway, the Three Heroes of Waterloo, Riding on Fleas, and a Variety of other Feats equally surprising. The little Insects are Dressed and Harnessed for their respective Tasks.
THE CELEBRATED
Perpetual Motion
By Magnetism, is also exhibited without any additional charge. A Variety of Optical Illusions causing Roars of Laughter.
Open from 10 till Dusk. Admittance 1s.
Beware of Imposition at 209.
E. & J. Thomas, Printers, 6, Exeter Street, Strand.

THE CELEBRATED & EXTRAORDINARY
EXHIBITION,
Patronized by the Royal Families of England,
France, Belgium, &c. &c. &c.
OF THE INDUSTRIOUS
FLEAS,
From Regent Street, is now Exhibiting at
Somerset Gallery, Strand
Next door to Somerset House.

A BALL ROOM
In which two Fleas dressed as Ladies, and two as Gentlemen
Dancing a Waltz: twelve Fleas in the Orchestra playing on
different Instruments of proportionable size, the Music is audible.
Four Fleas playing a game at whist.
A MAIL COACH
drawn by four Fleas, completely harnessed, the Coachman
and Guard, (also Fleas) dressed in the Royal Livery, the former
holding a Whip belabouring his four CHESNUTS; the latter
blowing the Horn.
By General Desire the much admired first-rate Man of War,
120 Guns, drawn by a single Flea! being 420 times the weight
of the insect.
The Marquis of W—driving a Tandem two spirited Colts, his
Lordship being represented by a Flea in a pea-green coat and
white trousers; the groom and horses are also Fleas.
The GREAT MOGUL, seated under a splendid palankin borne
by an Elephant, attended by slaves, who fan him as he proceeds
on his rout smoking his *Hookahs.*
The GAME OF THE RING will be executed by *four young
sparks,* and set in motion by a steady hand.
The Three Heroes of Waterloo!
The Duke of Wellington,
Napoleon Bonaparte,
And PRINCE BLUCHER,
Riding on Fleas, with Gold Saddles, &c.
Two Fleas deciding an Affair of Honour, sword in hand; another
Flea, dressed with a Blue Petticoat, pulling up a Bucket from a
Well; and several other objects, including Microscopes, Long
Faces, Broad Grins, &c.
Any comment on the merit of this Exhibition would be use-
less; the unparalleled success it has obtained during the last
three years, is sufficient proof that it deserves (as it has obtained)
the public patronage.

Open from 10 *till* 8.——*Admittance Sixpence.*
Collis, Printer, 104, Bishopsgate Street Within.

Run Little Cockroach Run! A New Craze Hits America,
Cockroach Racing. A natural for concessionaires, sideshows—
museums—parks—fairs—clubs—anywhere. A riot of fun—
see them run—holds the crowd—gets the money. Direct
from Europe—first time in America.

This outfit, provided by the International Mutoscope Reel Company of New York, featured "an actual
racetrack, 10 live cockroaches running hell for leather
from starting post to finishing line. . . . All you need is
the track with its patented starting device and a supply
of special racing roaches only obtainable through us.
Anyone can operate it. Life of average roach is 5 months.
New roaches can be supplied promptly."

I am pleased to report that the International
Mutoscope Reel Company is no longer in existence.

I continue to unearth astonishing amounts of material on these tiny performers. The resourceful Steve
Weissman and the gifted illusion designer John Gaughan
both provided me with rare bills on the exhibition of
fleas. Other correspondents replying to the issue included the indefatigable Professor Senelick, who sent a copy
of a lovely French bill for the Ubini Flea Circus (pa-
tronné par la Famille Royale d'Angleterre) at the
Pavillon Français; and David Mamet, who wrote:

> . . . scarce the width of a hair
> in this vale of despair
> between the Biter and Bitten
> But what is the Use
> to Write of the Puce
> After the Master has written?

Mamet introduced me to the remarkable Shel
Silverstein, one of three special friends who helped with
Parasites for Sore Eyes. All three have sadly died. Shel
drew the delightful cartoon on page 44, the writer Jo-
seph Mitchell discussed with me his observations on
Heckler's Flea Circus in Times Square, and T. A. Waters
delivered the flea pitch at that very institution. I marked
Waters's passing with an article in *The New Yorker* on
September 14, 1998. They are all greatly missed.

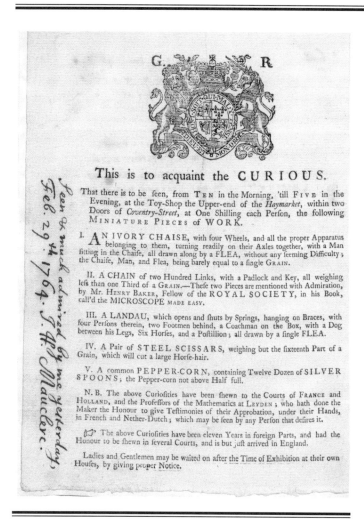

Seen & much admired by me yesterday, Feb. 29th 1764. J. H. Mauclerc.

This is to acquaint the CURIOUS.

That there is to be seen, from TEN in the Morning, 'till FIVE in the Evening, at the Toy-Shop the Upper-end of the *Haymarket*, within two Doors of *Coventry-Street*, at One Shilling each Person, the following MINIATURE PIECES of WORK.

I. AN IVORY CHAISE, with four Wheels, and all the proper Apparatus belonging to them, turning readily on their Axles together, with a Man fitting in the Chaise, all drawn along by a FLEA, without any seeming Difficulty; the Chaise, Man, and Flea, being barely equal to a single GRAIN.

II. A CHAIN of two Hundred Links, with a Padlock and Key, all weighing less than one Third of a GRAIN.—These two Pieces are mentioned with Admiration, by Mr. HENRY BAKER, Fellow of the ROYAL SOCIETY, in his Book, call'd the MICROSCOPE MADE EASY.

III. A LANDAU, which opens and shuts by Springs, hanging on Braces, with four Persons therein, two Footmen behind, a Coachman on the Box, with a Dog between his Legs, Six Horses, and a Postillion; all drawn by a single FLEA.

IV. A Pair of STEEL SCISSARS, weighing but the sixteenth Part of a Grain, which will cut a large Horse-hair.

V. A common PEPPER-CORN, containing Twelve Dozen of SILVER SPOONS; the Pepper-corn not above Half full.

N. B. The above Curiosities have been shewn to the Courts of FRANCE and HOLLAND, and the Professors of the Mathematics at LEYDEN; who hath done the Maker the Honour to give Testimonies of their Approbation, under their Hands, in French and Nether-Dutch; which may be seen by any Person that desires it.

☞ The above Curiosities have been eleven Years in foreign Parts, and had the Honour to be shewn in several Courts, and is but just arrived in England.

Ladies and Gentlemen may be waited on after the Time of Exhibition at their own Houses, by giving proper Notice.

6.
Grinners, Gurners & Grimaciers

Following the publication of *Grinners, Gurners & Grimaciers*, Laurence Senelick and Stephen Minch both reminded me that I had neglected one of the most famous of fictional grinners, Quasimodo, the Hunchback of Notre Dame. Hugo's character inadvertently wins a gurning contest at the Feast of Fools when he sticks his head through a hole in the wall and, without twitching a muscle, vanquishes all competition. Senelick also mentioned that "grinning through a horse collar" is a nineteenth-century expression meaning comic overacting.

One exhibition of facial irregularity mentioned in the issue featured a child with the words *Deus meus* imprinted on his eye (the other eye had a Hebrew translation). Two authoritative witnesses mentioned seeing such a child, I can now report. James Paris du Plessis, a

servant to Samuel Pepys, included the child in his manuscript record of anomalies on view in London and John Evelyn, the famous diarist, noted that he saw the boy in 1701.

In the early nineteenth century, Mr. Fitz-James was known for a performance combining ventriloquism and facial contortion. After a review of my files on ventriloquism, I can introduce several of his predecessors. Particularly blessed with these skills were an eighteenth-century Frenchman, Thimet, and a seventeenth-century performer known as Sannigus (from the Latin, "one who mimics or grimaces"). Because of his close relationship with James I, he was called the "King's Whisperer."

Through the kindness of the capable Bennett Gilbert I was able to examine an unpublished manuscript from the eighteenth century, *L'Art de Bien Grimacer, ou Le Secret d'Emploier, Les Mimes les plus épouventables avec grace*. "The Secret of Making the Most Awful Faces, Presented Graciously" is a tongue-in-cheek manual of grimaces for the acting profession. The dedicatory paragraph proffers the work to the "Queen of Disdain" and extols the royal prerogative of making "the most awful and horrible of looks thereby attracting grand applause." The anonymous author explains various means of altering one's countenance to resemble animal or human progenitors. Among the latter are "the Roquelonne," based on the face of Roquelaure, who, with his withdrawn nose, "combined the most unbelievable face in the world with a spirit as lively and penetrating as any man could have." Also featured was "the Bertholdine," derived from its inventor, called Bertholde, "one of the most deformed and villainous pieces of meat that nature ever created: this facial expression has enough merit that it deserves the attention of any curious reader who wishes to master this great art form." Bertholde was chronicled in numerous eccentric biographies. His monstrous face is vividly described in *The New, Original and Complete Wonderful Museum and Magazine Extraordinary* (London, 1807):

Bertholde had a large head, as round as a foot-ball, adorned with red hair very strait, and which had a great resemblance to the bristles of a hog; an extremely short forehead, furrowed with wrinkles; two little blear eyes, edged round with a border of bright carnation, and over-shadowed by a pair of large eye-brows, which, upon occasion, might be made use of as brushes; a flat red nose, resembling an extinguisher; a wide mouth, from which proceeded two long crooked teeth, not unlike the tusks of a boar, and pointing to a pair of ears, like those which formerly belonged to Midas; a lip of monstrous thickness which hung down on a chin, that seemed to sink under the load of a bear, thick, strait, and bristly; a very short neck, which nature had adorned with a kind of necklace, formed of ten or twelve small wens. The rest of his body was perfectly agreeable to the grotesque appearance of his visage; so that from head to foot, he was a kind of monster, who, by his deformity, and the hair with which he was covered, had a greater resemblance to a bear half licked into form than a human creature.

Any association with villainy was purely physiognomic. Bertholde was extolled for his wit and sagacity, and even served as prime minister to the King of Lombardy. According to the *London Magazine* of 1753, quoted by Edward Wood: "Though nature had treated him so ill with respect to his body, she had recompensed him by the subtlety, the agreeableness, and the solidity of the mind she had united to it." Michael Zinman favored me with a few depictions of Bertholde from the *Americanischer Stadt und Land Calender*, a German-language almanac published in Philadelphia in various years early in the nineteenth century. I include for your delectation a woodcut of the little man from the 1814 imprint. I am also able to include another representation of the grimacier pictured on page 50.

Berthold, der Witzling.

7.
Isaac Fawkes:
Surprizing Dexterity of Hand

I have unearthed several intriguing items on Fawkes, the great conjurer of the early eighteenth century who established a benchmark for contemporary performers. *Bartholomew Fair: An Heroi-Comical Poem* (London, 1717) contains a detailed celebration of a conjurer that is very mindful of Fawkes:

A famous Trixter next invites my Eyes,
By Sleight of Hand he could the World surprize;
The Cards alive, to flying Birds are chang'd,
And on the Table numerous Eggs are rang'd.
A living Hen appears upon the Board,
By W.... created, if you'll take his Word:
Gilt Balls they move by Motion of his Wand,
And jump a Mile with only his Command:

The large Half-Crown his magick jaws can blow
Unseen, unfelt, into the Sleeve of Beau;
A thief he makes in the majestick Row.
All this he does, a thousand Things beside,
His Fame's proclaim'd beyond the Ocean wide.
The Mob amaz'd, with Admiration stand,
And view the Great Copernicus's Wand:
Senseless they view, and on his Band they stare;
No thought had they his living Imps were there.

I have located an unidentified cutting hand-dated October 18, 1729, advertising a production in Fawkes's Theatre at the Tennis Court. It announces one signature effect, "The Artificial view of the World," and a performance by Anthony le Blain:

The Famous Balance Master From Paris who poizes several Pipes in a perpendicular Position on his Nose: Also several Glasses of Wine one upon another, with which he Dances, lies down on his Back and rises again without spilling the Wine; He carries a Ladder on his Forehead, with a Child of three Years old on the Top thereof, playing on the Violin at the same time. Also several Chairs one on another. Likewise a Coach Wheel edge-ways on his Forehead, to the Admiration of all Spectators. Note, He performs all this without the Use of his Hands, and several other Curiosities too tedious to insert; there being no Person in these Kingdoms does the same but himself.

I have been helped in my quest for material about Fawkes by kind friends at Bernard Quaritch, who alerted me to a curious pamphlet entitled *A New Scheme for the Lottery* (London, 1732). It satirizes get-rich-quick schemes, such as the recently burst South Sea Bubble and the Charitable Corporation, with a facetious proposal for selling fifty thousand lottery tickets. I was delighted to discover a reference to Fawkes, and he is apparently shown presiding over the schemers from a second-story window. As the monograph was published the year after Isaac's death, however, the illustration may well feature his son, who inherited his "mantle of magic." A Hogarth drawing in the series *Masquerades and Operas* shows a figure similarly posed, overlooking a crowd from a second-story window. Although a sign reads, "Faux, Dexterity of hand," the figure has been identified as John James Heidegger, later the Master of the Revels to George II. As noted in the issue, Fawkes was featured in Hogarth's famous engraving of Southwark Fair, published in 1734 (also published after Isaac's death, this may have pictured his son as well). I have obtained what is probably the only known playbill of the younger Fawkes. In a richly varied entertainment he presented: an automated musical clock, optical views of the world, a machine which simulated perpetual motion, a young posture-master and slack-rope performer, new magical effects of his own devising "never shewn before in public," and the blooming tree mystery made famous by his father.

Notice is hereby given to the Quality, Gentry, and Others,

That every *Monday*, *Wednesday*, and *Friday*, during *Lent*, the Town will be diverted with the following surprising Entertainments, at *FAWKES's Theatre*, adjoining to the old *Tennis-Court*, in *James-Street*, near the *Hay-Market*, being the same Place that his Father Perform'd at for many Years before his Death, viz.

1. IS *FAWKES's* diverting and incomparable Dexterity of Hand, wherein is perform'd several curious Tricks, never done by any one living but himself; particularly he causes a Tree to grow out of a Flower-Pot on the Table, which Blossoms and bears ripe Fruit in a Minute; likewise a Man in a Maze, or a perpetual Motion, whereby he makes a little Ball to run continually by the Word of Command only, which would endure for Ages; this curious piece has surpris'd the greatest *Mathematicians* in *Europe*; he has had the Honour to perform before the Royal Family, by which he gain'd the greatest applause; he has Invented several new Tricks, never shewn before in publick, and he is allow'd to be the greatest Master of this Art in the World, by all that have seen him.

2. Is his famous young Posture Master of Nine Years old, that far exceeds all others of the Kind: He shews a great variety of surprizing Postures quite Different from any in *Europe*; and he performs them with so much Ease and Pleasure, that render it highly Delightful and Pleasant to the beholders of it.

3. The surprizing vaulting of the Rope, by a young Lad, that surprizes all that sees him, and far exceeds all of the Kind in *Europe*.

4. Is the amazing Musical Clock, which has two most beautiful moving Pictures, and performs on several Instruments, a vast Variety of fine Pieces of Musick, compos'd by the best Masters.

5. The Temple of Arts, which is the finest and most perfect Piece of Workmanship in the World, the Machinery consisting of moving Pictures, and Variety of other inimitable Curiosities.

6. The Artificial View of the World, wherein is naturally imitated the Firmament; also a Representation of the Ocean, with Ships under Sail, saluting each other with their Guns, the Report and Eccho of which are heard in Proportion to the Distance they seem to be at: To which are now added many Improvements, never seen before in publick, and every Week are shewn different Prospect; and every Evening of shewing this Week, will be Represented the four following, viz:

  1. A fine Prospect of *Constantinople* in *Turkey*.
  2. A fine Prospect of *Windsor-Castle*, likewise a View of the River of *Thames*.
  3. The City of Grand Cairow in *Egypt*.
  4. The City of *Tripoly* in *Barbary*.

He hopes that Gentlemen and Ladies will honour him with their good Company, as they did his Father, he making no doubt of giving the same Satisfaction.

Also, Gentlemen and Ladies may be accomodated with a private Shew, giving but Notice over Night.

N. B. The Place is made very commodious, for the better Reception of Gentlemen and Ladies.   Pit 2s.   First Gallery 1s.   Upper Gallery 6d.

The Doors will be open'd at Five, and begin exactly at Seven o'Clock.

Vivant Rex & Regina.

SALON ÉLECTRIQUE.
L'HOMME MARCHAND AU PLAFOND.

8.
Dancing on the Ceiling

This issue paused to admire a number of films with upside-down turns. I was recently taken with such a sequence from the Marx Brothers' *At the Circus* (1939). Eve Arden plays "Peerless Pauline," a ceiling walker. In one scene, Groucho dons suction shoes to join her for an Antipodean spin.

While studying these inversions, I have been fortunate to draw upon the expertise of John McKinven for a number of technical details on ceiling-walk patents. Stuart Thayer has documented the circus performance of ceiling walks, and has graciously checked specific details for me. From the rich variety of depictions of these effects, I include illustrations from the Pedanto playbill, Hopkins's *Magic*, and an unidentified nineteenth-century engraving.

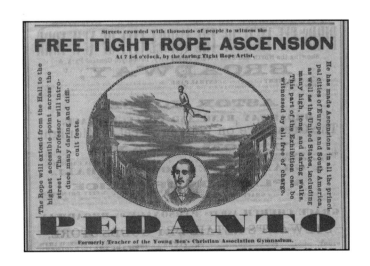

9.
Magical Mayhem: or,
The Celebrated Nose Amputation

Magical nose piercing with an awl – rather than a dagger – was discussed and displayed in *Evening Amusements, or Merry Hours for Merry People* by Henry T. Williams and S. Annie Frost (New York, 1878). The routine necessitated switching a legitimate awl for one with a spring that allowed the tool to recede into the handle. The description is quoted in full to allow the reader the flavor of the performance:

After handing round the perfect awl and making one of the company prick some holes in a card, you offer to pierce ears for nothing, and produce sundry large and tawdry ear-rings, to be given away to all who will have the operation performed (none are likely to step forward, but if they should they may easily be dismissed with a good pinch). You must then pretend to turn cross, and propose to puncture your own nose. Your confederate must try to dissuade you from this folly; you will, however, ask his assistance, and proceed to apply the "sham" awl to your nose, whilst he holds a plate, sponge, and cloth to receive the blood. Your confederate will make a great fuss, as if staunching the wound, and if the plate had been smeared with some perchloride of iron, and the small bit of the sponge contains a little sulphcyanide of potassium, by dexterously squeezing the liquid out of the sponge it will give all the appearance of blood, whilst your groans will improve the delusion. The horror of the audience will rise to a climax when another instrument is produced by which the supposed hole through the nose is to be provided with thread.

This device is similar to the nose pillar pictured on page 82. Pulling the thread between his nostrils, the performer was urged to exclaim that his "nose is ruined

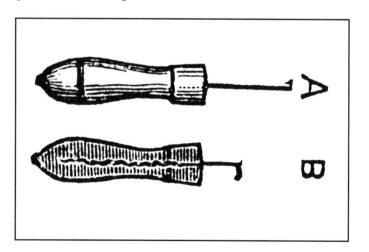

forever, when shouts of laughter will be provoked by the assistant producing a new nose of gutta-percha with which he should solemnly invest you, as also with a huge wig and spectacles." It is difficult to envision a more amusing evening.

Mervyn Heard, the showman and scholar of the magic lantern, wrote to remind me of the famous slip slide featuring a nose amputation. He continued: "As you'll be aware there are many lantern slides showing noses in various states of perishability, including entire successions en route to the grindstone." He kindly included a slide illustration of a human subject cutting off his nose to spite his face from "John Plowman's Pictures," which he describes as "a series of overly literal homilies taken from the popular printed lectures of the popular moralising evangelist C. H. Spurgeon."

A Dr. Valentine is united with Harrington, the much-heralded American magician and ventriloquist, on a broadside in the Milbourne Christopher collection. Valentine is billed as a mimic imitator and delineator of humorous character, and he is likely the person who performed the "dissertation on noses." While looking through slides of Tom Ewing's collection I found the lurid cut of Wyman's nose amputation from 1854 (see page 78) used sixteen years later on a gift show playbill of the conjurer Rubini for an appearance at the Opera House in Bellefontaine, Ohio.

Those fascinating purveyors of anomalous literature Eric Korn and Jeff Towns provided me with Frank Campbell's *Memoranda on Noses* (London, 1874). A curious compendium, it is subtitled "the nose as an index to character, and its other uses." This approach to the organ quotes a variety of sources, such as the seventeenth-century writer Giovanni Baptista Porta ("a very large nose indicates a man who seizes on the property of others. . . . he who has a nose thick at the end is lazy, like a cow"). The work reminds me of an even more curious volume in my library, Timothy Burr's 1965 classic, *Bisba*, a large octavo of almost five hundred pages devoted to "why and how women's breasts reveal their character." Long before Barry Humphries delighted theatergoers as Dame Edna Everage or subscribed to this journal, he produced a wonderfully eccentric compendium called *Bizarre* (New York, 1965). Among the many choice tidbits is a brief exegesis on artificial noses molded from caoutchouc.

10.
The Wizard of the North and the Aztec Lilliputians

Representations of John Henry Anderson with the children from Iximaya continue to surface. I was very pleased to obtain three variants of the early chapbook history of the "Aztecs" from the resourceful William Reese, one of which – written in French, printed in green ink, and published by A. H. Van Gorcum in Amsterdam – features a full-page plate of Anderson (who is not identified) with his young wards. A similar grouping appeared in a nineteenth-century volume compiled by Edmund Fillingham King and modestly titled *Ten Thousand Wonderful Things Comprising the Marvellous and Rare, Odd, Curious, Quaint, Eccentric and Extraordinary in all Ages and Nations, in Art, Nature, and Science Including Many Wonders of the World Enriched*

with Hundreds of Authentic Illustrations (see page 183). The impressive scholar and collector Volker Huber kindly sent a copy of a large broadside for the Aztec exhibition in Germany, complete with cuts I had seen only as full-page pamphlet illustrations. As Anderson did not participate in the German tour, he is not pictured.

I have also uncovered two contemporary articles that further register the awestruck credulity that greeted the early exhibition of the children. *The American Whig Review* of April 1852 noted that they were taken from "the newly discovered and Idolatrous City of Iximaia, in Central America, where they have been kept with superstitious veneration, distinct and secluded, as a Caste of their Priesthood, and employed as mimes and bacchanals in their pagan ceremonies and worship." A feature by "Australis" in *Graham's American Monthly* concludes that the interest in "these little beings . . . has been unparalleled in the history and production of those natural phenomena which have in this or any other age been presented to the world."

The anthropological phenomenon that was Carlos Castaneda provided the conclusion to this issue. Obituaries stated that he died on June 18, 1998, but the death certificate, cited by Celeste Fremon in her article "Dreaming Castaneda" (*LA Weekly*, June 30, 1998), evidently gave April 27. Adrian Vashon, the son of his exwife, was quoted as saying: "In keeping with the terms of legalities and record-keeping that the world of everyday life requires, Carlos Castaneda was declared to have died." A recent search for "Castaneda" on the Internet confirms a cyber-afterlife of more than eleven thousand references.

11.
The Gnome Fly

I am convinced that the irrepressible Hervio Nano is deserving of an in-depth reprise. His confident self-promotion is newly evident in a letter I have acquired, written to an emissary of the Frenchman LaFontaine, whom Nano had engaged to compose some sketches for the Continental tour he envisioned. He wonders if an English piece entitled *Jack Robinson and His Monkey* would be suitable for the French stage, and beckons, "If you will be kind enough to write to Rouen, Havre de

Grace and Bourdeaux and all the theatres in that direction, I shall be bound to take any engagements that you make in the beginning of next month and continue one after the other."

Helen Smith of the Jarndyce firm of booksellers and London's Theatre Museum kindly wrote to inform me of her research on Harvey Leach, as he was known before he acquired his Italianate epithet. Leach is portrayed in two episodes of the series *Tales of the Drama*, published in the 1830s. He is featured as *The Demon Dwarf, or The Vampire Bat* in no. 55 and as *The Gnome Fly* in no. 6, where he is depicted as he appeared at the Adelphi in 1838. Theater manager Frederick Yates had to outbid competition to book Leach and, according to a snide blurb of February 17, was "exciting a strong sensation in the neighbourhood of the Adelphi, by the exhibition of what he calls *his Adelphi Fly*, but this wonderful Fly is, after all, only a *Leach*, who formerly endeavoured to get a bite at the good folks round the Victoria." The reviewer declared the performance "very surprising, but not particularly edifying," and further denigrated the spectacle.

The response to Nano continued to be mixed. Laurence Senelick wrote to apprise me of the jingoistic diatribe to which Nano was subjected in *The Town* during this very run: "Harvey Leach's very *imposing personifications*, or rather transmigrations into the carcasses of blue-bottle flies and blue-faced monkeys, have been stretched to the extreme of public favour. One more step, and that must be from the sublime to the ridiculous; for it is impossible that such practical impositions, however ingenious, can be endured after the Greenwich Fair has commenced. We shall therefore advise *Signor Nano* to pack up his wings and decamp, no matter whether to ancient Rome or the Cape of Good Hope, ere the end of the passion-week. Such an exhibition may serve to kill time in the Vatican, whilst the Cardinals are making mouths for the roast lamb and asparagus, for which they have fasted since Shrove-tide; or it may afford some matter for conjecture to the long-armed apes and pongoes in the other settlement."

The *Times* of London offered emphatic praise for his sheer athleticism: "He climbs . . . along the side of the theatre, gets into the upper circle in a moment, catches hold of the projection of the ornaments of the ceiling of the theatre, crosses to the opposite side, and descends along the vertical boarding of the proscenium. . . . In a word, [he] performs some of the most astonishing feats ever exhibited within the wall of a theatre." According to Alicia Kae Koger, who cited the *Times* review in the online Adelphi Theatre site, Leach appeared fifty-four times that season, and in that exhibition Yates had "hit upon one of his greatest successes."

The always helpful Jenny Lee, now of Columbia University Library Special Collections, drew my attention to a Currier and Ives political cartoon of 1860, held at the New York Public Library. It showed Lincoln and Horace Greeley flanking another diminutive "What Is It?" with a poster for Barnum's exhibition faintly visible in the background.

Monsieur Gouffe was another famous man-monkey who found respectability elusive despite professional acclaim. According to an unidentified newspaper cutting of May 27, Gouffe complained to a magistrate in 1828 that he had "one of the most incorrigible wives in the canopy of heaven. She goes out, says he, and gets drunk as an owl, and I attempt to remonstrate with her on the impropriety of her conduct and . . . the cups and saucers are smashed in ten thousand pieces. . . . I have lost several good engagements owing to the conduct of my wife and if something is not done to prevent the annoyance, I shall be a lost man." The threat to his dignity was imminent, as she planned to appear at Drury Lane Theatre and "present herself drunk at the stage-door, and if she was refused admittance she would kick up such a disturbance as would raise the whole theatre." The judge replied, "You have taken her for better or worse, therefore I cannot help you." Since the magistrate was unmoved by mere rowdiness, Gouffe continued, "Your worship, I have caught her in bed with another man, cannot you take cognizance of that?" The magistrate proposed that Gouffe provide her with a separate dwelling, but he replied that this remedy, too, would only compromise his reputation: "That would be the delight of my heart to get clear away from her; but she refuses to go, declaring that she will stick to me as long as I have got a shirt to my back. When I threatened to turn her out the other night, added he, after having caught a big fellow in bed with her, she swore she would get a basket and hawk perriwinkles about the different public-houses in the neighbourhood of the Theatre, and every one who purchased one from her should know that she was the wife of 'Monsieur Gouffe, the performer.'"

12.
Subterfuge at Skittles: or, Bowling for Blacklegs

The third chapter of Olivier Gouyn's *Le mespris & Contennement de tous jeux de sort*, published in Paris in 1550, contains a very early reference to cheating at bowling. In cataloguing amusements that could be altered by deception Gouyn reports that even ninepins, or skittles, "is not exempt." He indicates that both the balls and the alleys may be altered to aid the hustler, and changed by the day to confound even the savviest player: "What was lowered will be raised, and what was raised will be lowered, and some other time he will put stones sharp as diamonds in the alley in which you play, in order to make your ball go to the cabbage, meaning out of the alley." I am indebted to Bill Kalush, whose impressive research into early conjuring books led me to this passage.

I am pleased to note that the Bowling Hall of Fame Web site now lists Washington Irving, rather than Jonathan Swift, as the author of *Rip Van Winkle*. It is gratifying to realize that one's tenure on the planet is not devoid of meaning.

13.
The Ultimate Diet: The Art and Artifice of Fasting

I was happy to obtain another impression of the scarce pamphlet *The Very Extraordinary Life and Singular Characteristics of Mr. Cavanagh the Celebrated Fasting Man*. A virtuosic but not untypical example of book-selling ingenuity, it bears a slightly altered title page adding the topical banner line "the Fasting Man Committed to Prison."

Garrett Scott provided an eighteenth-century account of extreme abstention that I had not seen, *The Case of Mr. John Ferguson of Argyleshire in Scotland Who Hath lived above Eighteen Years only on Water, Whey or Barley-Water*, and Gordon Bruce presented me with an autographed "before and after" postcard depicting Guiseppe Sacco-Homan, whose mustache waxed more luxurious as his visage waned. The formidable Steve Finer located a copy of *The Welsh Fasting Girl*, a short and,

by my harsh standards, unproduceable four-act play by W. F. Lloyd, published in Swansea in 1928. It takes its place on my shelves next to Dr. Robert Fowler's classic of fasting deception turned tragic, *A Complete History of the Case of the Welsh Fasting-Girl* (London, 1871).

Martin Gardner generously shared his file on Breatharianism, and a brief account of the subject appears in Andrew Weil's bestseller *Eating Well for Optimum Health* (New York, 2000). Dr. Weil supplies an appendix, "The Possibility of Surviving Without Eating," and notes that he became interested in the subject after reading of the guru Giri Bala, an aged woman who claimed to live only on "Eternal Light," in Paramahansa Yogananda's *Autobiography of a Yogi*. In South America during the 1970s Weil happened upon some Breatharians, "a supposed sect of noneaters, who

THE NEW SOCIETY OF CAVANERITES, Who Live without Eating!!

"We want no food any more, We scorn the butcher's door." *The Cavanerite's Song.*

Just Published, Price One Penny, A CORRECT AND UNABRIDGED ACCOUNT OF THE WONDERFUL SOCIETY OF CAVANERITES, OR, Human Nature Conquerors,

Who meet every Monday and Saturday Evenings in Watt Street, Whitechapel, to illustrate their views by analysing with spirits, Legs of Mutton, and other joints, and thus showing the mortification in the bone, &c.; also to enroll Members, by signing a declaration that they will LIVE WITHOUT FOOD INCLUDING A REPORT OF THEIR SPEECHES, and the manner they refresh themselves with Common Bran and Hot Water! ALSO, THE GREAT DR. BREWTREE'S Certificate of the excellent health of the members of this extraordinary Society, with the "CAVANERITES APOLOGY" For Eating no Food.

COMPILED BY THEIR FOUNDER, HUGH CAVANER, Son of the great Fasting Man, Barney Cavaner.

PRINTED BY W. DEVER, 18, GREAT ST. ANDREW STREET, AND PUBLISHED BY G. SEABROOK, 36, BROAD STREET, BLOOMSBURY.

Before. After.

GUISEPPE SACCO-HOMAN.

∾ THE WORLD'S FAMOUS FASTING MAN. ∾

had their headquarters in a hidden monastery near the shore of Lake Titicaca, where they lived on air and cosmic energy, having passed through the preliminary stages of vegetarianism and fruitarianism. No one I met had found this place, but some years later I was amused to learn of the exposure of a self-proclaimed Breatharian guru in California captured on videotape stuffing himself with candy bars between lectures."

Dr. Weil then reports what he is careful to call "secondhand information" on a phenomenon called "bigu," a technique of abstention from food taught by a Chinese "qigong" master, Yan Xin. Weil interviewed one of Yan Xin's disciples, an electrical engineer named Jun Wang, who claimed that she had been "in the abstaining from food state for eight years." She learned the technique after attending Yan Xin's lecture at the University of Connecticut. Unfortunately for us, she informed Weil, "I have been told not to reveal it."

14.
Dental Deception

The early-nineteenth-century conjurer Ingleby was so pompous in performance that he invited parody. It is difficult to believe that the following hyperbolic lines come from his own playbill of 1814 and are not the work of a satirist. They appeared under the incomprehensible heading "Hiliodmactrics": "The Performer will allow any person in the Room to break New Laid Eggs, and out of one of them he will produce, to the conviction of the whole Company – from the one A Recipe for the Cure of the Tooth-Ache which he wishes them not to expose, as he charges five Guineas for the Recipe." From the other egg he promised to extract a complete set of children's bed linen, child included.

One strongman who caught a bullet in his teeth in a performance of 1817 was graced by a strong-woman wife, introduced in the issue as Mme Gobert. I failed to mention at the time that among the prints in *Spectacles en Plein Vent* by Courtin is the only known likeness of her, which is reproduced here, probably for the first time.

The broadside of Jacob Philadelphia reproduced below came to me through the kindness of Volker Huber, who also introduced me to Marion Philadelphia, a direct descendant of the great conjurer. Bill Helfand, the expert on the iconography of medical quackery, responded to the issue with apposite commentary. He enlisted the aid of Ben Swanson, who graciously forwarded material on dental fraud, which, if slightly outside the purview of this discussion, nonetheless informed and pleased me greatly.

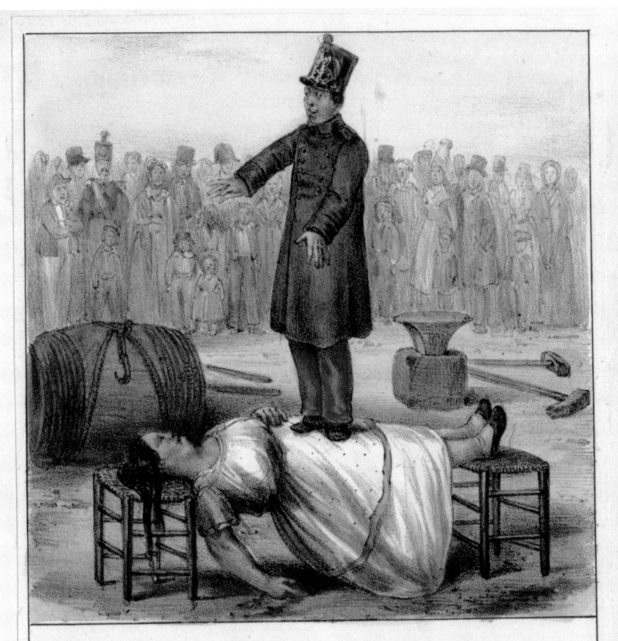

LA FEMME FORTE.

Chacun peut s'approcher et vérifier que madame Gobert, première femme forte de Frrrance!, qui a reçu des marques de bienveillance de S.M. l'Empéreur autocrate de toutes les Russies! n'use point de vains et fallacieux subterfuges, et ceux qui en douteraient encore sont invités à venir lutter avec elle.

15.
Suspensions of Disbelief

Upon receipt of this issue Laurence Senelick sent a copy of a lovely *carte de visite* of an unidentified woman suspended on stage and gently took me to task for misusing the Shakespearean phrase "mortal coil" in my characterization of the Asrah suspension. "Perhaps," he suggested, the draped maiden may be "shedding her corporeal envelope." I am consequently relieved to be able to identify the photographic subject as Mary Young, wife of the well-known American conjurer Professor William Henry Young (1821–74). I can also now share lithographic representations of Alexander Herrmann's wife, Adelaide, "Asleep In Mid Air" [see page 163] and Servais Le Roy performing a beautiful levitation.

In the posthumously published *Magie et Physique Amusante* (Paris, 1877), translated into English in 1881 as *The Secrets of Stage Conjuring*, Robert-Houdin describes a suspension markedly different from his "etherial" presentation, detailed in the issue. This version was intended as a spiritualistic effect. A woman carrying a bouquet comes from the wings and sits in a chair. The medium places the flowers on a nearby table (which is the only other furniture on the almost bare stage) and, "with imperturbable gravity, makes passes, more or less mesmeric in the direction of his subject." Now in a trance the woman, still sitting in the chair, begins levitating. "She then in a dreamy sort of way, extends her hand towards the table, and forthwith this in its turn rises in the air, and comes near enough for her to take her bouquet, which, indeed, spontaneously offers itself to her hand. The table then returns to its former place, and in due time, the lady, gently sinking to the ground again, wakes from her trance, rises from her chair, and leaves the stage."

16.
The Automaton Chess Player, The Invisible Girl & The Telephone

The letters I received after the last issue offered little in the way of rejoinders or new information but rather expressed sadness over the journal's conclusion. These letters gave me the opportunity to reflect on all of the issues, each chronicling idiosyncratic episodes in the history of entertainment, yet all fundamentally connected by the bizarre logic of performance.

I take unabated pleasure in the efforts of showmen to educate and entertain their audiences. I love the interaction and competition of rival promoters. I love the efforts of performers to develop improbable and original creations.

I love deception. I love the ways in which "the mind is led on step by step to ingeniously defeat its own logic." I love the way that P. T. Barnum, who eventually exhibited Faber's Talking Machine and the automata of Robert-Houdin, inaugurated his career by presenting Joice Heth, the 161-year-old nurse to George Washington. I love it that Johann Nepomuk Maelzel was forced to hold his automaton chess player in abeyance until the Heth furor had quieted. To entice spectators to return to his attraction, and almost certainly based on

GREAT ATTRACTION
JUST ARRIVED AT CONCERT HALL.
FOR A SHORT TIME ONLY.
JOICE HETH,
NURSE TO
Gen. George Washington,
(The father of our country,) who has arrived at the astonishing age of 161 years! will be seen at Concert Hall, corner of Court and Hanover streets, Boston, for a SHORT TIME ONLY, as she is to fill other engagements very soon.
JOICE HETH is unquestionably the most astonishing and interesting curiosity in the World! She was the slave of Augustine Washington, (the father of Gen. Washington,) and was the first person who put clothes on the unconscious infant who in after days led our heroic fathers on to glory, to victory and freedom. To use her own language when speaking of the illustrious Father of his country, "she raised him." JOICE HETH was born in the Island of Madagascar, on the Coast of Africa, in the year 1674 and has consequently now arrived at the astonishing
Age of 161 Years!
She weighs but forty-six pounds, and yet is very cheerful and interesting. She retains her faculties in an unparalleled degree, converses freely, sings numerous hymns, relates many interesting anecdotes of Gen. Washington, the red coats, &c. and often laughs heartily at her own remarks, or those of the spectators. Her health is perfectly good, and her appearance very neat. She was baptized in the Potomac river and received into the Baptist Church 116 years ago, and takes great pleasure in conversing with Ministers and religious persons. The appearance of this marvellous relic of antiquity strikes the beholder with amazement, and convinces him that his eyes are resting on the oldest specimen of mortality they ever before beheld. Original, authentic and indisputable documents prove however astonishing the fact may appear, JOICE HETH is in every respect the person she is represented.
The most eminent physicians and intelligent men both in New York and Philadelphia, have examined this *living skeleton* and the documents accompanying her, and all *invariably* pronounce her to be as represented 161 *years of age!* Indeed it is impossible for any person, however incredulous, to visit her without astonishment and the most perfect satisfaction that she is as old as represented.
A female is in continual attendance, and will give every attention to the ladies who visit this relic of by gone ages.
She was visited at Niblo's Garden New York, by *ten thousand persons* in two weeks.——Hours of exhibition from 9 A. M to 1 P. M. and from 3 to 10 P. M.—Admittance 25 cents—Children 12½ cents. Over

his new acquaintance with Maelzel, Barnum personally started the rumor that Heth was not a human being but a mechanical simulacrum. I love it that when Heth died, Barnum charged fifty cents apiece for doctors and members of the press to witness her autopsy, which confirmed that Heth had reached perhaps half her advertised age. I love the image of Robert-Houdin's son suspended gracefully above his stage in Paris, so befuddling observers that some thought the child was not human but a sophisticated machine. I love it that the chess-playing Turk, presented as the first true thinking machine, was not a marvel of science but a clever magician's illusion. And I love it that the sagacious sow, the eponymous sapient swine from *Learned Pigs & Fireproof Women*, was exalted with this billing:

[The Pig] far surpasses in mystery and real merit any thing ever exhibited in England, and like the Automaton Chess Player, always leaves the astonished spectators in doubt to determine whether the object before them is real or imaginary – a living animal, or a machine scientifically and imperceptibly actuated by the power of human intellect.

I really do love this stuff. ◎

ILLUSTRATIONS

ANIMAL SAGACITY,
AND NO DECEPTION.

THE
MYSTERIOUS
CALCULATING PIG,

*Patronized by their Royal Highnesses the Duke and Dutchess of Gloucester,
and Her Royal Highness the Princess Augusta, and most of the
Nobility in England.*
IS NOW EXHIBITING AT
No. 29, Old Bond Street,
Nearly opposite the Western Exchange, a few doors further up.

Among the Exhibitions claiming and receiving public patronage, it is universally acknowledged by the tens of thousands of visitors, Ladies and Gentlemen of high rank and talent that the Pig Souchanguyee, far surpasses in mystery and real merit any thing ever exhibited in England, and like the Automaton Chess player, always leaves the astonished spectators in doubt to determine, whether the object before them is real or imaginary---a living animal, or a machine scientifically and imperceptibly actuated by the power of human intellect. Notwithstanding all the speculation among the learned relative to the mystery of this incomprehensible animal, there are Ladies and Gentlemen, and those possessing great curiosity, who, for the want of ocular demonstration, content themselves with saying, "It is all fabulous! what can a Pig do? I have seen the Pig at Spring Gardens, and he sadly disappointed me!" But let such unbelievers be told that this is not the Spring Gardens Pig, nor was he ever shown at Fairs, but is as far superior to any thing of that kind, as Sir Isaac Newton, would be to a mere Idiot; and we are convinced, should such Ladies and Gentlemen gratify their curiosity, they would make use of the general exclamation, "Well, we would not have believed it without seeing it!" or ten to one, in some measure doubt the truth of their own optics.

Hours of Admittance at any time of the day from 11 in the Morning till 6 in the Evening.

Ladies and Gentlemen one Shilling, Children Six Years of Age, Half-price

INDEX